DECISION ANALYSIS

GRID SERIES IN INDUSTRIAL ENGINEERING

Consulting Editor
WILLIAM MORRIS, The Ohio State University
Moore & Kibbey, *Manufacturing: Materials and Processes*
Morris, *Decision Analysis*
Giffin, *Queueing: Basic Theory & Application*

DECISION ANALYSIS

William T. Morris
Professor of Industrial and Systems Engineering
The Ohio State University

Grid, Inc., Columbus, Ohio

Printed in the United States

I.S.B.N. 0-88244-131-0
Library of Congress Catalog Card Number 76-15720

2   3   4   5   6 ▨ 2   1   0   9   8

Decision Analysis *was edited by Jane C. Foss; stylized by Lois L. Yoakam.
Cover design was by Marcie Clark. Production Manager; Elaine Clatterbuck.
The text was set in 10pt. Times Roman with a 1pt. leading by Fyldetype Ltd.,
Kirkham, Lancs., PR4 3BJ, England.*

CONTENTS

HOW TO USE THIS BOOK

This book, successor to two previous editions of *The Analysis of Management Decisions*, has benefitted from numerous comments and suggestions made by both students and teachers over the years. Many of these are reflected directly in the book, and many deal with ways in which the book might be used. On the hypothesis that the way in which a book is used is at least as important as what the book contains, several specific suggestions are outlined below.

1. To return from time to time to the instructional objectives given in Chapter 1 may be useful. These reflect the basic viewpoint of the book—that applied, working, decision analysis needs to be seen from three directions:

   a) The logic of decision making, including mathematical models

   b) The general psychology of decision making, including what we know of the broad regularities of human choice behavior

   c) The style of individual decision makers, the psychology of individual differences, on which hangs the question of whether the decision aids we design will actually be used

2. A number of the problems suggest experiments involving the actual encounter with human decision makers. This experience is important for the serious student of decision analysis. No book can transmit the subtleties of actually helping a practicing decision maker.

3. The reader is urged to keep in mind the goal of becoming more self-perceptive concerning his own personal style of decision making. The key to understanding the choices of others lies partly in objectifying one's own decision-making processes.

4. Pedagogic strategy requires the discussion of simplified, abstracted decision situations. The reader should question these simplifications, supply the complexities of reality from his own experience, and extract general principles from these simplifications that will be robust in the face of actual application.

5. At the end of Chapter 1, suggestions for a field study or research project are provided. This activity has been well received by students who often believe that, given time, doing is the most effective method of learning.

6. The calculus is occasionally used, but can be avoided without serious loss. Probability theory, however, is more central to both the logical and the psychological understanding of decision making.

7. A large number of problems have been included, about which several suggestions may be made:

   a) The reader is encouraged to glance through the problems, since in many cases they are the medium for the introduction and exploration of ideas not included in the text itself.

 b) While numerical answers for many of the problems are given in the Appendix, the reader should avoid the compulsion to "get the right answer." Instead he should see problems as simplifications that may usefully be enriched from one's own experience, and most importantly, view the problems as starting points for discussion, argument, analysis, and experimentation.

 c) Only infrequent references are made to the computer since computation is not really central to the instructional objectives of the book; yet the reader should keep in mind that the computer typically plays an important role in the actual application of the decision aids one may design.

8. While working with the book, the reader is encouraged to attend to his own decisions, those of persons with whom he is in contact, and those described in the business and professional press. These concepts and methods need to be continually tested for relevance, for usefulness, and for their fruitfulness in the production of decision aids which will actually be used. Acceptance of the printed word is no substitute for doubting, testing, and experiencing.

William T. Morris

DECISION STRUCTURES AND DECISION AIDS

Decision analysis is the study of human decision-making behavior. It involves the development of models or structures and the experimental study of these models.

WHAT DECISION ANALYSIS MEANS

Decision analysis has many uses but two basic purposes. The psychologist and social scientist are chiefly interested in decision analysis as a way of predicting how people and groups of people will make decisions. The engineer and the management scientist are interested in decision analysis as a basis for designing decision aids. A decision aid is a model, method, technique, or process designed to enhance the decision-making process. Our emphasis will be on this latter purpose. We will consider decision analysis from the viewpoint of the decision aid designer who wants to offer decision makers assistance in the improvement of their choice behavior. The reader should be warned at the outset that there are at least two nontrivial issues in this simple statement of objectives. Just what we will mean by the "improvement" of decision-making behavior will need considerable subsequent attention. Whether practicing decision makers will accept the aids which the designer offers is a second matter of some subtlety which will require a close look.

It is sometimes helpful to think of decision-making behavior as characterized along a continuum from random decision making at one extreme, through inspirational decision making, to systematic behavior at the other extreme. By random behavior we might mean decisions with no detectable pattern, order, logic, or consistency. Random decisions are those which we, as observers, find impossible to model, to explain, or to predict. Inspirational decisions are those which feel "good" or "right" to the decision maker himself, but to the observer the explanation of the choice seems highly oversimplified, leaving out most of the obvious considerations present in the situation and placing excessive weight on one or two factors. Systematic deciding implies that the decision maker and the observer can fully see the logic, the pattern, the process that explains choices. Systematic behavior has a sort of consistency, predictability, and clarity that indicate the decision maker knows what he is doing when he decides.

There is a strong belief, and considerable evidence to support the belief, that systematic decision making increases the probability of achieving a good outcome. There is evidence that almost any systematic method of deciding, even though highly simplified, is better than none. The objective of this book is to suggest ways to design decision aids that will be useful in systematizing the decisions sufficiently important to warrant the effort required.

INSTRUCTIONAL OBJECTIVES

This book aims at four objectives—to assist the reader in developing the ability

1. To give structure to, or model a variety of real decision-making situations
2. To apply to actual decisions the modern concepts of preference analysis and uncertainty analysis
3. To become more fully aware of one's own decision-making style in both personal and professional decisions and to create decision aids for enhancing that style
4. To design decision aids for clients in various fields of activity to assist these clients in more fully attaining their own standards of reasonableness in deciding

The meanings of these objectives will become clearer as we become further involved in the study of decision making. The best way to begin, however, is by looking at an example of a typical decision.

A TYPICAL DECISION PROBLEM

The management of a manufacturing firm is undertaking the production of a new product it hopes to sell both commercially and to the military services. Much effort has gone into the study of the market for this product, its design, its production, and the possibilities for profit. At an advanced stage in this effort, the management of the firm must make a decision as to what type of lathes should be purchased to carry out one stage in the production of the product. A staff analyst is asked to study this problem and make a recommendation to management. He undertakes a study of the lathes available from various machine tool manufacturers, getting as much data as possible on the prices, operating costs, performance characteristics, maintenance costs, service lives, and salvage values of the various machines. His objective is to find the type of machine that will perform the anticipated operations on the product with the required precision as economically as possible.

As he accumulates and studies the information, it becomes clear that the machines fall into two general groups. There are special-purpose lathes which can do a limited variety of production operations, but do them very economically at a high rate of output. There are also general-purpose lathes which can do a greater variety of operations, but for any given set of operations their output rate is lower than that of the special-purpose machines. On the basis of various considerations such as price, precision, and reliability, he is able to select what seems to be the best of the special-purpose machines and the best of the general-purpose machines. Let us refer to these as machine A and machine B, respectively.

In studying the relative desirability of machines A and B, the staff analyst decides to compute the unit production cost for each type. Using the data he has obtained, he comes up with the following result. If the product is to be produced at an annual rate of 20,000 units or more, machines of type A will have the lower unit production cost. If less than 20,000 units per year are produced, machines of type B would be cheaper on a unit cost basis. He reports this conclusion to the head of his staff group who adds the following idea. If for some reason the firm eventually ceases to make the product, machines of type B would be more useful for making other products than would those of type A.

The two analysts then present their findings to a meeting of the firm's management. At this meeting many other factors are discussed, such as the availability of capital, the reputations of the machine tool manufacturers, the possibilities of getting a substantial military contract for the product, plans for other new products in the future, and so on. The orderly thought processes of the analyst may become a little confused at the variety and vagueness of the considerations discussed. Finally a show of hands is called for, and the majority of the managers favor type B machines. A small but vehement minority argues on in favor of type A. Time passes, tempers are lost, but eventually those in the minority reluctantly agree to type B machines. At this point the president of the firm directs the treasurer to make the necessary funds available and the purchasing agent to begin negotiations to buy the equipment. This little drama represents the kind of situation examined in this book.

Decision making is such a prominent management activity that it is seldom considered analytically by those who do it regularly. Indeed, managers are seldom capable of explaining their own decision process. As one prominent manager stated, "You don't know how you do it; you just do it." One may begin to understand the process, however, by turning an analytical eye to the little episode just described. The events might be organized as follows:

1. **Explicit Recognition of a Decision Problem.** As plans and preparations for the new product advanced, the decision about lathes required management attention. Fortunately there was time to study the decision before any forced action.
2. **Seeking Staff Assistance.** Management decided that this decision required the assistance of the staff.
3. **Search for Alternatives.** The analyst searched for various courses of action which management might choose. His task was to predict the consequences of various acts. He could not search indefinitely but had to get on with the problem.
4. **Prediction.** The analyst attempted to predict what would happen if various alternatives were adopted. This was difficult because of such uncertainties as future sales rates, military contracts, and product life.
5. **Evaluation.** The analyst tried to calculate the value or worth of the action in the light of various future events. He did this in terms of production cost but recognized that this might not capture such considerations as reliability, flexibility, availability of capital, and so forth.
6. **Production of an Explicit Model.** The result of the analyst's effort was the production of an explicit model or conceptualization of the decision problem.
7. **Application of Managerial Judgment.** Management recognized that the analyst's efforts were a considerable help but not an exhaustive statement

of the problem. They added factors not included in the model, weighing and combining them in an implicit judgmental process.

8. **The Management Decision Process.** The final conclusion was reached by pooling the judgments of the management committee, ostensibly by a vote. When the vote failed to be unanimous, efforts were made to reach a consensus. A great deal of bargaining and persuasion may have been involved here, often quite difficult to understand.

TWO BASIC CONCEPTS

Two fundamental ideas kept in mind may help considerably with a study of decision making.

By a decision we mean a conceptualization of a choice situation, whether in the form of a mental image or an explicit model.

Each of us perceives a choice situation differently and thus has different concepts, models, or images of it. Although the scientifically trained analyst attempts to express his conceptualization as an explicit model, what goes into this model is necessarily a function of his experience, the selective character of his perception, and his judgments as to what should or should not be included.

All decision making involves the simplification of reality. Because of the limited capacity of the human mind (and of the computer) all conceptualizations of choice situations are produced by abstracting from the rich complexity of reality. This is true for both the experienced manager and the analyst, although they may simplify to different degrees and in different ways. When we examine models of decision situations, keep in mind that they are necessarily simplifications and that the way in which the situation has been simplified is a product of the analyst's perception and judgment. The key to understanding any decision process is to understand the way in which it reduces the unmanageable complexity of the management situation. We begin with an example of a decision to illustrate the elements of one of the basic decision models that will be used throughout the book.

A MODEL OF A DECISION

Consider the decision problem encountered by the roulette player who wishes to place a one dollar bet on either red, black, or zero and double zero. The rules of the game are simple. If the wheel is spun and the ball stops at a position which corresponds to his wager, he wins. Otherwise he loses. For winning bets of one dollar the house pays as follows:

$$
\begin{array}{ll}
\text{Red} & \$\ 2.00 \\
\text{Black} & 2.00 \\
\text{0 and 00} & 18.00
\end{array}
$$

In approaching this decision the player observes that there are 38 possible positions on the wheel, 18 of which are red, 18 of which are black, and the remaining two are labeled 0 and 00. Although no wheel is absolutely perfect, the imperfections are usually so slight as to become evident only after extremely long periods of study. Thus, the usual view taken by the player is that the ball is equally likely to stop at any position on the wheel. Using this opinion, the probabilities which encode this uncertainty are:

$$
\begin{array}{ll}
\text{Red} & 18/38 \\
\text{Black} & 18/38 \\
0 \text{ and } 00 & 2/38
\end{array}
$$

It is helpful to summarize all this information about the decision in a matrix. The rows of the matrix correspond to the alternative bets among which the player must choose. The columns correspond to the various results of a spin of the wheel, with the probabilities noted for each possible result. The cells of the matrix then indicate whether the player wins or loses and the corresponding net money return.

The net return in each case is obtained by subtracting the dollar wagered from the amount which the house pays. Thus, if the player chooses red and the ball stops at red, the house pays $2; but he wagered $1, so his net return is $2 - 1 = \$1$. Having displayed a good deal of information about the decision in this matrix form, the player is ready to actually make his choice. How should he place his bet? As we shall see later on, a number of arguments could be advanced to answer this question. At present we will consider only one such argument, which suggests that the player should choose so as to maximize his long-run average or expected return. Thus we might compute the average or expected return for each possible choice and select the one for which this quantity is the largest.

		The Ball Stops at:		
		Red Prob. = 18/38	Black Prob. = 18/38	0 and 00 Prob. = 2/38
	Red	WIN $1	LOSE −$1	LOSE −$1
The player chooses	Black	LOSE −$1	WIN $1	LOSE −$1
	0 and 00	LOSE −$1	LOSE −$1	WIN $17

The expected return for a bet of $1 on red is

$$(18/38)(\$1) + (18/38)(-\$1) + (2/38)(-\$1) = -\$.053.$$

This means that if we bet on red a large number of times, the net return each time tends toward an average loss of 5.3 cents. The prospect of such a loss is not attractive, but if the expected returns for bets on black, and 0 and 00 are computed, they turn out to be precisely the same. The decision maker may then draw several conclusions:

1. Using expected return as an index, it makes no difference how he places his bets.

2. No matter how he bets, this sort of gambling will not be profitable in the long run.
3. There is no way of improving his analysis of the decision unless he can study the wheel for a very long time to check the probabilities more carefully.

A similar study of other commercial gambling games would show that all have negative expected returns; otherwise gambling houses would soon go out of business. Our point is not to dwell on the folly of gambling but to suggest that the elements of this decision are typical of many decisions and that a model can be set forth making these elements explicit.

In any decision of interest, there are two or more alternative courses of action among which the decision maker must choose. (In the foregoing example, bets on red, black, or 0 and 00.) We will use the symbol a_i to represent the ith alternative course of action. The actions are listed in a mutually exclusive and collectively exhibitive manner. The result of deciding upon a course of action depends on other events beyond the control of the decision maker. (Where the ball stops.) We shall call these other events "possible future states of the world" or simply "possible futures." In many decisions it turns out that the possible futures may be described very simply. (We can summarize the very complicated series of events which take place when the wheel is spun and describe the relevant possible futures as "the ball stops on a red position," etc.) The symbol S_j will stand for the jth possible future. The result of selecting a particular course of action and having a particular possible future happen is an event which we will refer to simply as an outcome. (Win or lose.) The outcome of choosing alternative a_i and having possible future S_j happen, is the event θ_{ij}. In studying the outcomes, the decision maker will wish to evaluate them or measure their worth in terms of his objectives and value system. Often the value of an outcome may be expressed in terms of dollars of profit or loss which it may represent, but sometimes intangible considerations will enter. (How can we evaluate the pleasure the player obtains from playing roulette and winning?) If we can evaluate an outcome, we write $V(\theta_{ij})$ for the value of θ_{ij}. (Net dollar returns to the player.) We may now present our matrix representation of the elements of a decision in symbolic terms.

	S_1	S_2	S_3		S_j		S_m
a_1	$V(\theta_{11})$	$V(\theta_{12})$	$V(\theta_{13})$	$\cdots$	$V(\theta_{1j})$	$\cdots$	$V(\theta_{1m})$
a_2	$V(\theta_{21})$	$V(\theta_{22})$					
a_3							
.							
.							
.							
a_i				$\cdots$	$V(\theta_{ij})$	$\cdots$	$V(\theta_{im})$
.							
.							
.							
a_n						$\cdots$	$V(\theta_{nm})$

If the probabilities of the possible futures are used, the symbol p_j may be used to stand for the probability of S_j. In terms of these symbols, the expected return from a_i may be written:

$$E(a_i) = \sum_j V(\theta_{ij}) p_j$$

This is one kind of model which may be used to represent the elements of a decision.

MULTIPLE POSSIBLE FUTURES—TERMINOLOGY

The reader familiar with the literature of decision analysis, with management terminology, or with previous editions of this book will be aware of a basic change in terminology which has taken place in recent years. Classically, the presence of probabilities in a decision model has signaled the model as one of a decision in the face of risk. If multiple possible futures were considered but probabilities were not included in the model, the situation was referred to as a decision in the face of uncertainty. This terminology goes back at least to the economist, Frank Knight, whose work appeared in the early part of this century.

More recently, decision analysts have adopted the viewpoint that probabilities are always present and that *all* decisions in which multiple possible futures are considered are to be called decisions in the face of *uncertainty*. We will follow this more modern usage, dropping the word risk in this context and referring to the consideration of several possible futures and their probabilities as *uncertainty*.

STRUCTURING DECISIONS

There are in common use among decision analysts, four basic ways of structuring or modeling decisions. One is the matrix form we have just examined. A second type of model consists of one or more mathematical equations which have the general structure

$$\text{Payoff or value of } a_i = f(a_i, S_1, ..., S_m, p_1, ..., p_m)$$

We have already encountered an instance of this structure in the form

$$E(a_i) = \sum_j V(\theta_{ij}) p_j$$

This is a particularly compact and useful type of model for a decision, since it often permits one to take advantage of a wide range of mathematical or deductive operations to find the most desirable course of action.

A third type of structure is the "decision tree," a diagramatic representation of a sequence of decisions interspersed with a sequence of "chance" events, or events beyond the control of the decision maker. A simple decision tree is shown in Figure 1-1. The squares represent decision nodes, or points at which

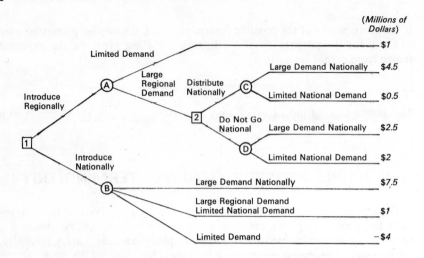

Figure 1-1 New Product Marketing Decision Tree

the decision maker is able to make a choice. Emanating from the decision nodes are the alternative branches which represent the courses of action among which the choice may be made. Each alternative branch leads to a chance node (sometimes called an event node or a probability node) which symbolizes events beyond the decision maker's control. Chance nodes, symbolized by circles, give rise to outcome branches representing the various ways the event may turn out. If the probabilities of these outcomes are to be considered, they are usually written alongside the outcome branches. The tree terminates in outcome branches leading to "terminal states," which are really points at which the analyst summarizes the subsequent series of decisions and events by writing a single payoff, value, or outcome.

Any path through the tree consists of

- A specific set of contingent alternatives chosen by the decision maker
- A specific set of events beyond the control of the decision maker

The specific set of alternatives might be characterized as a single complex alternative or strategy, and the specific events might be represented as a single possible future. The probability of the resulting possible futures might be computed by taking the product of the event probabilities. The values of the terminal states might be considered to be the payoffs associated with each strategy or alternative and each possible future. Thus any decision tree could be summarized in terms of the matrix model outlined above. Similarly, any matrix could be expanded in the form of a decision tree. The two are logically equivalent. The advantage of the tree lies in its clear exposition of the multiple stages or sequences of decisions which often characterize complex choice situations. We shall look more carefully at these multi-stage decisions in Chapter 7.

Finally, decisions may be structured in the form of a process diagram or process flow diagram. An example of such a model is shown in Figure 1-2.

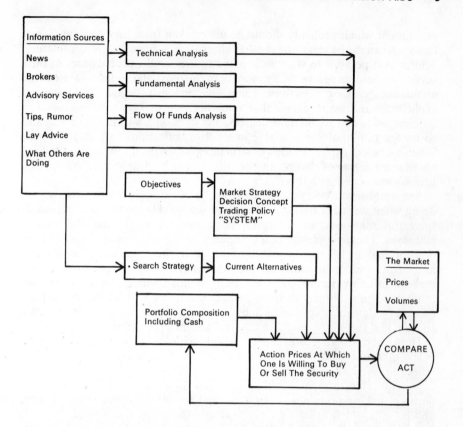

Figure 1-2   Process Flow Diagram

Process diagrams sometimes take the precise form and adopt the conventional symbolism of computer program flow charts, indicating at least by implication, that the decision process is similar to the sorts of processes which a computer may be programmed to carry out. Sometimes process flow diagrams are less formal and consist of "boxes and arrows" which represent the dynamic sequence of events, information flows, information processing steps, and decision-making steps which constitute a complex choice process. The process flow diagram, often less formal, less precise, and less quantitative than the previous structures we have described, is most useful in displaying the dynamics of the decision process in a particularly rich way. We will use such a diagram shortly to make a first analysis of the general dynamics of the decision process.

EXPLICITNESS

To attempt to say clearly the way one sees a decision, to put as much of it down on paper as possible in a reasonable time, is a useful and sobering experiment which probably should be undertaken from time to time. Sometimes we cannot be clear about what alternative actions we are considering. Seldom is it possible to state anticipated futures or the probabilities of their occurring. Seldom can we make more than the most platitudinous statements about our goals or objectives. There are obviously degrees and kinds of explicitness and we recognize that some decision makers will be explicit in different ways and to different degrees. Yet data on goals, probabilities, and so on are not routinely available in most organizations to a *useful* extent. When we talk of explicit models or structures for decisions, we are thus talking about some degree of change, and we will want to be clear about the costs and benefits associated with this change.

Any enthusiasm we might develop for knowing more about what we are doing when we make decisions is likely to be quickly tempered by a look at successful managers, or successful physicians, or even successful mathematicians. These people are not, it appears, very explicit at all. Most of their decision making is better described as intuitive. More than that, they seem to know (intuitively) the limits of their own effectiveness as intuitive decision makers, to know (intuitively) what decision aids to seek, and to know (also intuitively) how to integrate the assistance they receive with their own experience and judgment. Explicitness does not seem to be a necessary condition for success, and there is no evidence that it is a sufficient condition.

Thus when one advocates clarity, verbalization, and communication, there is less than unbounded enthusiasm among those more given to action than reflection. Any such proposals must be examined in the light of realistic expectations as to what could come from an examination of one's own decision-making processes. They must lead to actions, costs, resource uses, and benefits which fit into the constraints imposed by the context in which decisions are really made. In short, such proposals must be practical. In fact, they must be more than practical; they must be irresistible. It is too easy to avoid the realization that we don't know what we're doing when we make a decision and too easy to accept the idea that since we know all about decision making from first-hand experience there could hardly be any payoff from getting explicit. Before we go further, we need to develop realistic expectations about what is possible.

Efforts expended on understanding decisions and the development of decision aids are rewarding, but there is often confusion about what form these rewards will take. Will we be happier, more successful, less worried, less fraught with conflict? To reduce the possibility of disappointment and disenchantment, it seems best to throw a little cold water on these expectations by stating what might and might not be reasonably achieved.

THE RIGHT DECISION

Some managers are not curious about the nature of their decision-making behavior. They want a simple "practical" recipe that "will work." They do not want to be the first to try anything, but prefer things tested and proven. They are easily put off by the first blush of failure which has accompanied the introduction of many successful innovations in decision making in recent years. They are not willing to make an effort to understand, having picked up the notion that it is the responsibility of others to communicate with them, to "sell" them. These individuals, many of whom are successful managers, are not likely to enjoy the subtleties we will encounter. They had best "drop the course" immediately.

On the other hand there are those who seem to cherish a vague feeling that someday there will be the simple mechanical system for making decisions that will virtually guarantee success. The vigorous sales of books about gambling or the stock market which offer simple mechanical systems is testimony to this lingering hope. Managers sometimes manifest a similar yearning when they demand the "right decision," and they seem disappointed when it is suggested that only God knows the right decision. All that men can offer is the possibility of decisions that are in various senses "better," but no guarantee of success in specific choice situations. What managers often mean by the "right" decision may be, in fact, the "right" outcome, a distinction which is fundamental to all thinking about decision making.

The tough, no-nonsense view of American industry is that a person is paid and promoted on the basis of results. Little sympathy attaches to the manager who can say that because of factors beyond his control, because of things which he could not reasonably foresee, he did not produce the expected results. The troublesome thing about the manager who has "produced" results is the question of to what extent he is personally responsible for the results, to what degree it was "luck" and to what degree "skill." There is the suspicion that some managers whose decisions have produced good results might have risen to the top, but these results are largely a matter of chance, of circumstance, or of fortuitous conditions which nobody could reasonably have foreseen. Many wealthy, powerful, and otherwise successful men have had nothing to do with decision analysis, have achieved success without the aid of formal training in decision making, and thus decision analysis cannot be shown to be a necessary ingredient. Is it even a sufficient ingredient? In its present state the answer is that it is neither necessary nor sufficient.

LUCK AND SKILL

To make sense of the ancient luck versus skill question, there must be a basic distinction between a good decision and a good outcome. It is particularly interesting that experienced managers seem to have difficulty in accepting this fundamental notion. A decision, in the sense of the choice of a course of action, is within the control of the decision maker. If he chooses according to some standards of reasonableness, having the information reasonable to have at the time of choice, then we will say that he makes a good decision. The outcome which follows from the implementation of the choice is to some extent beyond the decision maker's control, and of course, the outcome may or may not be good. If I must get to New York as quickly as possible and money is not a serious consideration, flying is a good choice. As I boarded the plane I would probably feel that, knowing what is reasonable to know at that moment, I was implementing a good decision. If, however, the plane is disabled and forced down en route, the outcome is not good. It is an outcome which I could foresee as a posibility, but not an event subject to my control. The key to understanding the distinction is to be able to leave the disabled plane, regretting the outcome, but not regretting the decision. The good decision stands up from a hindsight point of view, no matter what the outcome. It also stands up when, given a good outcome, you ask yourself, "How would the decision look if the outcome had been otherwise?" If we select a stock to buy on the basis of decision processes that meet out own standards of reasonableness, then whatever the stock does, we should not regret the decision, however much we may regret the outcome. If, on the other hand, we buy a stock on the basis of a tip, a vague hunch, or a blind plunge, a dramatic rise in that stock may give us a good outcome; but, if this important distinction is to be honored, we cannot congratulate ourselves on making a good decision. We cannot say how much the outcome depended on luck and how much on skill, but we can say something about how much skill went into the decision.

STANDARDS

Setting realistic standards as we evaluate our own decisions is thus a serious problem. We cannot know or control the future. We want to know things reasonable to know, to think reasonably about our experience, and to act in ways consistent with what we know and think. This may or may not produce success, but we have an abiding faith that this is the way to do things, and this faith is well supported by our examination of experience.

We are disappointed, frustrated, or angry when a decision does not lead to a good outcome, but it is sensible to ask whether we could reasonably have chosen otherwise. If the answer is "no," then we have probably made a good decision. As much as we may regret the outcome, we do not need to regret the decision-making behavior. It is not a trivial distinction, for it is often difficult to get "practicing" decision makers to feel comfortable with it. It may be that the conceptual separation of the decision from the outcome is unnatural for them.

Some of us will wish to act, at least in serious and consequential decisions, so that we can see whether our actions are consistent with our objectives and our beliefs about the future. This may sound simple, but consider the varieties of poker players. Many players will agree that it is reasonable to play with an eye to the odds or probabilities of various cards being drawn and various hands occurring. Many will agree that it is unreasonable not to do this. If one is willing to make some assumptions about the shuffling and dealing of the cards, the mathematical theory of probability may be used to calculate these quantities. The calculations can, however, rapidly become complex. Yet which of us requires that these calculations actually be carried out? We might regard the player who did so as having very high standards of reasonableness for his decisions, or we might see him as quite unreasonable. He spends far more time and effort calculating probabilities than is warranted by a game of poker, and he plays with such deliberation that he takes the fun out of it.

Some of us will be content to know, however vaguely, something about the relative magnitude of the probabilities on the basis of our experience. Others will think themselves reasonable to consult the little wallet cards salesmen give out with a few of the odds printed on them. The point is that each of us decides what degree of coherence among goals, experiences, and expectations will satisfy our own criteria for reasonableness. Each of us judges for himself when he has acted to avoid blunder, blind choice, or random behavior. Probability theory could be used by the reflective player to police his decisions for incoherence and lead him to reconsider. Some reflective players have found the theory, taken with a grain of salt, to be compelling, but others have not. Decision analysis generally provides similar logical guides for policing behavior, but we must choose our own standards of enforcement.

RATIONALITY

Rationality, or rational choice, is not really a mysterious concept in the hands of most students of decision making. What we mean by rational choice is choice for which we have a model or explanation, choice in which we know what we are doing. Rational decisions are knowing, seeing decisions, rather than blind or random decisions. To choose rationally is to choose in an explainable way, explainable to ourselves and to others.

To be scientific in one's decision making is not to be superhuman, clairvoyant, or always right. Science involves transforming casual experience into more carefully designed experiment. It means being more efficient in learning from what happens. Science implies an explicit realization of what we do not know and an explicit realization that we must stipulate and act on an incomplete, imperfect, uncertain view of the future. We have no choice but to *act as if* our limited view of things were in fact true, and the important implication of science in decision making is the deliberate recognition of this. In this way, science suggests we will be able to test our imperfect conceptions against reality, constantly revising and correcting them. There may be one best way of making decisions, but we are unlikely to find it or to realize what we had if we did discover it. In summary:

1. A good decision does not guarantee a good outcome. A good outcome does not necessarily indicate a good decision.
2. A good decision is one consistent with the information which the decision maker can reasonably have available at the time the decision must be made; consistent with the decision maker's beliefs about the future; and consistent with the decision maker's preferences, goals, or objectives.
3. The objective of decision analysis is to design decision aids which will *increase the probability* that good outcomes will result.

COSTS AND BENEFITS

It is of some use to pursue the notion of decision-aid design as a sort of constrained optimization problem, without taking the time for structure of the problem too seriously. Efforts to alter decision-making behavior are costly. Cost here is used in a broad sense to include not only dollars but time, cognitive energy, staff effort, and the opportunity of failing to do the other things which a manager might do with his energies. It makes less sense to ask if these efforts "work" than it does to try to identify the various results which they produce, some beneficial and some not, some limited and some extensive. As with cost, we will want to think of benefits in a broad sense. We would like to maximize some function of the benefits and costs, say the difference between benefit and cost, or the ratio of benefit to cost. If we find it difficult to take seriously the tools of the systems analyst in the context of our efforts to modify decision making, perhaps we would at least be willing to say something like, "We would prefer the more beneficial of two decision-aiding programs having about the same cost, or the least costly of two efforts having about the same benefits." The structure of the problem provides the important insight, not its careful quantification. The options available to us for working toward this sort of maximization are constrained or bounded in important ways. The apparent lack of success of some past efforts to influence management decision making may be seen both as failures to meet the constraints, as well as failures to show with sufficient clarity a favorable cost benefit relationship.

The time available to get the decision made is obviously a key constraint. The problem is how to make better decisions in the time we have without being left behind by the pace of affairs. The greater one's ability to anticipate a decision, the greater the opportunity for careful explication, detailed staff studies, and intelligent delegation of parts of the decision. The greater also are the opportunities to develop and use decision aids.

A companion constraint arises out of the fact that most decisions come to managers in the context of situations that appear vague, confused, ill-defined, full of contradictions, and incomplete. Those who have actually engaged in the hard work of translating ill-structured, management-decision situations into well-structured research problems agree that this is possible in a limited number of instances. It can be achieved with a favorable cost-benefit relationship in an even more limited number of situations. It is not presently reasonable to make every management decision over into a well-structured subject for analysis.

These kinds of constraints arise largely out of the nature of the situations in which the manager must work. There are, of course, other constraints which seem to arise more nearly out of the nature of the manager himself.

Our efforts to develop more satisfying decisions must recognize, first of all, that we are creatures of habit. We develop our own ways, our own personal styles of doing things, including making decisions. There will be decision aids that will seem natural and acceptable and easy to integrate into our behavior. Others will seem unnatural and are not for us. Here, again, may be one of the sources of failure for previous efforts to bring about changes in the behavior of practicing decision makers. We must recognize also that we are constrained by the human cognitive capacity. Each of us has a limited ability to hold ideas in our short-term memory, to manipulate those ideas, to reason, and to calculate. We can remember more and think more extensively if we have some structure or concept which relates ideas, but we are seldom clear about our own cognitive capacities nor about how to improve them. It will be futile to invent decision-aiding methods too complex to be taught and learned with reasonable effort. Finally we should recognize differing degrees of experience among managers and the sort of constraint this implies. The more experienced a decision maker, the less he needs or values decision-aiding schemes. In what we do, we must make some attempt to account for the more experienced and less experienced decision makers.

INTUITION

When a manager makes what we usually call an intuitive decision we think of him as deciding with confidence but without knowing very clearly how he is doing it. We should say this without prejudice, however, since effective and competent professionals in mathematics, medicine, science, and many other fields are highly intuitive decision makers. It might thus be wise to pause before attempting to replace intuitive managers with computers, or attempting to exclude science from management by insisting the real decision making can only be an art. Reasonable men may be those who prefer to make decisions so they can see what they are doing, but there are other paths to success, other standards of reasonableness. If we are to understand the whole man or the whole manager, we should expect to find him sometimes intuitive, sometimes explicit, sometimes well aware of what he is doing, and sometimes not. The ways in which we use or neglect our intuitive capabilities are among the most basic aspects of personal style.

Intuition is a term for which there appears to be no widely accepted operational definition. It is a concept which we only vaguely understand, and perhaps we should admit that we understand it only intuitively. It is probably wise and certainly honest not to insist too much on drawing hard distinctions between intuition and explicitness in our personal patterns of choice. Clearly, however, if we want to look introspectively at our decisions, if we want to pursue the development of awareness of ourselves as decision makers, we must try to suggest some of the things one might mean by intuitive behavior. We will describe it in a variety of ways, hoping to strike a responsive note of understanding, before considering any attempts to change it.

To describe an intuitive decision many of us would use words or phrases like

- *Hunch*
- *Jump to a conclusion*
- *Top of the head decision*
- *Seat of the pants decision*
- *Judgment*

- *Flash of insight*
- *Gut feeling*
- *First impression*
- *Snap reaction*
- *Shot in the dark*

We might find some agreement on the following properties of intuitive decisions:

- *A "feeling of rightness"*
- *Not explained very well*
- *Product of subconscious, preconscious, or prelogical thought*
- *Private, implicit, and undelegated*

Intuitive thinking can mean that kind of thinking which cannot be verbalized. Intuition suggests the immediate leap to a decision, rather than a process involving careful, well-defined, conscious steps. The intuitive thinker is unable to report what aspects of the situation his perceptual processes have selected, what portion of the contents of his memory he is using, or the inferential methods that lead him from these inputs to a decision. He responds to a total conception of the problem, his thoughts moving in seemingly nonlogical fashion through all kinds of shortcuts to a decision. The mode of thought is obscure, scarcely formulated, and inarticulate. We may see intuitive deciding as involving a kind of total immersion in the decision situation, steeping the self in all of its details. After the steeping process has gone on for a while, a choice is made—more than a wild guess, but something less than a verbalizable, justifiable, deliberate decision.

Managers admit readily enough that there are many decision situations which leave them quite unable to be explicit. It is not their habit to verbalize unless required to follow the choice with justification and persuasion. Part of the difficulty is certainly connected with a lack of language and structure. It is difficult, for example, to be very clear about risk if one must verbalize without the help of the language and concepts of probability. It is a revealing test of self-objectification to ask a decision maker to write down the policies he uses in a particular situation so that his successor could carry on in substantially the same manner. Many of us find it very difficult to do this in a way which inspires confidence in the result. Indeed we suggest that if a person is unable to explain decision-making methods to a successor, he is using intuitive methods.

EXTERNAL EXPLICITNESS

There are interesting and important differences between being clear and explicit internally, with ourselves, and being explicit externally, with others. To reflect on the contents of one's own mind, to think about one's thoughts, to be introspectively perceptive is subject to not so obvious difficulties. Our memories are selective, our recollection of our thoughts is influenced by our needs, and we tend to justify ourselves through a certain amount of unintentional distortion. We are not objective observers of our own decision-making behavior. It will be important for us to explore these difficulties and develop a compensating vigilance.

External explicitness is required to justify or to delegate. Here, of course, we become involved in the combination of trying to be clear about our decisions and trying to influence others by what we say. To those who admire logic we portray our choice as logical. Keeping an eye on these difficulties, we might say that when the decision maker does not make a decision explicit, he is acting intuitively.

If one can make some aspects of a decision explicit to himself, if he knows his own mind in some respects, we will say that these parts of the decision are not intuitive. To the extent we "know what we are doing" we are not deciding intuitively. If we can and will make some aspects of the decision explicit for others then these aspects as well are not intuitive.

Being unable to verbalize is clearly different from being unwilling. A manager may, of course, reserve to himself the decision to verbalize or not. He may, more or less consciously, render pseudo-verbalizations which serve his own purposes in the organizational context. He may offer socially approved reconstructions of his decision process ("See how logical I am." or, "That was decided strictly according to company policy."). If he were so inclined he might look for verbalizations to suggest that the blame for possibly bad results fall on others, while reserving for himself the credit for any successes.

Thus when we are dealing with others we find ourselves involved in some long-standing psychological problems. If a decision maker does not make his choice explicit, is it because he cannot or because he will not? If he does make it explicit, is the report knowingly or accidentally distorted? Will he really do what he says? Our definition suggests that there is little we can do about the first two problems, being limited as we are to listening to what decision makers say and watching what they do.

PREFERENCE FOR IMPLICITNESS

Experienced decision makers typically have a strong preference for their own implicit decision processes. Given a choice, they will not elect to be explicit, at least in areas where they feel strength or competence based on experience. They will probably resent attempts to impose explicit methods on them.

Intuitive, implicit, or judgmental decision making is after all the mainstay of the experienced decision maker, and for good reasons. Intuitive, unaided methods have typically served the decision maker well, and he can reflect on some considerable personal history of productive reliance on his developing intuition. Until very recently there has been little to choose from except implicit methods, and even now aids tend to be available only in well-defined situations to those with special training. Effective managers are usually highly implicit deciders and find this way of working not only reliable and habitual, but satisfying since it utilizes their unique skills and sensitivities. It is especially important that intuitive methods appear well suited to meet the pressure of ongoing affairs, permitting rather immediate responses on the basis of limited information.

There is considerable evidence to suggest that unaided, implicit human decision making is reasonable, effective, and reliable within at least a modest range of decision-making problems. One objective of decision aiding is to extend the capacity of the human mind to remember and perform simple logical operations. Much of the mathematical analysis and computer application of recent years has been an attempt to extend the "logical" limitations of the decision maker in extensive repetitive tasks involving storing and processing information. We wish, however, to turn in a somewhat different direction, facing other difficulties which might be characterized as "psychological," rather than "logical," limitations on perceptual and cognitive activity. These difficulties appear when intuitive methods lead us astray, trap us, and, sometimes to our great surprise, fail to merit the confidence we have come to place in them. The particularly difficult situations are those wherein the limitations of intuitive methods are not obvious to us, but occur at the subconscious level of decision processes. It is difficult to know when we are passing from "ordinary" problems where intuitive, common sense methods work to extraordinary problems where these methods are likely to be unsatisfactory. Our intuition fails without giving fair warning.

A DYNAMIC MODEL OF THE DECISION PROCESS

There is much more to the process of decision making than confronting a model of the decision with a principle of choice and producing a recommendation for action. In the ongoing context of affairs, this may be a very limited aspect of the decision process in terms of the time, expense, and difficulty it involves. We hypothesize that the problem of how managers make decisions or how they "ought" to make decisions is primarily an empirical problem. Most of the effort consists of developing the conception or model of the decision through the processes of searching for the alternatives, predicting the outcomes, and evaluating them in terms of the decision-maker's objectives. Once all this is done, one may turn to the question of applying a principle of choice to obtain a preferred course of action.

To understand something of the dynamics of this process, we will raise some hypotheses in the form of a simple model of decision making. We will suppose that the process begins with some events which stimulate or trigger decision-making activities. A machine breaks down, leading management to raise the question of whether it should be repaired or replaced. A competitor proudly announces the installation of a large computer, leading to an inquiry from management as to whether the staff would recommend similar action. A critical shortage in the inventory of a particular product brings about a review of the inventory policies throughout the firm. These are but a few examples of the endless variety of such events which appear to trigger decision-making activity. The manager may, of course, respond to the stimulus events in his own way, without the assistance of the analyst. If, however, he seeks help in the form of staff analysis, we may think of the staff as forming an initial model or conception of the decision situation. This initial model may be incomplete, confused, filled with doubts and uncertainties, and felt by the analyst to be totally inadequate as a basis for recommending action. Alternatively, the stimulus events may suggest a decision problem with which the analyst has had considerable experience, leading to an immediate suggestion of a preferred choice.

The major question which we confront in considering the dynamics of the decision process is the question of what response or pattern of responses will be elicited by the initial conception and by its subsequent modifications. A possible view of these responses is suggested in Figure 1-3. They include:

1. **Immediate Choice.** The initial model or some later modification will be judged by the analyst to be an adequate basis for choice. He will apply a principle to produce a recommendation. The interesting and difficult question is how much effort must be devoted to developing the decision model or conception before he is willing, or forced by the pressure of affairs, to make a recommendation.
2. **Search for Alternatives.** Instead of immediate choice the analyst may respond by deciding to search for alternative courses of action beyond those currently being considered. The result of this search may be to modify the decision model; thus we have the feedback arrow in Figure 1-3.
3. **Data Gathering for Prediction.** The analyst may find his doubts and uncertainty as to the possible futures and outcomes so great that he is

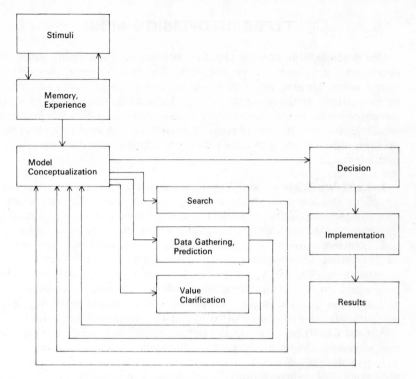

Figure 1-3   Decision Process Dynamics

unwilling to suggest a choice. He sets out on a program of data collection and analysis, leading to predictions which in turn modify the decision model. Here we are considering the whole range of empirical scientific procedures involved in experimental design, statistical analysis, and the development of prediction techniques. Again, the basic question is how much data gathering will be done, or should be done, before turning to another response.

4. **Evaluation of the Outcomes.**   Finally, we hypothesize that the analyst may find his image of the decision problem unsatisfactory because of doubts and uncertainties about the objectives which management seeks and the values of the outcomes in the light of these objectives. Here we try for realism by looking beyond our simple profit-maximizing hypothesis. This is perhaps the most important, and at the same time, the most difficult problem in the analysis of management decisions. We have chosen to approach it in two stages, permitting the reader to move gradually out toward the research frontier. In Chapter 3 we examine the special problems of evaluation which come with the explicit recognition of uncertainty in the analysis of a decision. In Chapter 12 we attempt to recognize and structure the problem of multiple, conflicting management objectives. As before, a basic question for the analyst is how much effort to devote to attempts at explicit evaluations of outcomes before turning to another response.

TYPES OF DECISION AIDS

One needs to think broadly about the possibilities for decision aiding. By a decision aid we mean any method, technique, tool, concept, pattern of behavior, computer program, staff assistance, or mathematical model which can be assimilated into the decision-making style of a client and serves to enhance the effectiveness of decision-making behavior. To give some impression of what is included in this broad range of possibilities, we might roughly classify decision aids according to their primary function (most decision aids serve multiple functions).

1. **Extending Memory and Cognitive Capacity, Coping with Complexity.** This includes the whole range of files, records, information storage systems, and very prominently, computer-based systems for supplementing the memories and cognitive limitations of decision makers.

2. **Structure Giving, Ambiguity Coping, Simplification.** The sorts of structures or models for decisions introduced in this chapter fall in this category. We will go on to develop a variety of models for decision situations, the central function of which is to give structure to choice situations, to aid in the reduction of confusion and ambiguity, and to simplify the vast complexity of reality to manageable dimensions.

3. **Goal Clarifying.** One of the prominent difficulties in being explicit in choices is the uncertainty which surrounds objectives or goals. What a person really wishes to achieve, how to make trade-offs in the face of multiple conflicting objectives, how to know what compromises are acceptable, and similar questions often block the decision process. Utility analysis, multiple-criterion decision-making models, and the formulation of principles of choice are efforts that we will examine to help decision makers become clearer about these difficult aspects of the process.

4. **Uncertainty Coping.** Perhaps the single most prevalent and troublesome source of difficulty in the decision process is the need to cope with uncertainty about the future. We are always faced with incomplete knowledge, imperfect information, inadequate vision as to what will actually happen if we undertake a particular course of action. Sometimes we cope with this uncertainty by suppressing it. Sometimes, however, decision aids may be useful in making the uncertainty explicit, in deciding how much effort might reasonably be devoted to the reduction of uncertainty, and in choosing in the face of whatever residual uncertainty remains. Probability theory provides the most widely used language for expressing uncertainty and brings to bear considerable deductive power useful in illuminating the questions of uncertainty reduction and choice.

5. **Enhancing Cognitive Activity.** Finally there are a wide range of decision aids useful for the maintenance and improvement of the decision maker's cognitive functioning, whether intuitive or explicit. We know that our thinking and decision making are impaired by frustration, anxiety, and ego involvement, and thus there is considerable interest in decision aids which seek to relieve these psychological stresses. We know that fatigue, interpersonal friction, and habit have an impact on our choice behavior

and are thus interested in aids which mitigate these effects. In similar fashion, much of our perceptual and cognitive activity is need-directed, conditioned by our own fears and wishes. Thus we often seek aids which will protect us from the selective nature of memory, from wishful thinking, and from the tendency to see things not as they are, but as we would like them to be. We know also that one of the most fundamental characteristics of human decision making is its variability, its inconsistency, its sensitivity to irrelevant cues, characteristics, and conditions. Many of the aids we will develop will function chiefly to protect decision makers from the widely shared human attribute of inconsistency.

PROBLEMS

1–1.   One of the basic skills of the decision analyst is that of moving from a description of a decision situation provided by a subject or a client, to a first rough structuring or model of the situation. Freely supplying details from your imagination and experience, create a preliminary model for each of the situations described below. Think of the preliminary model as a starting point for understanding and as a possible guide to further information which might be sought. It need not be seen as a finished, validated representation of the client's choice problem.

Situation A

After considerable development work, a new product has arrived at the point where the client must decide to put it on the market or to scrap the program. Some discussion occurs in a meeting of involved persons called to consider this decision. Someone says that the way the economy is going, the product does not have a fair chance. Another expresses the view that if Washington can prevent a recession and keep personal income rising, the product should do very well indeed. Still another view is that all the money sunk in development costs prohibits giving up the program at the present stage. The subject is clear that the marketing results of the product are closely tied to the movements of the economy through changes in personal income. He begins to reason that if there is a recession the product will be a serious loser. If there is a renewal of boom and inflation, it will make a good deal of money. If the economy goes into an extended period of stable growth, there will be a modest return from marketing the product.

Situation B

The client, product development manager in a firm continually attempting to bring forth new items in the consumer field, is asked to describe the process by which a new idea may eventually reach the market. His response is summarized here:

Stage 1:   The basic idea is conceived and developed to the point at which rough design costs and potential demand estimates are available.
Stage 2:   The design is refined and a test model built. A more carefully conceived study of available marketing data is made. The production engineering group is asked for detailed estimates of production costs.
Stage 3:   A small production run is made, and the product is submitted to a consumer panel test.

Stage 4: A pilot production run is made. Several market areas are chosen for initial introduction and promotion.

Stage 5: Full-scale production facilities are brought into operation and national distribution is undertaken.

The client notes that only about one in one hundred ideas worked on in *Stage 1* eventually make it to *Stage 5.* Of those products which go into national distribution on a full scale, only about one in five is really successful.

1–2. In the ensuing case problem entitled "The Promotion" you have an opportunity to attempt to structure a variety of decision situations. It may help you to create simple preliminary models of these situations if you try looking at them both from the viewpoint of the experienced decision maker and from the viewpoint of the young person hoping to get real insight into the decision process. Many of these situations will reappear in the analysis to be developed in subsequent chapters.

The Promotion

Your supervisor, Avery Adams, calls you into his office on Monday morning to let you have the good news. The promotion you well deserve has come through, and you will be moving to a new job at a new salary very soon. Like a lot of good news, however, this has a hook in it. Adams says he just cannot release you until he feels confident that you have prepared your replacement to carry on making decisions the way you have. You both agree that young Baker is the logical person to take over. He is bright, interested, energetic, and well liked. He understands the technical aspects of your operation very well, but unfortunately he has no management experience.

Adams suggests rather pointedly that if you want to get on to the new job, you had better take young Baker in hand and give him a crash program in how you make decisions. Adams' idea is that you should have Baker working side by side with you for a period of time so he can see how you handle the various decision situations that come along. Adams, an engineer by training, is particularly strong on one point; "Don't just tell Baker what you decide in these situations. He must learn about your methods, *how* you decide, *how* you figure out what to do, and *how* you justify it."

During the period that Baker is with you, the following situations must be dealt with:

The Hiring Freeze. Just after you have been informed that personnel funds are extremely tight and no further hiring can be done, one of your five key subordinates leaves to take another job. In spite of your pleas, Adams indicates that the hiring freeze extends even to the replacement of key resignations. He goes on to point out that at least for the remainder of the fiscal year, some nine months, you will simply have to divide up the workload and responsibilities among the other four key subordinates.

Since Baker will have to live with the results of this decision, he is especially interested in how you go about deciding who will do what.

The Lagging Project. You have two really important programs under your supervision, and two of your key subordinates are assigned to each of them. One of these programs has been gradually falling behind schedule and always for reasons that seemed beyond anyone's control. The situation has now reached the point that the project is three months behind schedule, and Adams is firm in his demand that the work absolutely must be completed in six months.

Baker, seeing that this sort of thing is likely to happen from time to time, is anxious to learn all he can about the methods you use in deciding how to attempt to get the project back on schedule.

The Computer. You must decide which of two proposals for a computer installation to accept for your operation. You hope to computerize two basic parts of your activities—the routine functions now performed by accounting and the management functions of planning and monitoring your major programs.

XBM, the outstanding leader in the computer industry, makes a very impressive and comprehensive proposal that would handle both the accounting and the management functions at a total cost of about $120,000 per month. Adams has given you a budget of $90,000 per month and has made it very clear that that is it. Once you make this clear to XBM, they indicate they can provide a system that would handle the accounting functions alone for $80,000 per month or a system that would handle the management functions alone for $60,000 per month. XBM has a very strong reputation, a fine record of success, and can clearly do what they say.

YBM, a new, innovative computer firm, is very anxious to get your business. They have a limited number of installations with customers who are moderately satisfied. Their systems have experienced some bugs, some serious delays in getting on line, and in at least two cases, they have had to admit outright failure. Still, their proposal is creative, involves some interesting new equipment, and they are perfectly honest about their newness in the business. Best of all, they propose to accomplish both the accounting and the management functions for $90,000 per month.

The Secretary. Since your secretary has agreed to go with you to your new position and since Baker does not presently have one, he is very concerned about the decision he will have to make in choosing a secretary. Since you will not be available while he is interviewing and since he has never done anything like that, he is particularly concerned that you be explicit in outlining how you make such a decision.

Baker is especially conscious of the fact that it is most unlikely he will find all of the good qualities of the ideal secretary embodied in one person, and that each person he interviews is likely to have both strengths and weaknesses.

Bidding on the Big Job. You are responsible for deciding what to bid on an important opportunity. The estimating department has worked up an estimate of what it will cost to perform the work, but you know that they are usually off in their estimate, sometimes a little bit, sometimes quite a lot.

This is a very competitive opportunity, and the award is likely to be made almost exclusively on price considerations alone. You typically find four or five competitors bidding against you, but you cannot be sure just who will be bidding on any particular opportunity. Some of your competitors are hard up for work and are likely to come in low, while some are pretty busy and likely want work only if they can get it at a fairly good price. Some of your competitors have technical skills, experience, and facilities which you do not have. Yet, you are, in certain ways, in a better position than others of your competitors.

Adams says he would like to see you win the competition but sees no reason for any unusual price cutting.

Rising Costs. Watching carefully the costs per unit of output for the three sections under your management, you notice that the costs for section B are rising significantly faster than those for the other two sections. The head of section B is your immediate subordinate, and you have made every reasonable effort to fully inform him of the importance of controlling costs.

In Baker's view this is typical of what he expects to face when he becomes a management decision maker, but he has no clear idea of how you decide what to do in such cases.

Empire Building. It becomes clear to you that another organizational unit is trying to take the lead in a new program which clearly falls within the scope of your own operations. Since the new program appears likely to be successful, to promise future growth, and to have high visibility, you are reluctant to let it go to the other unit. It seems clear, however, that if you raise a strong objection, a good deal of time, unpleasantness, and ill will are certain to be involved in the process of settling the dispute. This is especially difficult since you must have the cooperation of the other organizational unit in moving forward with many of the programs you now have under way.

If you simply let the program go, others may seek to take advantage of you in the future; if you fight and lose, you suffer a considerable loss of face and reputation; if you fight and win, the other unit will surely be looking for a future opportunity to even the score.

Young Baker finds this situation particularly difficult and emotionally charged. His ideas of what should be done seem to change almost hourly.

Funding New Programs. Your two most promising subordinates have each proposed to you a new program. Each is enthusiastic about his proposal, has worked out the details carefully, and become quite personally involved with his ideas.

You have enough money and people to undertake one, but not both of the proposed programs. There seems to be no sensible way of reducing the scale of either proposal to permit doing both at a lower level of effort, so it will have to be a choice of one or the other.

The two proposals are roughly summarized by the following descriptions:

	Proposal A	*Proposal B*
Resources required	max. available	max. available
Chances of moderate success	high	moderate
Chances of big payoff	low	moderate
Time to first results	1 year	3 years
Chances of a real disaster	moderate	low
Staff support and enthusiasm	low	high
Upper management support and enthusiasm	high	low

Inventory Crisis. You are responsible for establishing the stock level for a critical and expensive item used in your operation. You get a delivery only once each month, and no interim supplies can be obtained. When you run out, considerable difficulty and inconvenience is experienced, people are idled and must be transferred, and operations fall behind schedule. If, however, you stock too much, finance gives you trouble for keeping too much of the chronically short working capital tied up, and you experience some inventory shrinkage through loss and damage.

The number of units actually required in each of the last six months is indicated below:

Month	1	2	3	4	5	6
Units required	52	64	57	52	50	69

In your past discussions with Avery Adams you have both agreed that it is bad to run out of stock, but it is also bad to have too much. In fact, you have agreed that it is two or three times as bad to run out as it is to have too much in stock.

1–3. One of the essential aspects of developing skill as a decision analyst is gaining experience working with human subjects in experimental efforts to understand their choice behavior. The field study outlined below has as its primary objective some initial experience of this sort. It has proven especially insightful to those without previous experience in working with decision makers in direct, face-to-face situations. It is designed to require a minimum of resources and should be begun after the reader has completed the first three chapters of the book.

Field Study

1. Arrangements should be made to obtain at least three subjects for your experiment. One subject should be used for the pre-test or pilot study, the other two for the main experiment.

2. A brief clear report is required, possibly the equivalent of three to four double-spaced typed pages. The report should indicate:

   a) Your conclusions with respect to the subjects tested

   b) Your hunches as to what would happen if more subjects were run

   c) Your suggestions for improving the program of experimentation if it were to be extended

   d) A discussion of such points as are mentioned in item 3.

3. You may wish to give some thought to at least the following points:

   a) The questions suggested for research are not stated in the form of experimental hypotheses. You will need to refine these questions and state them explicitly in behavioral terms, indicating the relationship between the general questions and the specific hypotheses tested.

   b) In the selection of subjects, what will be the effect of age, decision-making experience, motivation, education, and so on?

   c) What are the key controls that should be built into the design? What about learning on the part of the subjects?

   d) What was learned from the pre-test or pilot study that was useful in modifying the design?

   e) What sort of experimental task should be used? Some suggestions: stock market trading, portfolio selection, inventory management, bidding, purchasing, gambling, insurance buying, production management.

4. A persistent difficulty surrounds the basic need to make the hypotheses studied both explicit and operational. The topics for investigation suggested below are not in shape for experimental study, and are offered only as potential areas of research.

Every important concept in a person's experimental hypothesis must be made operational. That is, one must state the operations to be carried out to bring the concept within one's experience. More informally, he must say what subject behaviors are to be observed, measured, or identified, or what actions on the part of the experimenter are to be associated with each major concept in the hypothesis.

For example, "decision time" is made operational by indicating two specific behaviors whose time separation is to be measured.

Somewhat more effort may be required to operationalize concepts such as:

Personal style	Ambiguity
Ease of deciding	Expression of risk
Apprehensiveness	Personal decision
Consistency	Learning effect

The effectiveness of this sort of experiment seems to rest importantly on one's skill, ingenuity, and imagination in making interesting hypotheses operational.

Suggested Research Areas

1. Appreciating One's Personal Style of Decision Making

   a) What can be learned about a subject's style by means of an open-ended unstructured interview?

b) What are the most important dimensions (most useful dimensions) that might be used to describe decision-making style?

c) What can be learned from an interview in which the subject is prompted, the questions are well structured, and he is given some guidance in describing his style?

d) What can be learned from observing a subject's behavior in a decision-making task?

e) What are the benefits of making the subject more explicitly aware of his decision-making style?

f) What specific suggestions could be made for enhancing a subject's style?

2. Self-Developed Decision Aids

Instead of having an "expert" design decision aids for a client, it might be interesting to have the client design decision aids for himself. What would be the advantages of this? In a specific choice situation, what types of decision aids do people invent for themselves? How can subjects be trained or motivated to design decision aids for themselves? What is the role of mathematical or logical models as self-designed decision aids?

3. The Explicit Expression of Uncertainty

a) Do subjects find some ways of expressing uncertainty easier, more natural, or more useful than others?

b) Does the explicit expression of uncertainty have any observable effect on decision-making behavior?

c) Do people feel better, less anxious, less apprehensive, or more confident when they have been explicit about uncertainty?

d) Does the explicit expression of uncertainty make decisions more consistent?

4. The Unaided Human Decision Maker

How "good" is the unaided human decision maker (in some specific decision-making task)? Can his behavior be usefully compared to the decisions made by a digital computer using a mathematical model of the choice situation? In what ways is the unaided human "better" or "worse" than the computer? What can be said about such hypotheses as:

a) The unaided human decision maker's ability is seriously degraded by the pressure of time and the anxiety of personal involvement.

b) The unaided human decision maker does well enough as long as his capacity to handle information is not exceeded. When he becomes "swamped" with information, his performance declines in effectiveness.

c) The way to get a decision made is to give the human those parts of the job he can do best and the computer those parts of the job it can do best.

5. Utility Analysis

a) How reliable is a subject's utility function over short periods of time?

b) Are some ways of obtaining his utility function easier, quicker, more natural, or more predictive than others?

c) How well does a subject's behavior agree with that predicted from his utility function?

d) What are people's attitudes toward decision aids of this sort?

1–4. Listed below are thirty-five declarative statements about decision making. It is often useful for people to consider these statements, to discuss them, to form opinions about them, and then to see to what degree these opinions might change as one progresses through the book. The statements should not be assumed to be conclusions subsequently advocated by the book, but rather provocative assertions with which some people agree and some do not.

1. The way one makes decisions is not very important. What counts, what one gets paid for, is how they turn out. Results are what it's all about.
2. In making a decision, it is possible to get too much information as well as too little.
3. One ought to make decisions in such a way as to know what one is doing.
4. The advice of others should usually be sought in important decisions.
5. Really good doctors diagnose largely on the basis of intuition. No computer could ever come close to rivalling the performance of an experienced human diagnostician.
6. Most decisions involve subtle, judgmental, complex considerations which just cannot be written down or talked about. One has to feel them.
7. Most of the really effective professionals in the stock market rely entirely on intuition.
8. Deciding among wines, works of art, or books is entirely a matter of taste. Nothing could be done to assist one in making such choices.
9. One should work at a decision until he gets a strong, clear feeling of the right course of action.
10. The clearer one is about one's objectives, goals, or targets, the better the decision.
11. The more objective a person can be, the better the decisions he makes.
12. All decisions involve emotions to some extent and there is no use trying to avoid emotional involvement.
13. An action should never be taken until all possible alternatives have been considered.
14. In making a decision, it is important to avoid leaving out any consideration or simplifying the situation.
15. Decisions should not be made hurriedly.
16. Everything possible should be done to obtain all the relevant information before making a decision.
17. In making a decision, one cannot go on too long trying to find additional alternative courses of action. There comes a time when it makes sense to choose the best of those so far identified.
18. It usually pays to define clearly what one wants to achieve before making a decision.
19. The criterion for a good decision is the degree to which one can look back on it without regret, no matter how it turns out.
20. Good decisions often involve intuitive, seat-of-the pants, top-of-the head methods which cannot really be explained.
21. Generally speaking one should discuss a decision with somebody else before going ahead.
22. A person should be able to explain or justify his decisions to himself as well as to others.
23. The best way to make a decision is to immerse one's self in the situation until one gets a feel for what should be done.
24. The more a person can write down about a decision, talk about it, explain it, or seek the advice of others, the better the decision.
25. Decisions that are important should involve some use of paper and pencil to write down the relevant considerations.
26. The human mind is capable of considering, in ways which we cannot yet explain, a vast array of complex aspects of any decision situation.
27. Important decisions should be avoided when one is very tired, distracted, or emotionally upset.
28. As long as there is any possibility of finding a better course of action, one should keep on looking.

29. To the extent that decisions involve calculations, it is very important to avoid mistakes in arithmetic.
30. The objective of any decision-aiding tool or expert advisor is to guarantee that the right decision is made.
31. Really good decision makers are never uncertain about how things will turn out.
32. It is not unreasonable for people to be able to choose a course of action without being able to say clearly what their goals or objectives may be.
33. All decisions involve some degree of risk. What is important is to take sensible, calculated risks.
34. Uncertainty about the results of one's actions is unavoidable, but it makes sense to do what is necessary to reduce that uncertainty to a reasonable level.
35. One should always write down, or discuss explicitly the alternative courses of action among which one is choosing.

SUGGESTIONS FOR FURTHER STUDY

Bross, I. D. J. *Design for Decision*. New York: The MacMillan Company, 1953.

Chernoff, H., and L. E. Moses. *Elementary Decision Theory*. New York: John Wiley & Sons, Inc., 1959.

Luce, R. D., and H. Raiffa. *Games and Decisions*. New York: John Wiley & Sons, Inc., 1958.

Schlaifer, R. *Probability and Statistics for Business Decisions*. New York: McGraw-Hill Book Company, 1959.

"Special Issue on Decision Analysis." *IEEE Transactions on System Science and Cybernetics*, Vol. SSC-4, No. 3 (September 1968).

Tribus, Myron. *Rational Descriptions, Decisions, and Designs*. New York: Pergamon Press, 1969.

DATA, EXPERIENCE, AND ENCODING UNCERTAINTY   2

The key to understanding any decision-making process is to discover the ways in which the decision maker simplifies the complex fabric of the environment into workable conceptions of his decision problems.

SIMPLIFYING REALITY

The human mind has limited information-handling capacities; thus both analysts and managers deal with decisions in terms of conceptual simplifications or models of reality. Perhaps the most obvious of these simplifications is that of suppressing the necessary ignorance of the future and considering a decision as if only one possible future could occur. This is not to pretend that one knows the future with certainty but is simply an act of conceptual simplification. It allows an answer to the question, "If this particular set of circumstances were to occur, what would be the reasonable course of action for management?" If a manager undertakes the course of action which results, he is acting as if the set of circumstances in question were sure to occur.

Likewise, when an analyst suppresses uncertainty in making a management decision explicit, it does not imply that he claims knowledge of the future. It is one of the many ways in which science may simplify the real world in order to study it. None of us can know the future, but it is often useful to ask questions about how we would act if we did.

On the other hand, consider a decision as to which of two arbor presses to purchase. If, after reasonable investigation, we conclude that the two machines are equal in terms of output, operating costs, service life, and salvage value, then perhaps the only remaining consideration is price. In such a decision prices are quoted firmly and there is little uncertainty involved. The assumption that we have complete information and can consider the decision as being made under conditions of certainty is a reasonable and acceptable one. Just what level of information completeness to achieve or assume in a decision is a matter largely of judgment, although later the problem will be discussed in terms of some guiding principles.

It is traditional to study the great majority of managerial decisions as decisions under assumed certainty. Thus, in the selection of equipment, materials and designs, the choice of operating methods and policies, and so on, the assumption of certainty is widely used. The underlying reasons for its use may be:

1. The amount of uncertainty involved in the decision may appear to be so small that the analyst feels safe in neglecting it.

2. Uncertainty may be importantly involved, but the difficulty or expense of including it in the analysis of the decision may suggest that it be left to the managerial judgment to be applied after the analysis has been completed.
3. The decision may be such that, even if the uncertainty were explicitly included, the choice would depend only on average values of the outcomes. For example, in estimating the cost of using a particular machine, its salvage value at some future time may be important. While the salvage value may not be exactly known, the analysis can be carried out by using the average salvage value for such machines.

Clearly, all of these reasons include the judgment or common sense of the analyst to a great extent.

SUPPRESSING UNCERTAINTY

One of the most widely observed phenomena of management decision making is the general suppression of uncertainty. In the vast majority of instances, it would appear that uncertainty is not dealt with in any explicit fashion. This does not necessarily mean that uncertainty is entirely neglected, only that it does not receive explicit consideration. Point estimates, single valued forecasts, and the consideration of one possible future are the norm, although this is gradually changing. The change may be due in part to the work of decision analysts. The reasons for the suppression of uncertainty probably include the following:

1. Most forms, procedures, and management information systems are not designed to accommodate explicit expressions of uncertainty. Single values are almost always called for.
2. Uncertainty suppression is clearly the long established habit of the majority of decision makers, a habit most difficult to alter.
3. Certainty represents the traditional academic view of most engineering and management decisions, and its continuation may reflect a tendency to fit things into academic formulas and modes of thought.
4. Certainty may be associated with personality characteristics such as boldness, aggressiveness, confidence, success, self-assurance, and feelings of power.
5. Suppression of uncertainty may be associated with the need to preserve a self-image of the assured, confident, successful man of affairs.
6. The suppression of uncertainty is clearly connected with the lack of a readily available language for expressing it. One of the most useful contributions of the decision analyst is to supply such a language.
7. Certainty may in part explain the appeal to all manner of hunches, cues, habits, and rules of thumb with which a decision model may be simplified.
8. Most important, certainty may help to explain some of the nonrational relationships psychologists have pointed out between evidence, experience, and beliefs. Facts alone are seldom sufficient to change people's

minds. We are dealing here with a widely observed human tendency to convert assumptions into facts, doubts into certainties, and to revise images of decision situations to meet the need for certainty.

THE LANGUAGE OF UNCERTAINTY

Decision analysis regards uncertainty as a state of mind, state of knowledge, or level of information which characterizes the decision maker. To express uncertainty explicitly is thus to encode the decision maker's knowledge, attitudes, or opinions about the likelihood of various events. Modern decision analysis proposes that uncertainty be encoded in the language of probability theory and whenever we use the term probability in this discussion, it refers to such an encoding of the decision maker's state of knowledge. It is of great importance to grasp the basic concept of probability as the term is used in decision analysis:

Probability is a property of the decision maker, not of the phenomenon.

To understand this, we consider first "probability theory," by which is meant a particular body of abstract, formal mathematics. One can study probability theory without being concerned with its applications, and without trying to puzzle over the operational meaning of statements such as, "the probability of the event A is P" or "X is a random variable." Probability theory is then concerned with analytic truths only, and like other branches of mathematics does not ask nor answer questions about the empirical confirmation of its conclusions. The theory includes statements such as:

- The probability of either A or B equals the probability of A plus the probability of B, if A and B are mutually exclusive.
- The probability of either A or not A is one.
- The probability of both A and B is the probability of A multiplied by the probability of B given A.

To apply probability theory is to ask first what operational meaning is to be attached to the term "the probability of the event A." Given an answer, one then attempts to investigate whether the corresponding operational interpretations of the deductive hypotheses are in agreement with observed events. Through toughmindedness, the scientist tries to form synthetic statements which can be verified. The trick is to do this in a way which will be of some use in decision making, capturing, and modifying the decision maker's feelings of uncertainty.

Interpretations of probability theory, attempting to make it operational, have always gone rather well, so it would seem, as long as they were addressed to problems involving coins, cards, and dice. In decisions having to do, say, with the merger of two airlines, things do not go so well, if at all. Operationalizing probability is not a problem on which all agree or have a ready answer. In fact, it usually comes as a considerable surprise to the student to discover how much the question is being discussed in the literature and how active the controversy is. Surely, it seems such a fundamental question must long ago have been settled, considering the wide use of the subject.

For our purposes it will suffice to consider two rough types of interpretations of the term "probability," although there are more.

1. **Relative frequency.** The probability of an event A is the limit of the relative frequency with which A is observed when an experiment is repeated an indefinitely large number of times. This is ordinarily what is meant when it is asserted that the probability of heads is one half when a fair coin is flipped. It is an unhandy kind of an operational definition since the notion of a limit is quite imaginary. In practice, however, we are perfectly willing to make an induction from a large number of replications as to what would happen in the limit. The class of all possible experiments or instances is called a reference class, and the occurrences of the event A form a subclass of the reference class. Sometimes the reference class is finite (the number of customers now served by the firm) and the probability of an event (sales of \$1,000 or more to a customer) can in principle be learned by examining every member of the reference class. The trouble comes, as we shall see, not when we want to make statements about large or infinite reference classes, but when decision making requires something be said about very small reference classes containing perhaps one or two members.

2. **Personalistic or subjective.** The probability of the event A in this view is a measure of a person's "degree of belief" in the statement, "The outcome of the experiment will be A." It measures his confidence in the assertion or his conviction of its truth. This interpretation is itself the subject of considerable confusion. We will shortly explore more carefully its meaning and the ways in which it may be made operational. Personalistic or subjective probabilities are not, in spite of their name, products of unbounded flights of whim and fancy. The interpretation is appealing because of the possibility of dealing with a manager's confidence in assertions like, "Our chief competitor is coming out with a new model this year." Managers have feelings of certainty or uncertainty about such assertions, and these feelings can in no useful way be dealt with by means of the relative frequency interpretation.

MANAGEMENT RESPONSES TO UNCERTAINTY

At any stage in the evaluation of an investment proposal, management's attitude toward the predicted cash flows reflects their evaluation of the uncertainty surrounding these future events. The critical question is whether evaluation has sufficiently reduced the uncertainty so that management may now make a decision, or whether further efforts to reduce uncertainty are needed. Thus at any stage in the proposal's development management may feel prepared to make its decision, or more effort may be devoted to collecting data and making judgments. In the latter case we will suppose that the objective of the firm's management information system is to make the uncertainty explicit, perhaps by expressing it in terms of probabilities. If the uncertainty can be made explicit then several advantages follow:

1. Uncertainty can be communicated, checked, and refined throughout the system. Without explicit expression, it tends to be suppressed and highly uncertain estimates produced at the operating levels are accepted as certain statements of the future at higher levels in the firm. It is important to have a method of transmitting uncertainty.

2. The logic of probability theory can be used to help management make consistent decisions in highly complex situations. That is, from explicit expressions of uncertainty about simple events well within one's experience, probability theory can be used to obtain logically consistent expressions of uncertainty in complex events beyond one's immediate experience.

3. If uncertainties can be made explicit, rather than remain exclusively a matter of implicit managerial judgment, then management will be far more willing and able to delegate important aspects of the decision-making process.

Thus it is supposed that the aim of the firm's management information system is to collect data or obtain judgments from experts or experienced managers which will lead to an explicit evaluation of the uncertainty in a decision. By this means, future events are to be predicted in terms of probability distributions, and the resulting decisions will be what have been traditionally called decisions in the face of risk.

THE MANAGEMENT INFORMATION SYSTEM

Hopefully the firm's information system will provide data, both from its own experience and from outside the firm, which will permit the prediction of cash flows in terms of probability distributions. This may prove to be a difficult and expensive undertaking.

Suppose a firm is considering the purchase of one of several alternative production machines and that experience and preliminary investigation reveal that the following information is needed for each alternative:

Price	Output
Installation cost	Scrap rate
Operating costs	Service life
Maintenance cost	Salvage value

Assuming this decision is important enough to warrant a rather detailed analysis, we will suggest some of the sources from which basic information might typically be obtained, and in the next chapter illustrate some of the techniques which might be used to process this information for inclusion in the analysis.

The price of each machine would most likely be obtained through a direct quotation from the manufacturer. The installation cost might be the result of a detailed estimate by the plant millwright based on data obtained from similar jobs done in the past. If the installation is to be performed by the manufacturer or by an outside contractor, quotations might be obtained from these sources.

If the major difference in operating costs among the alternatives will arise out of differing direct labor requirements, the firm's time study department might be consulted. Either from performance times observed on similar machines doing similar operations, or from a system of synthetic time values, an estimate of the direct labor requirements might be obtained. From the personnel department or the accounting department an estimate of the wage rates from the skill levels involved could be obtained, which would yield a direct labor cost estimate when combined with the performance-time estimates. Maintenance costs might be separated into costs associated with regularly scheduled maintenance activity or preventive maintenance, those costs which result from breakdowns, and repairs which require unscheduled maintenance effort. Once a preventive maintenance program is estimated, the times, skills, wage rates, and thus the costs may be estimated by recourse to the information available from the time study department, the accounting department, and the records of the maintenance department itself. The frequency and severity of breakdowns are much more difficult to estimate, and are typically obtained either from records of the firm's experience with similar machines or from data furnished by the manufacturer describing the failure patterns of his equipment under operating conditions similar to those which exist within the firm.

The estimated output of each alternative is usually based on the manufacturer's specifications of feeds, speeds, power, and capacity for his equipment, in combination with estimates from the time study department of human performance times wherever they are involved. The scrap rate of each machine may be difficult to estimate, but some basis may be obtained from the manufacturer's claims as to precision and accuracy and from the records of the quality control department for similar machine and job situations. The service life depends heavily on the firm's policy with respect to machine replacement. How does the firm decide when to replace a machine and when to continue its use? Once this policy is clearly established, data from the firm's own records or from those of the manufacturer may provide a basis for estimating service life from the study of similar machines. Salvage value is usually a function of the age of the machine, as well as its condition and degree of obsolescence. Often the best one can do is to obtain data on current and past market prices for used machinery as a basis for estimating the salvage values of the alternatives under consideration.

Given this sort of data, the techniques of inferential statistics may be brought to bear. The basic tactic is to formulate probabilistic or random models for the cash flows and then test to see if the models are reasonably consistent with the data. For example, given a sample of salvage values for five-year-old machines of a certain type, one might raise the hypothesis that this salvage value could be viewed reasonably as a normally distributed random variable with some specified mean and variance. Statistical techniques then may be used to test the reasonableness of this model in the light of the data. In this way, one comes to view future cash flows as random variables.

In many cases it is difficult, very expensive, or even impossible to obtain the relevant data. Investment decisions often involve contingencies, or future events which cannot readily be forecast by means of available data. Events such as research discoveries, technological innovations, the emergence of new competitors and so on may not yield readily to predictions based on past data. In these cases expert judgment and management experience must be sought, but again it will be supposed that the uncertainty associated with these judgments is to be expressed in probabilistic terms. These expressions are subjective or personalistic probabilities.

SUBJECTIVE PROBABILITY

Just how such expressions of uncertainty in the language of probability theory are to be obtained and how they can be logically manipulated are matters of some subtlety. The use of random models as ways of expressing a manager's uncertainty about future events is today a hypothesis whose effectiveness must be tested in practice, rather than an established feature of many management decision systems. Yet it is a hypothesis which promises some very considerable benefits and thus seems worth investigating to many systems designers. The basic issues are roughly outlined below.

Suppose we assume that a manager chooses in uncertain situations so as to maximize his expected or average profit, an assumption we will shortly consider in detail. Suppose further we described to this manager a lottery in which there were one hundred tickets to be sold, and the prize is K dollars or something which has for him a utility equivalent to that of K dollars. We offer him any one of the tickets and, if the decision maker was indifferent as to which ticket he held, we could then say that the drawing of any ticket was an event with which he associated the subjective probability .01. This lottery may be used as a measuring device in the following manner. To find the subjective probability he associates with the event "he will win a certain contract" we ask him, "How many tickets in the lottery would you find equivalent to the prospect of winning a prize of utility K in the event that you win the contract?" If he is able to answer this question, after due consideration, by saying that he would be indifferent between twenty tickets in the lottery and the prospect of winning the prize if he is awarded the contract, then we would call .20 his subjective probability of the event "he wins the contract." We could start with a lottery of 1,000 tickets and perhaps learn that his subjective probability is .203.

It would be convenient to be able to use the theorems of probability theory to make calculations of the subjective probabilities of complex events based on the subjective probabilities of simple events. The theorems are used in this way in the case of relative frequencies. To make this reasonable, we assign subjective probability zero to any event which the decision maker believes is impossible, and subjective probability one to any event which we feel is certain to occur. Further, we insist that the sum of the probabilities of a mutually exclusive and collectively exhaustive set of events must be one. For any two mutually exclusive events, we insist that the subjective probability of either one or the other be equal to the sum of their individual subjective probabilities. If the results obtained from a decision maker are not in agreement with these axioms, then we must ask him to reconsider and correct his "inconsistency." If his subjective probabilities do agree with them, then we have some justification for using them to predict consistent choices according to the theorems of probability theory. Recommendations based on subjective probabilities would be predictions of consistent choices for the decision maker.

Several important points should be noted about the notion of subjective probability.

1. The decision maker must be able to think about his attitudes toward uncertainty and answer the sort of questions which have been suggested. Without doubt this is difficult to bring off in actuality. Inconsistencies may arise, the results may be unreliable, and the whole thing may appear quite "fuzzy" to the manager.
2. Reasonable men could be expected to have similar subjective probabilities for events with which they have had similar experience. Thus subjective probabilities should not be matters of widely divergent attitudes, when some experience is available.
3. In many routine situations, a manager's subjective probabilities will be determined by routine data collection and analysis methods. In these cases, the determination of probabilities can be delegated to the analyst, and the manager may be freed for the more difficult decisions.
4. Relative frequencies (sometimes called objective probabilities) are themselves the product of considerable subjective judgment by the analyst. They differ mainly in that the data on which they are based and the rules for processing the data are made more explicit.
5. If a manager's experience is not considered most extensive and most relevant on a particular question, then an expert may be brought in. The expert is someone believed to have considerable knowledge and experience on the matter in question. He is then integrated into the decision process by obtaining from him his subjective probabilities. One could suggest certain qualifications that might be used as tests to determine a person's admissibility as an expert. For example, we might require that he
   • Have personalistic probabilities which are reasonably stable over time, providing he receives no new evidence
   • Have probabilities which are affected in the right direction by new evidence
   • Be selected for his past predictive performance, his demonstrated record of success and accuracy

A good deal of what is most subjective about subjective probabilities would be removed in the case of the expert. He is in fact treated as a kind of powerful computer in the decision process. He digests rich and complex past experience, producing the probabilities as his output.

Thus we suppose that either by explicit methods of data collection and statistical analysis or by means of subjective probability, or by some combination of the two, the uncertainties surrounding future events can be expressed in probabilistic terms.

MULTIPLE POSSIBLE FUTURES—AN EXAMPLE

A research and development organization is considering the problem of its budget for the coming year. A number of proposals for projects have been submitted by the staff, and a decision must be made as to which will be funded.

Each proposal, as is typical in many firms, describes only a single possible future. Single values are given for the cost, duration, facilities requirements, manpower requirements, and perhaps for the ultimate net profit contribution. This description of the possible future seems to many clearly inadequate. Some projects have a higher chance of success than others. When this is taken into consideration, what now appear to be the best projects may turn out to be somewhat less desirable. Thus it seems natural to enlarge the possibilities and add the probabilities of success and failure, since there is a good chance that this would change one's mind and change the resulting expectations. Perhaps it will seem worthwhile, by the same rough logic, to go further and develop a richer conception of the possibilities for each project. We might for example move toward a view which considers:

- Significant success
- Moderate success
- Break even
- Moderate failure
- Serious failure

A still richer view might include categories of net profit contribution such as

More than $1 million
$.5 to $1 million
$.1 to $.5 million
And so on

We could continue even further developing views of the future which rendered the categories finer and finer and added similar categories for the other dimensions such as manpower consumption and duration. To be helpful, this progression also carries the task of forming a corresponding conception of the probabilities associated with these possibilities. Somewhere along this line of enrichment, experienced people will have a sense that things have been carried far enough. They will make the judgment that the effort involved in going further is not going to be matched by the possibilities of altering their budgeting decisions and the advantages that might result. We would simply urge that there be some awareness that such a judgment is being made, and that it be made with some deliberation. To see something more of what might be involved, let us continue the process in terms of the research and development budgeting situation.

A significant aspect of our conceptualizations of various futures is the planning horizon or the degree of "look ahead." Some research and development budgeting looks ahead six months or a year, while in other firms the consequences of various proposals are explored five or ten years into the future. It is sometimes, but not always, true that the further into the future an event, the more uncertain we are about it. Likewise it is sometimes, but not always, true that the further into the future an event, the less its relevance and the smaller its consequences for decisions we are presently making. Thus there are at least two effects, as we extend the planning horizon, which tend to limit the payoff from the effort required. Eventually things appear so uncertain and of such small importance to present plans that we are clearly willing to neglect them. We are saying that to extend our view of the future beyond some planning horizon is not likely to be warranted because there is little chance that it would result in an alteration of our present preferences or a significant change in our expectations. Again we would argue not for a careful calculation of some sort of optimum planning horizon, but a sort of deliberateness in selecting one, rather than leaving it to custom, chance, or irrelevant considerations.

It is widely observed that the elaboration of futures as practiced by many decision makers stops short of becoming explicit about probabilities. This is a matter which warrants some special attention because the payoff from such an effort may be higher than is generally supposed. Let us illustrate. Suppose we are concerned about the time to complete a certain research program and find ourselves dissatisfied with a single-valued estimate. Too often in the past the actual completion times have varied importantly from such estimates, and the consequences of this variation have been matters of some concern. An elaboration of this aspect of the future might change our minds to an interesting degree about the projects we will fund in the current budget. There are several ways to undertake this elaboration.

We might produce an optimistic time, a pessimistic time, and a most likely time, together with some qualitative probabilities for each. We might produce such statements as "The chances of completing within a year are less than the chances of requiring more than a year," or "The project is about as likely to be completed in less than fifteen months as it is in more than fifteen months." We could go on to develop richer categories of outcomes with which to associate qualitative probability expressions.

Duration	Probability
0 to 9 months	very low
10 to 12 months	low
12 to 15 months	high
15 to 18 months	very high
more than 18 months	low

Finally, we could refine the qualitative statements into quantitative ones and continue to make the categories finer and finer.

DIFFICULTIES

As we have said, such elaboration is uncommon and this suggests the inference that many of us find the effort required unwarranted. There are at least two difficulties involved; it is a matter of considerable effort to produce such statements or expressions, and it is not entirely clear to many of us how we would respond to them once they have been produced. A part of the usefulness of a view of the future must be the degree to which it permits natural, easy, direct, expressions of uncertainty. One of the things we must consider in the elaboration of our conceptions is their relation to the way we habitually or intuitively think about uncertainty. An uncertain state of mind is so much a part of our cognitive stance and such a central problem in all sorts of decision making, that it deserves a closer look.

To express an opinion, to summarize experience, to give judgment in the language of probability, is both difficult and useful. There are many choices in which it is reasonable to go forward with conceptions such as:

- The chances of success for this project are good.
- There is a strong probability that the market will go up.
- Failure of that system is probable.
- There is a better than 50-50 chance that we will get the contract if we bid x.
- The odds are in favor of a sales increase for product y.

There are, however, other choice situations in which further explicitness and refinement are both needed and justified. If we are considering the choice between two projects, both of which have good chances of success, other similarities between them may leave us indecisive. We will want to develop some more precise expression of the chances for success. If we are trying to establish an inventory policy for a product and are considering the possibility of getting more data which might be used to reduce our uncertainty about its future demand, qualitative expressions of our uncertainty may not always be helpful. If information which will permit substantial uncertainty reduction is cheap, clearly we will want it. If it is very expensive, clearly we will not. In the difficult middle ground between clearly cheap and clearly expensive information, only a more careful encoding of our present state of mind is likely to help us toward a reasonable determination of how much additional data should be obtained.

To confidently, naturally, and comfortably express the view that the probability of success for a project is .80, is not a part of everyone's style. It is a habit which will have to be cultivated. We need to find simple, natural ways of encoding experience and to motivate ourselves to think habitually in such terms. A great part of the difficulty in being explicit about uncertainty is simply that we have little experience. The whole idea seems to be a questionable attempt to be overly precise about some "vague" and uncertain opinions; opinions, incidentally, which we use readily enough when we decide but seem reluctant to render explicit. We are distracted by the fact that there is no right answer when it comes to expressing our uncertainty. There is no correct value, no test of validity, only a feeling that what we have expressed does or does not reflect our own state of mind or degree of belief. We often let ourselves wander into the paradox of insisting that such expressions of uncertainty are only subjective (which is correct) and therefore inadmissable in the decision process. They are in fact, significant expressions of what is intuitively and implicitly involved in most of our daily work of deciding.

CREATIVITY

Making uncertainty explicit is a creative act. It involves more than simply summarizing "what is there." It requires an intuitive combination of one's experience and the translation of the result into an explicit communication. It is also an experimental act and is usefully thought of as raising an hypothesis about one's state of knowledge. We must try out our expressions of uncertainty to see if we like them. Do their logical consequences seem reasonable? Do the decisions into which they lead us seem intuitively satisfying. At the outset, most of us have little "faith" in the judgments we have expressed in the form of probabilities and are hardly willing to act on them. We are not accustomed to behaving in this way and are likely to have little confidence in the effectiveness of such a strange way of dealing with uncertainty. We scarcely believe what we have said when we encode our incomplete knowledge in probabilistic terms. A little practice, however, is likely to change all this. There is substantial reason to hope that with some effort, one can find natural ways of arriving at probabilistic expressions of uncertainty. Once this becomes customary the results grow more satisfying. They help us toward the achievement of standards of reasonableness which are otherwise elusive.

Expressing uncertainty, like other novel and creative acts, can be encouraged by the provision of some structure. In this case, the structure is the language and logic of probability. Many of us must first get over the idea that probability is exclusively limited to the expression of the relative frequency of various results in experiments involving cards and dice.

We need to open ourselves to the possibility that probability could be used to express uncertainty, degrees of belief, or opinions based on imperfect information. More basic than this, many of us need to accept the possibility that uncertainty is a legitimate and expressible state of mind. To regard something as uncertain, is to regard its truth as something in which we may have *degrees* of belief. If we are certain something will happen, we may express our degree of belief by associating with it a probability of 1. If we regard something as certain not to happen, we associate with it a probability of 0. If we are neither perfectly certain that it will happen, nor perfectly certain that it will not, we may express our degree of belief in its happening using a probability somewhere between 0 and 1. Notice two very basic and perhaps surprising aspects of this medium of expression. Probability is not a property of the event, but a property of the decision maker's knowledge of the event. Probability is not descriptive of the phenomenon, but of the observer. Whether or not the event happens neither proves nor disproves the belief which was expressed in terms of probability. If we feel that our degree of belief in the statement "It will rain tomorrow" is .40, this is neither validated nor invalidated by what tomorrow's weather actually turns out to be. All of this is worth some reflection.

METHODS

Considerable experimentation has been carried on to find good ways of helping people express their uncertainty, but as yet, not much progress has been made. In some experiments subjects have been asked to express directly in the form of graphs, the probability that a candidate will receive various portions of the vote in a forthcoming election. This seems surprisingly easy for many people, once they get the notion of what the opportunity implies. Some find it easier to deal in cumulative expressions, drawing curves showing their opinions that the candidate will get "between 0 and *x* percent of the vote" or curves expressing their view in terms of the probability that the candidate will get at least x percent of the vote. Still others find it more natural to express their uncertainty in the form of odds. They find it easy to make such statements as "The odds are fifty-fifty that candidate A will get at least 45 percent of the vote," and "The odds are three to one against him getting more than 52 percent of the vote." It really makes little difference in which of these formats one encodes his experiences. One is as useful as another, and the one to be preferred is that which seems most natural.

THE REFERENCE LOTTERY

Somewhat more complex schemes for helping people express their uncertainty involve comparing one set of events for which uncertainty seems easily expressible with another set for which it seems more difficult. The "reference lottery" briefly described earlier, is a good example of such a method. Imagine a lottery in which one hundred tickets are to be sold and in which the prize is substantial enough to attract one's interest. If we find one ticket in the lottery just as desirable as any other, then we might agree that all tickets are equally likely to be the winning ticket. Keep in mind that this is an expression of our uncertainty. We might find it perfectly natural to say that our degree of belief in the statement, "A ticket bearing serial number x is the winning ticket" is one in one hundred or .01. This is a rather acceptable quantitative expression of our uncertainty. We might also find it natural to say that if we have k tickets, the probability that we have the winning ticket is k divided by one hundred. Now we may compare other events with this lottery in the following format. Consider two opportunities:

A: A substantial prize if one of k tickets is the winning ticket.
B: The same substantial prize if it rains tomorrow (or if the market goes up next week, or if we get the contract, etc.).

One is then asked to find the value for k which will make these two opportunities equally desirable. If this value of k can be found, then there is some well-developed underlying theory which suggests that it would be reasonable to express our uncertainty about rain tomorrow by saying its probability is $k/100$. More precisely, the theory suggests it would be consistent to express our degree of belief in the statement "it will rain tomorrow" by the number $k/100$. The interesting result is that when people get used to the idea, the expression turns out to be an appealing and satisfying one, quite independent of the import of the underlying theory. This standard gamble method may seem cumbersome and difficult, but several experiments show that it is quite useful, even for naive and untrained subjects. Obviously when one becomes more accustomed to this mode of thought, the lottery may be abandoned and direct expressions of uncertainty will be easy and natural.

The point of course is not so much the methods which others have suggested, but the methods a person might devise for himself. More satisfying decisions are likely to emerge if we learn what we can from the work others have done, but feel very free to develop our own methods of expressing uncertainty. We need methods which will seem natural, usable, and worth the effort.

All this must begin with a willingness to test the hypothesis that uncertainty is a legitimate and expressible state of mind which is exceedingly common. It is important as well, to get used to the idea that there is no way to be proven right or wrong about one's expression of uncertainty in the light of what actually happens. It is hard for many of us to be accustomed to the idea that to have the opinion that the market is more likely to go up than down, is not in fact tested, proved, validated, or justified by what the market actually does. This is not to say that all opinions are equally good. Indeed, we test our expressions of uncertainty as well as we can by using the notion of "the reasonable man." Our reasonable man has several properties which may turn out to be acceptable standards for our own conceptualizing. Reasonable men, we often say, who have been exposed to similar experiences and similar evidence, will hold similar opinions. One tests one's opinion about the chances that a coin will come up heads on the next flip, by comparing one's uncertainty with that expressed by those who have lots of similar experience with similar coins. Indeed, this is the very grounds on which we come to accept so readily the notion that the coin is equally likely to come up heads or tails on the next flip.

We find reasonable men in some disagreement about the history of the moon because they have not been exposed to large amounts of similar experience and data. Thus we find those who have had the most experience to be those whose expressions of uncertainty we may wish to use. They are, in short, the experts. We also expect that reasonable men will not change their opinions unless confronted by relevant evidence. If evidence does appear, we expect their opinions to change in a reasonable direction. That is, we would not find it reasonable for a man, seeing a large number of successive heads when a coin is flipped, to change his mind in the direction of feeling that heads is less likely on the next flip than he had previously believed.

Expressing uncertainty is one thing and is perhaps useful by itself. To make a choice which is responsive to, consistent with, or reasonable in terms of the expressed uncertainty is often quite another thing. We know what to do if the market is almost certainly headed up and what to do if the market is almost certainly headed down. Most of us, however, feel a lot less clear about how to behave if the market is, in our opinion, a little more likely to go up than go down. If we have gone to the trouble of expressing the demand for a given product in the form of a table of quantities and their probabilities, it is not at all clear how to plan the production or inventory levels for the product. Much of life seems to come to us in terms of choices between a high probability of something pretty good and a low probability of something very much better. The financial environment seems to abound in opportunities that present a high probability of modest returns and opportunities which have a low probability of very high returns. Once we have made these uncertainties explicit we immediately become conscious of our style (or lack of it), for choosing in the face of alternatives thus structured. The fact that we often experience blocking in such situations tends to favor the suppression of uncertainty and the adoption of simpler views of the future more easily related to compatible and consistent courses of action. Our conceptions are naturally conditioned by the views to which we can readily respond, and few of us are naturally equipped to respond to probabilistic expressions of our uncertainty.

The payoff from explicitness comes from three more or less related possibilities which emerge from the rendering of our uncertainties. First, we can
be perceptive about our tolerance for uncertainty and test it for reasonableness. This fundamental aspect of style is closely related to the satisfaction we
take from our choice behavior. Second, we can begin to learn or change our
minds more reasonably by being somewhat clearer about the strength of our
original opinion and the corresponding weight which should be given to
additional information. These matters we have examined in some detail
already. Finally, we can develop a more explicit, and hopefully more coherent
style for deciding in uncertain situations. How do we actually make a commitment when we face uncertain alternatives?

There is no way best for all of us, only those ways which reflect our individual
attitudes, objectives, and standards. Sometimes we may simplify a complex
conceptualization of an uncertain choice by computing the average or expected
payoff for each opportunity and then choosing so as to maximize this quantity.
Mathematically, this implies computing the product of the probability of each
outcome times the payoff for the outcome and then summing the products over
all outcomes. If we consider a stock equally likely to go up ten points or down
two points, then its expected gain is

$$\tfrac{1}{2}(+10) + \tfrac{1}{2}(-2) = 4 \text{ points}$$

We might consider this a better buy than a stock whose expected payoff is 1
or 2 points in the same holding period. This is a fairly conventional way of
summarizing the desirability of a course of action, but one must be careful in
two respects. If the average or expected number of children per couple is 3.2,
there is no family that has this exact number. The average or expectation is an
index of desirability, not a statement of what will actually happen nor a
prediction about a single choice. It is true that if we made the same decision a
very large number of times and divided the total payoff obtained by the number
of choices, the result would likely be close to the average. Usually, however,
we make a decision a small number of times and this interpretation is not
especially satisfying. We notice this, for example, when we buy commercial fire,
automobile, or health insurance. The average or expected payoff to the policy-
holder is negative. The insurance companies, when all policyholders are considered, take in more in premiums than they pay out in claims. Yet in our own
individual case, this may be quite beside the point. We may need to be insured
in spite of the negativity of the expected return. Our objectives may be better
served if we can reduce the probability of a large loss which we can ill afford.
This is actually what the typical insurance policy does. We agree to accept a
certain small loss, the premium, in return for protection against an unlikely
large loss. This sort of reasonableness may be better described by imagining
our style to be couched in terms of aspiration levels. We try to minimize the
probability of having our loss exceed some chosen amount, or maximize the
probability of having our profit exceed some level of aspiration.

THE VARIABLE INTERVAL METHOD

This is one of the two most widely used methods of eliciting probabilities.
Essentially it involves the analyst subdividing the continuum into intervals of

varying width which are seen by the client as containing equal probability. Such an interview might go as follows:

Analyst: What sales volume would you say is as likely to have next year's sales fall above it as below it?

Client: Well that's hard to say. If I had to say something it would be about 5,000 units.

Analyst: Good. Now let's consider only the possibility that next year's sales will be above 5,000 units for a moment. Given that next year's volume is greater than 5,000 units, what level is equally likely to have actual sales above or below it?

As this process goes on the analyst is systematically dividing the continuum into unequal intervals which contain equal probabilities. As the interview progresses it may be useful for the analyst to feed back to the client some of the logical consequences of his responses as a way of checking for consistency, of giving the client an opportunity to learn about his own beliefs, and to assure the client that the object is to develop an encoding of uncertainty which he can live with. "Living with" here means being willing to make decisions in actual situations which are logically consistent with the consequences of his encoded uncertainty. It is clear that this sort of process is expensive and time consuming, thus we would want to undertake it only with those sources of uncertainty which are of central importance in any decision situation.

THE FIXED INTERVAL METHOD

In this method the analyst divides the continuum into intervals of equal length, and the client is asked to express his opinion about the probability that the variable in question will fall in each of the intervals. Suppose the analyst and the client find it comfortable to work with intervals such as

> less than 4000 units
> 4000 to 4200 units
> 4200 to 4400 units
> 4400 to 4600 units
> . . . and so on up to
> 5800 to 6000 units
> more than 6000 units

The interview might then continue as follows:

Analyst: Which of these intervals seems least likely to you?

Client: I guess it's least likely that sales will fall below 4000 units.

Analyst: Very good. Now what are the chances that such a low volume would occur as you see it?

Client: Well, only about one chance in twenty I'd say. About 5 percent chance.

Analyst: Fine. Now forget about sales below 4000 units for a minute. Which of the other intervals seem least likely to occur in your opinion?

Client: I'd have to think about that a little. I suppose the intervals 4000 to 4200 and 5800 to 6000 are about equal and less likely than the other ranges.

Analyst: That's great. Now, what are the chances of sales being in either one of those intervals?

Client: I'd say about one chance in ten for each of them.

Here again the analyst will want to feed back to the client some of the consequences of his responses from time to time to see if there is any desire on his part to change his mind. Decision analysts have accumulated considerable experience with these methods and find them to be generally satisfactory. It is to be strongly emphasized, however, that:

1. Encoding of uncertainty must follow considerable training, explanation, and clarification, especially with clients who have little relevant experience.
2. The client must be dealt with privately and patiently.
3. Considerable effort must often be invested in making clear to the client what is to be gained from all this effort, why he should make the effort, and what the payoff might be for him.
4. No encoding is likely to express the client's opinions the first time it is obtained. Every opportunity should be given the client to explore, check, revise, learn, and gradually develop an encoding he can live with.

GENERATING MANAGEMENT INTEREST

Experience suggests that some simple applications of uncertainty encoding are useful in obtaining management interest, in putting people at ease with uncertainty expression, and in providing an immediately useful result. One such application which may take a variety of particular forms is illustrated below. This application often elicits the response, "That's just what I'm doing in my own mind anyway." Such a response tends to dramatize to the manager that decision analysis is, to a great degree, the process of making explicit, clarifying, and giving consistency to decision processes which are naturally implicit.

One typical source of uncertainty is the many types of forecasts which managers routinely make in the conduct of their affairs. An extremely useful step in encoding this uncertainty is to compare past forecasts with actual events. This is done by the firm which follows up its capital investment decisions with a "post-audit," designed to see if their investments are performing in accordance with the forecasts on which the decisions were based. It is done by the company president who keeps track of his sales manager's forecasts and then compares them with actual sales data. This is espeically useful when forecasts are made repeatedly, and the actual events are observable within a reasonable period of time. Consider, for example, the jobbing foundry which forecasts the cost of producing various castings for its customers and then measures the actual costs of production. There are many instances in which firms forecast costs and then are able to observe the actual costs which result. In these situations it may be valuable to keep track of the effectiveness of the forecasts made as a basis for improving the process.

Let us suppose that it is possible in such a situation to obtain data on forecasted and actual costs for various jobs. Let

$$E_i = \text{forecast of the cost for job } i$$

$$A_i = \text{actual cost for job } i$$

$$e_i = \frac{E_i}{A_i} \text{ error ratio for job } i$$

Instead of using the ratio of forecast to actual cost as a measure of error, we might have used some other function such as

$$\frac{E_i - A_i}{A_i}$$

We will, however, proceed using e_i as previously defined. One might expect that, if e_i were obtained for a number of jobs and tabulated, it might be reasonably described by a probability distribution $f(e)$. Some statistical analysis would be necessary to support this supposition, since e_i might differ markedly among jobs of different sizes, types, or degrees of complexity. However, if we are able to obtain an $f(e)$ for the class of jobs under consideration, then it is useful to compute the mean and variance of the error ratio.

$$\bar{e} = \sum e f(e)$$

$$\sigma_e^2 = \sum (e - \bar{e})^2 f(e)$$

The mean of the error ratio, $\bar{e}$, provides a measure of the accuracy, bias, or validity of the forecasts. If the mean is equal to one, then we may say that our forecasts are accurate in the sense that, on the average, they are equal to the actual cost we are attempting to estimate. If the mean of the error ratio differs from one, the amount of this difference is a measure of the bias in our forecasting process. If, for example, $\bar{e} = 1.05$, then we may say that, on the average, our predictions are 5 percent too high. If this is the case then it would be sensible to correct our forecasts in the future to adjust for this bias. We might then work with a corrected forecast, E_i', computed from the relation

$$E_i' = \frac{E_i}{\bar{e}}$$

The alternative to this method might be to investigate the process in an attempt to trace back the source of this bias and correct it where it originates. This can be done only if the prediction process is explicit.

The variance of the error ratio is a measure of the precision of process. It reflects the pattern of dispersion of our forecasts in terms of the average of their squared deviation from their mean. This is also referred to as the reliability of the process.

There is no simple short-run way to overcome lack of precision. It may be taken directly into account in decision making. It may also be possible to review the process, looking for the steps which are the major contributors to the variance of our predictions, and seek to reduce this variance at its source. Time, experience, and the accumulation of larger samples of data should improve the precision of our predictions.

The point, however, is that very often the variance of the error is neglected entirely. When this happens, we have a typical example of the suppression of uncertainty and the resulting tendency to assume that the forecasting process is free of error. This, indeed, suggests the way in which many decisions under assumed certainty arise.

The considerable experience which decision analysts have accumulated in the difficult task of encoding probabilities clearly leaves much more to be learned. It is useful, however, to summarize what is generally known about this process on the basis of research so far reported.

1. The process must begin with a training step, especially for those clients having limited association with the concept of probability and the process of making their attitudes and judgments explicit. Training may vary all the way from formal class sessions to brief, personalized instructions relating probability to the encoding of uncertainty in the context of an immediate application.

2. Attention must be given to the prior step of motivating the client to take the effort seriously by indicating to him what the benefits might be.

3. The client must be given every opportunity to revise, to respond to feedback, and to realize that any given expression is not in any sense final.

4. The client should be clear that both data and experience are typically involved in encoding uncertainty. He should be aware of all the relevant data which can cost-effectively be made available. He should grasp the possibility of letting the probabilities be determined exclusively by the data, determined exclusively by his unaided experience in the absence of data, or, more commonly, by some combination of explicit data and experience.

5. The client should be given the opportunity to work with standard gamble methods, with the fixed interval or variable interval method, or with whatever method he finds most comfortable and most natural.

PROBLEMS

2–1. Assess your own probabilities and those of one or two other subjects in some of the contrasting situations listed below. What suspicions about the encoding process are generated by these situations?

a) A source of uncertainty with which you have considerable experience and one with which you have very little experience.

b) Before and after obtaining a small amount of relevant data about a source of uncertainty.

c) Before and after obtaining a large amount of relevant data.

d) A source of uncertainty modeled as a discrete random variable and one modeled as a continuous random variable.

e) An uncertain past event and an uncertain future event.

2–2. Assess the probabilities of three or four subjects with respect to some source of uncertainty for which you have available considerable relevant data. Then ask the subjects to examine the data and reassess their probabilities. What would you predict about their probability distributions as the amount of data increased?

2–3. Giving people forms to fill out as a method of eliciting their probability distributions has generally been quite ineffective, although it is appealing because of its low cost. What hypotheses would you suggest as potential explanations of the ineffectiveness of this method?

2–4. Listed below are several methods of probability elicitation. Design an experiment to determine which of these methods is the most effective. How should effectiveness be defined and measured? Would you expect effectiveness (as you define it) to depend on the particular decision maker involved? Would it depend on the particular source of uncertainty being considered?

   a) *Choice-Between-Gambles Technique for Deriving Probability Density Functions.* This method varies the probabilities in the hypothetical gamble and the level of the variable of interest to obtain a discrete probability density distribution.

   b) *Choice-Between-Gambles Technique for Deriving Cumulative Distribution Functions.* This method derives a discrete cumulative distribution function using a hypothetical gamble versus real-world gamble betting situation in successive stages.

   c) *Standard Lottery.* Probabilities are inferred based on the selection of a number of hypothetical lottery tickets chosen by the client from a lot of fixed size. The number of tickets chosen by the client for each defined level of the variable directly infers the client's opinion for the probability of realization of that variable value giving a discrete probability density function.

   d) *Direct Assessment of Probabilities.* The client himself describes the probabilities or probability density function associated with the variable of interest.

   e) *Fit Values to Given Shapes of Probability Density Functions.* The client is given a number of standard distribution functions and chooses, from among these functions, the one he thinks best approximates his opinion concerning the variable of interest, assigning the applicable values to that distribution function.

2–5. A number of computerized probability encoding programs have been developed which permit the decision maker to interact with a computer terminal. These programs ask the decision maker to respond to questions, permit changes and adjustments as the process goes on, and print out in both tabular and graphical form the resulting probability distributions. Outline the basic form and structure of such a probability encoding program. What considerations should be foremost in designing a probability encoding program? How could the effectiveness of such a program be defined, measured, and tested?

2–6. Below are several considerations which experienced decision analysts feel should be kept in mind when conducting a probability encoding interview. What other considerations might usefully be added to this list? Design an experiment to test the significance of these considerations.

   a) Do not lead the subject.

   b) Be sensitive to shifts in responses.

   c) Be sensitive to structural problems.

   d) Do not impose consistency.

   e) Elicit all responses as choices between two alternatives.

2–7. One of the persistent difficulties in encoding probabilities is the tendency for people, consciously or unconsciously, to bias their assessments when it appears to be in their own self-interest to do so. For example, a number of development engineers whose proposals were competing for limited funds, were asked to indicate in their proposals not only the cost but also their assessments of the probability of success of the work proposed. Design a system of incentives which would make it a matter of self-interest to these engineers to avoid bias in the probability assessments.

2–8. A major government agency asks potential contractors to include in their proposals not only costs and completion dates for the work on which they are bidding, but also the probability distributions of costs and completion dates. The agency then wishes to examine these probability distributions to see "whether or not they are correct and valid." What would be your advice to the agency in this matter?

2–9. Some people refer to "subjective" probabilities as estimates. What are they estimates of?

2–10. One of the useful training instruments for introducing people to the notion of probability assessment is presented in Exhibits 1, 2, 3. It consists of a list of declarative statements, a probability scaling sheet, and an analysis sheet. The subjects are instructed that they are to encode their uncertainty for each statement by choosing one of the five scales on the scaling sheet (Exhibit 2) on which to express it. These scales are (left to right):

> A three point qualitative scale
> A five point qualitative scale
> A line calibrated from 0 to 100
> Number of tickets in an indifference lottery
> Direct expression in numerical form

For each statement, the subject is asked to select a scale, express his uncertainty, or elect to make no response if one appears to be unusually difficult.

The analysis sheet is designed for the recording of simple counts of the number of responses made on each of the scales for various categories of statements. The categories are designed to suggest from very rough analysis of the responses. For example:

a) Comparing response total on all statements among subjects gives each subject some idea of his "ability" or "sophistication" in the expression of uncertainty relative to the others.

b) Analyzing responses by statement subject raises the hypothesis that they may depend on the subject's experience, knowledge, interest, or biases.

c) Comparing responses on the first eight questions with those on the last eight raises the question of whether or not any learning took place during the exercise.

Other similar, simple analyses will occur to the reader. It is useful to administer this instrument both to one's self and a few others. What does it tell you about your own style as an uncertainty assessor? What did you conclude about the amount of explanation required to administer it to others? How could the effectiveness of such a simple device as a training method be measured?

Exhibit 1. Declarative Statements

1. San Francisco will play in the next World Series.
2. A lot of product is known to be twelve percent defective. If two items are sampled from the lot, one will be good and one will be defective.
3. I will receive a salary increase of at least three percent within the next twelve months.
4. Our company's sales during the next calendar year will be greater than during the current calendar year.
5. Ohio State will win more games than Michigan next season.
6. If I were to throw an ordinary pair of dice, they would come up double threes.

7. If I were to select a card at random from a well shuffled pack, it would be either an ace or a heart.
8. The next time I travel from my home to work (school), it will take me longer than it did the last time.
9. Over 95 percent of our customers are generally satisfied with what we do for them.
10. A lot of product is known to be 2 percent defective. If two items are sampled from the lot, one will be good and one will be defective.
11. The color of the speaker's underwear is green.
12. A manned landing on Mars will be achieved by 1986.
13. The crime rate will be higher six months from now than it is today.
14. In five years fusion will be a larger energy source than will fission.
15. All major types of cancer will be successfully treated within ten years.
16. The next person to enter this room will be female.
17. The median weight of persons in this room is more than 160 pounds.
18. Since January 1, 1969, mutual funds have outperformed the DJIA.
19. Housing stocks will perform better than airline stocks in the next twelve months.
20. The DJIA will close up on the next business day following today.
21. Jack Nicklaus will play in the next Master's Tournament.
22. The winner of the 1966 NFL Championship was Green Bay.
23. During the coming fiscal year our trade balance with West Germany will be in our favor.
24. The next president of the United States will be a Democrat.
25. At no time during the next two years will unemployment drop below 4 percent.
26. The presidential nominee of the next Democratic convention will be a governor.
27. The senior senator from this state is generally opposed to free trade legislation.
28. If I flip an ordinary coin three times, it will come up heads twice and tails once.

Exhibit 2. Probability Scaling Sheet

Statement Number	Scale 1	Scale 2	Scale 3					Number of Tickets	Number
1	H M L	VH H M L VL	0	25	50	75	100		
2	H M L	VH H M L VL	0	25	50	75	100		
3	H M L	VH H M L VL	0	25	50	75	100		
4	H M L	VH H M L VL	0	25	50	75	100		
5	H M L	VH H M L VL	0	25	50	75	100		
6	H M L	VH H M L VL	0	25	50	75	100		
7	H M L	VH H M L VL	0	25	50	75	100		
8	H M L	VH H M L VL	0	25	50	75	100		
9	H M L	VH H M L VL	0	25	50	75	100		
10	H M L	VH H M L VL	0	25	50	75	100		
11	H M L	VH H M L VL	0	25	50	75	100		
12	H M L	VH H M L VL	0	25	50	75	100		
13	H M L	VH H M L VL	0	25	50	75	100		
14	H M L	VH H M L VL	0	25	50	75	100		
15	H M L	VH H M L VL	0	25	50	75	100		
16	H M L	VH H M L VL	0	25	50	75	100		

17	H M L	VH H M L VL	0 25 50 75 100	_____	_____
18	H M L	VH H M L VL	0 25 50 75 100	_____	_____
19	H M L	VH H M L VL	0 25 50 75 100	_____	_____
20	H M L	VH H M L VL	0 25 50 75 100	_____	_____
21	H M L	VH H M L VL	0 25 50 75 100	_____	_____
22	H M L	VH H M L VL	0 25 50 75 100	_____	_____
23	H M L	VH H M L VL	0 25 50 75 100	_____	_____
24	H M L	VH H M L VL	0 25 50 75 100	_____	_____
25	H M L	VH H M L VL	0 25 50 75 100	_____	_____
26	H M L	VH H M L VL	0 25 50 75 100	_____	_____
27	H M L	VH H M L VL	0 25 50 75 100	_____	_____
28	H M L	VH H M L VL	0 25 50 75 100	_____	_____

Exhibit 3.   Analysis Sheet

Scale Frequencies		No Response	Scale 1	Scale 2	Scale 3	Tickets	Number
1. All Statements							
2. Direct Experience:	8, 11, 16						
Cards, Dice, Coins:	6, 7, 28						
Sports:	1, 5, 21						
Stock Market:	18, 19, 20						
The Company:	3, 4, 9						
Politics:	24, 26, 27						
The Economy:	13, 23, 25						
Science and Technology:	12, 14, 15						
Sampling:	2, 10, 17						
3. Past Events	11, 17, 18, 22, 27						
Future Events	1, 4, 5, 8, 12						
4. Statements	1–8						
Statements	21–28						

SUGGESTIONS FOR FURTHER STUDY

Aigner, Dennis J. *Principles of Statistical Decision Making.* New York: The Macmillan Company, 1968.

Lindley, D. V. *Introduction to Probability and Statistics from a Bayesian Viewpoint.* Cambridge: Cambridge University Press, 1965.

Morgan, Bruce W. *An Introduction to Bayesian Statistical Decision Processes.* Englewood Cliffs: Prentice-Hall, Inc., 1968.

Raiffa, H., and R. Schlaifer. *Applied Statistical Decision Theory.* Boston: Division of Research, Graduate School of Business Administration, Harvard University, 1961.

Schlaifer, Robert. *Analysis of Decisions Under Uncertainty.* New York: McGraw-Hill, Inc., 1969.

GOALS, OBJECTIVES, AND ENCODING PREFERENCES 3

When a decision maker does not suppress his ignorance of the future but makes it explicit in the form of probabilities, then he faces what we are calling a decision under uncertainty. When the analyst works with a model of a decision in which several possible futures are recognized and the probabilities of these are explicitly stated, then the model is one of a decision under uncertainty. The probabilities may be based on explicit historical or experimental evidence, or on implicit managerial experience, or, most often, on some combination of the two.

Suppose, for example, that a firm is considering whether to bid on a government contract. To prepare the proposal will require an expenditure of some $20,000. If the award is won, a profit of $100,000 will result. We will suppose that the analyst estimates the probability of winning is about .50 and that the manager whom he advises agrees with this estimate. To make the decision explicit, we return to our basic model. There are two alternatives, to bid or not to bid, and two possible futures, win and lose. Using profit as a measure of value for the outcomes, the matrix appears below.

	$p_1 = .50$ $S_1 : Win$	$p_2 = .50$ $S_2 : Lose$
a_1: Bid	$100,000	$-$20,000
a_2: Do not bid	0	0

Generally, the model of a decision under uncertainty will include the following elements:

a_i = ith alternative course of action ($i = 1, ..., n$)

S_j = jth possible future ($j = 1, ..., m$)

θ_{ij} = outcome resulting from selecting action a_i when the future turns out to be S_j

$V(\theta_{ij})$ = value of outcome θ_{ij} to the decision maker

p_j = probability that future S_j will occur

The general form of such a decision is then represented by the matrix notation:

	p_1 S_1	p_2 S_2	p_3 S_3	p_4 S_4
a_1	$V(\theta_{11})$	$V(\theta_{12})$	$V(\theta_{13})$	$V(\theta_{14})$
a_2	$V(\theta_{21})$	$V(\theta_{22})$	$V(\theta_{23})$	$V(\theta_{24})$
a_3	$V(\theta_{31})$	$V(\theta_{32})$	$V(\theta_{33})$	$V(\theta_{34})$

Here

$$n = 3 \quad \text{and} \quad m = 4$$

For convenience we have written the probabilities immediately above the futures with which they are associated. When such a decision has been made explicit, the next question is how to process the data into a recommendation or explanation for management action. In the bidding decision introduced previously, a natural and conventional response is to compute the expected profit associated with each alternative and recommend to management the action having the largest expected profit. If the outcomes have been evaluated in terms of profit, then $E(a_i)$ will stand for the expected profit for the ith action.

$$E(a_i) = \sum_j V(\theta_{ij}) p_j$$

In the example we have

$$E(a_1) = \$100,000(.50) - \$20,000(.50)$$

$$= \$40,000$$

$$E(a_2) = 0$$

We might then recommend a_1, bid, to the manager, since it has the higher expected profit. We might, however, find that the manager rejects this advice and does not bid. Yet several other firms (operating, we will assume, from essentially the same model of the decision) do bid on the contract. Can it be that all of the firms have acted reasonably? Can we offer an explanation which is consistent with these differing conclusions? Clearly, we must look further into the matter for more is involved than we have so far made explicit in the decision matrix.

RESPONSES TO UNCERTAINTY

The variety of responses which decision makers exhibit in uncertain situations is sometimes bewildering. Some people have life, health, accident, and collision insurance, and some do not. Those who have these types of insurance have them in greatly varying amounts. Some investors own "growth" stocks, some prefer bonds, and perhaps the majority invest in a diversified portfolio of securities. Young men with neither obligations nor experience go into business for themselves, while older men with experience but with family obligations as well, do not. Some people are willing to enter hazardous occupations in return for higher monetary rewards; some are not. Some will take every opportunity to gamble, some will never gamble commercially, and many gamble sometimes. Can we understand all of these decisions in a way which will make them seem reasonable and in the best interests of the decision maker?

The reader might gain more direct insight by asking himself how he would choose in the following risky situations:

1. Suppose you are stranded in Las Vegas with $20 and no immediate source of further funds. It is very important to you to get to Los Angeles,

but you must have at least $40 to pay your fare. Would you be willing to bet your $20 on "red" at the roulette table? (See Chapter 1 for a model of the roulette decision showing that the expected dollar profit is negative.)

2. Suppose you have just arrived in Monte Carlo with enough money to make a long-anticipated tour of Europe, providing you budget carefully. A friend suggests that you put all your money on red at the roulette table, pointing out that if you win you can make the trip in style. Would you take his advice?

3. You go to your boss with a new idea for a major change in company policy. You feel that the idea has a fifty-fifty chance of succeeding. Your boss is dubious but agrees to give it a trial if you will show your confidence in the plan. He will double your salary if it succeeds but expects you to resign if it fails. You feel that your present salary is rather good, and it is your guess that you would be able to find another job paying at most three-fourths of your present salary. What would you do?

4. You have won, during an evening of poker, x dollars. As the game concludes, one of the other players asks if you will bet the x dollars on a single flip of a fair coin. Your profits for the evening are shown below.

	.50 Win	.50 Lose
Bet	$2x$	0
Do not bet	x	x

What would be your decision for various values of x?

People often choose to bet in situation 1, not to bet in situation 2, but in situation 3 it may be difficult to find a clear majority opinion. In the fourth case, many people will accept the bet if x is small, but as x grows larger they become unwilling to bet. Thus it would seem that the expected profit, 0 in this case, does not explain their choices, but rather the value of x itself is involved. Our task is to provide an explanation or theory which will make these choices appear consistent with the objectives and beliefs of the decision makers from which they came. We must understand something of what is going on here before we can make recommendations to management.

MANAGEMENT RESPONSES TO UNCERTAINTY

We seek a principle of choice which will use the data in a model of a decision to determine a preferred course of action. One may approach the understanding of a manager's attitude toward uncertainty using the following program. If the analyst could get data on the manager's preferences, then perhaps a model could be developed which would "explain" or agree with the observations and serve as a basis for predicting his preferences among outcomes beyond those observed. The analyst could then use the model as a basis for making recommendations which he predicts are consistent with the manager's values. If the analyst and the manager agree as to the alternatives, futures, and outcomes involved in the decision, and if the analyst's model of the manager's preferences is successful, then presumably the recommendation will be accepted. In this sense the recommendation would be consistent with the manager's own attitudes. He would want to accept the result because it is the same conclusion he himself would have reached had he taken the time to do the analysis which has been done for him. The manager might then be willing to delegate (perhaps with only perfunctory approval) those routine decisions for which the alternatives and outcomes can be determined by routine methods and for which the analyst's model of his preferences is applicable. This relieves the manager to devote more of his time to those difficult decisions which really require his experience and judgment. The manager may further become willing to accept the assistance of the analyst in finding consistent preferences among complex outcomes which are perhaps beyond his immediate experience. The analyst, beginning with simple expressions of preferences reflecting the manager's experience, reasons with the aid of the model to reach deductively consistent preference statements for complex outcomes. The manager may find that this relieves him of many hours of difficult study in complicated decision problems.

The study of management responses to uncertainty may be approached with a program similar in principle to this. Now, however, it will be useful to study a manager's attitude toward actions which involve probabilistic combinations of outcomes rather than sure outcomes as before. As will become evident, it is difficult to divorce a manager's attitude toward profit from his attitude toward the chances of making various amounts of profit. By studying his preferences in risky situations we will try to capture in a model his attitudes toward uncertainty, profit, and loss. As before, we will try to make some observations which will serve as a basis for such a model of how he responds in the face of uncertainty. Assuming the manager wishes to be consistent in the sense of not contradicting himself, he would be interested in accepting recommendations based on such a model. For the analyst, the model becomes a principle of choice which he uses to process the data describing a decision under uncertainty into a recommendation for management action.

DEVELOPING A MODEL OF ATTITUDES TOWARD UNCERTAINTY

Let us begin with some data indicating the responses of a particular manager to some uncertain alternatives. Suppose we confront this manager with two contracts (or gambles, or business opportunities) which are very simply described so as to make it reasonably easy for him to state his preferences. Contract A requires an investment of $100,000 the results of which depend on three possible future events. Possible future S_1 will bring the manager a profit of $200,000 if he accepts contract A, while possible futures S_2 and S_3 result in a complete loss of the original $100,000. Contract B requires an investment of $40,000 which will be lost in the event of S_3, but which will yield a profit of $70,000 in the case of either S_1 or S_2. The manager's decision is whether to accept contract A or contract B (but not both), or to accept neither. For convenience we will label the action "accept neither contract" with the name, contract C. We will suppose that the analyst and the manager agree that the probabilities (whatever their basis) are

$$p_1 = .50 \qquad p_2 = .10 \qquad p_3 = .40$$

The decision is summarized in the matrix below.

	$p_1 = .50$ S_1	$p_2 = .10$ S_2	$p_3 = .40$ S_3
Contract A	$200,000	−$100,000	−$100,000
Contract B	$ 70,000	$ 70,000	−$ 40,000
Contract C	0	0	0

Now we will suppose that the manager, confronted with these three mutually exclusive actions, is able after due consideration to express his preferences. Suppose, for example, he reports that he would most prefer contract B and would choose contract C (accept neither) in preference to contract A. Thus he ranks these actions

1. Contract B

2. Contract C

3. Contract A

Considering this statement as our empirical evidence, can we develop a model or principle of choice which will agree with it or "explain" it? Conventionally in decisions under uncertainty it is suggested that we compute the average or expected profit associated with each action, and choose so as to maximize this quantity. Does this principle provide a model consistent with the results of our experiment?
Let

$$E(a_i) = \text{expected profit for alternative } i \text{ (dollars)}$$

For contract A

$$E(A) = (.50)(\$200,000) + (.10)(-\$100,000) + (.40)(-\$100,000)$$
$$= \$50,000$$

For contract B

$$E(B) = (.50)(\$70,000) + (.10)(\$70,000) + (.40)(-\$40,000)$$
$$= \$26,000$$

For contract C

$$E(C) = 0$$

Summarizing these results and comparing them with the manager's reported preferences we have

Action	Expected Profit	Manager's Ranking
Contract A	$50,000	3
Contract B	26,000	1
Contract C	0	2

Clearly maximizing expected profit fails as a model of this manager's preferences in this experiment. Seeking further clues, perhaps we discuss the matter with him. Possibly he suggests something like this; "I would rather do nothing than accept contract A because, with the limited working capital we now have, the loss of $100,000 would put the firm in very serious trouble. A 50 percent chance of making $200,000 is not good enough to offset the 50 percent chance that we will lose the $100,000. On the other hand, contract B is acceptable because we could weather the loss of $40,000 well enough, and the chances of a profit are better." This manager seems "averse to uncertainty" in a rather reasonable way. To understand his behavior, we will have to consider the actions available to him not simply in terms of expected profit, but in terms of the possible profits and losses, together with the probabilities of each. However, the expected profit principle would have been satisfactory if the choice had involved only contracts B and C. We will return to this point later.

Suppose we had been able to arrange three new contracts labelled A', B', and C' whose conditions were

A': a loss of $200,000 with probability .35
a profit of $400,000 with probability .65

B': a loss of $200,000 with probability .28
a profit of $400,000 with probability .72

C': a loss of $200,000 with probability .30
a profit of $400,000 with probability .70

If we had asked him to rank these three mutually exclusive actions, the decision would have been both easy for him to make and easy for us to explain. The dollar amounts of profit and loss are the same for each contract, and surely a reasonable man would choose the contract which maximizes the probability of a $400,000 profit and minimizes the probability of a $200,000 loss. Thus we would expect the contracts to be ranked

Contract	Manager's Rank
A'	3
B'	1
C'	2

Now we will show a rather remarkable thing. The original decision among contracts A, B, and C can be reduced to the easy one among contracts A', B', and C' in a way which makes them equivalent in the opinion of a logically consistent manager. Such a manager would find himself indifferent between contract A and contract A' and thus consider the two equivalent. He would hold similar opinions about B and B', as well as C and C'. Thus if he were consistent he would prefer contract B' in the easy, reduced decision and contract B in the original decision. This scheme for reducing decisions to equivalent ones, in which the manager would choose so as to maximize the probability of a given amount of profit (or the probability of "success"), provides the basis for our model of his preferences.

To do this, we approach uncertain decisions from a somewhat different viewpoint. Suppose we may eventually be interested in the manager's attitudes toward contracts involving losses as great as $200,000 and profits up to $400,000. We take these two extreme amounts and form a basic contract or "reference" contract which we will use as a sort of measuring device. The basic contract is one which promises a profit of $400,000 with probability p, and a loss of $200,000 with probability $1 - p$.

We then approach the manager with the following question, "If you had already incurred a debt of $100,000, and someone offered to take over your obligation if you would enter into a contract which promised $400,000 with probability p and $200,000 loss with probability $1 - p$, what would the value of p have to be before you would just be willing to do this?" We suppose that after considerable reflection the manager is able to say that he would be indifferent if p were .40. We will interpret this result by saying, "He is indifferent between a sure loss of $100,000 and our basic contract with p, the probability of making $400,000, equal to .40." Let us call p the probability of success in the basic contract, for short.

Next, we ask him to suppose that he is offered the basic contract and he must choose between it and doing nothing. We wish to learn what the probability of success in the basic contract would have to be, before he would be willing just to accept it. We will suppose that he is able to say that if p were .70 he would be indifferent just between the basic contract and doing nothing. We repeat precisely the same sort of question for a loss of $40,000 and profits of $70,000 and $200,000. In each case we ask him to compare the amount in question for sure, against the reference or basic contract, and to report the value of p for which he would be indifferent. Let us imagine the results are those summarized below.

Outcome	Value of p in Equivalent Basic Contract
− $100,000	.40
− 40,000	.60
0	.70
70,000	.80
200,000	.90

Using this scheme it would be reasonable to expect indifference between a loss of $200,000 and the basic gamble with $p = 0$. Similarly, we would expect indifference between the basic contract with probability of success 1 and a sure $400,000 profit.

Consider now the matrix in which we summarized the original decision together with the preference statements we have subsequently obtained. The manager has indicated that he is indifferent between our basic contract with probability of success .90 and a sure profit of $200,000. We now suppose that if we alter the original decision by removing the $200,000 and replacing it with our basic contract having a probability of success of .90, we do not alter the value of alternative A in the opinion of the manager. That is, we assume that if the $200,000 profit in contract A is replaced by the basic contract with $p = .90$, then the manager's attitude toward alternative A remains unchanged. If, after all, he is indifferent in the way in which he has reported, then we should be able to make this change without altering his view of alternative A. Using this important assumption, we continue substituting for the outcomes in the original matrix, the various basic contracts for which he has indicated indifference. The transformed matrix now contains the alternatives A', B', and C'. It appears below.

	$p_1 = .50$ S_1	$p_2 = .10$ S_2	$p_3 = .40$ S_3
A'	Basic contract with $p = .90$	Basic contract with $p = .40$	Basic contract with $p = .40$
B'	Basic contract with $p = .80$	Basic contract with $p = .80$	Basic contract with $p = .60$
C'	Basic contract with $p = .70$	Basic contract with $p = .70$	Basic contract with $p = .70$

We suppose, it is to be emphasized, that the values of the alternatives A', B', and C' in the transformed matrix are the same for the manager as the values of the contracts A, B, and C in the original matrix. This supposition defines in part what we mean by a reasonable and consistent manager.

Now if he chooses contract A', he will receive a profit of \$400,000 with probability given by

$$(.50)(.90) + (.10)(.40) + (.40)(.40) = .65$$

and suffer a loss of \$200,000 with probability

$$(.50)(.10) + (.10)(.60) + (.40)(.60) = .35$$

This is equivalent to saying that if he chooses contract A it is quite the same as choosing the basic contract with a probability of success equal to .65. If he chooses alternative B' it is the same as choosing to receive \$400,000 with probability .72 and lose \$200,000 with probability .28. That is

$$(.50)(.80) + (.10)(.80) + (.40)(.60) = .72$$

$$(.50)(.20) + (.10)(.20) + (.40)(.40) = .28$$

Again this is equivalent to saying that choosing alternative B' is quite the same as choosing our basic contract with probability of success equal to .72. This, in turn, we take to be equivalent in the manager's opinion to choosing the original contract B. He has already stated that accepting neither contract A nor contract B is equivalent to accepting our basic contract with probability of success equal to .70. As before alternative C' in the transformed matrix is taken to be indifferent with respect to the original contract C (accept neither).

Now the decision represented by the transformed matrix appears quite obvious to the manager. He chooses alternative B' in preference to A' or C' since this maximizes his probability of success in the basic contract, or gives him the largest probability of making \$400,000 and thus the smallest probability of losing \$200,000. If he is consistent with his own basic expressions of preference, he will also choose contract B in the original decision. This is, in fact, what we observed.

What we have done is to reduce the original decision to an equivalent one involving only our basic alternative. Having done this, it seemed reasonable that the manager would choose so as to maximize the probability of success. If we wish to, we may assign this probability of success the name utility. The utility of any alternative is thus the probability of success in the equivalent or indifferent basic alternative.

Our results so far are summarized below.

Contract	Expected Dollar Profit	Manager's Rank	Utility
A	$50,000	3	.65
B	26,000	1	.72
C	0	2	.70

Put another way, he already indicated that he would prefer to do nothing rather than accept our basic contract unless the probability of success is at least .70. For contract A we were able to substitute an equivalent basic contract with a probability of success of only .65. Thus, if he were consistent he would do nothing rather than accept contract A. Contract B, however, could be reduced to an equivalent basic contract with a probability of success equal to .72. Thus consistency would suggest that he would choose contract B in preference to no contract at all. Since maximizing the probability of success in the basic alternative seems to describe or explain his behavior rather well, we can if we wish call this probability a utility and say that the manager chooses so as to maximize his utility.

It turns out thus that the zero point on our utility scale corresponds to a loss of $200,000, while a profit of $400,000 has a utility of 1.00. We shall see shortly that it makes no difference where we take the zero point and what we take to be one unit of utility. We are developing an interval scale which will perform satisfactorily with an arbitrary zero point and with an arbitrary but constant unit of measurement. In this respect it is like temperature measurement with Fahrenheit or Centigrade scales.

We discover, then, that, although a model based on maximizing expected dollar return does not seem to describe his attitudes, a model which attaches utilities to outcomes and contracts in the way we have described does indeed agree with his preferences (so far as we have observed them).

UTILITY

Now let us make some general statements about this method of assigning numbers, called utilities, to outcomes and contracts. Notice that we have assigned numbers or utilities to sure outcomes, say a profit of $200,000 for certain, as well as to contracts which were in fact uncertain alternatives, such as contract A. Now let us adopt the term "prospect" to stand for either of these, and use the symbol $U(P)$ to stand for the utility of a prospect P.

Generalizing from our work so far, we could suggest that our method of assigning utilities has the property

$$U(P_1) > U(P_2)$$

if and only if the manager prefers the prospect P_1 to the prospect P_2. This is true on the basis of our observations so far, and if he acts in a consistent fashion, it will be true in general. Thus our model predicts that if he acts consistently, he will always choose the prospect which maximizes his utility.

Notice also a second property of this scheme. We have assigned the following utilities:

$$U(-\$100,000) = .40$$

$$U(\$200,000) = .90$$

$$U(\text{Contract } A) = .65$$

Now suppose instead of computing the expected dollar return for contract A, we compute the *expected utility*.

$$\text{Expected Utility of Contract } A = (.50) U(-\$100,000) + (.50) U(\$200,000)$$

$$= (.50)(.40) + (.50)(.90)$$

$$= .65$$

Thus, under this scheme for assigning utilities, the utility of a risky alternative is equal to its expected utility. While our expected dollar return model did not work, an expected utility model does. Thus we may reach the following important conclusion about decisions under risk: *A manager who wishes to act in a logically consistent way in any decision under uncertainty will choose the alternative which maximizes his expected utility.*

If we could measure a manager's utilities in this way, then the problem of a principle of choice for decisions under uncertainty would be solved. Before examining the possibilities of applying this scheme in actual management situations, let us sharpen our understanding of it.

First let us show that the zero point and the unit of measurement on the utility scale make no difference in the results. We chose $-\$200,000$ as the zero point and $\$400,000$ as the unit point because it was convenient. They represented the extremes of the range in which we expected to deal. Now suppose we change the unit of measurement by multiplying all the utilities by a positive constant and change the zero point on the scale by adding a constant to all the utilities. Under this transformation the utility of a prospect $U(P)$ becomes $a + bU(P)$. Under our method of assigning utilities, the utility of a prospect is equal to its expected utility. Thus

$$U(A) = (.50) U(-\$100,000) + (.50) U(\$200,000) = .65$$

$$U(B) = (.40) U(-\$ 40,000) + (.60) U(\$ 70,000) = .72$$

For the manager whom we studied we might transform the utility scale by multiplying by a positive constant b and adding a constant a. Calling the transformed utility scale U', we have

$$U'(A) = (.50)\{a+bU(-\$100,000)\} + (.50)\{a+bU(\$200,000)\}$$

$$= a + bU(A)$$

and similarly

$$U'(B) = a + bU(B)$$

Thus any decision consistent with the original utility scale will also be consistent with the transformed utility scale. Incidentally, one should note that the choice of the reference contract does not limit the range of amounts of money which can be considered. If we wished to measure the utility of $500,000 using the original reference contract which involved a loss of $200,000 and a profit of $400,000, we might confront the decision maker with the following choice:

a_1: a loss of $200,000 with probability $1-q$
a profit of $500,000 with probability q

a_2: a sure profit of $400,000

When the decision maker reported the indifference value of q, we could then set the utilities of the two actions equal.

$$U(a_1) = U(\$500,000)\,q = U(a_2) = 1.00$$

It would then follow that

$$U(\$500,000) = \frac{1.00}{q}$$

As we would expect, the utility assigned to $500,000 would be a number greater than one. Thus there is no logical limitation on the range of application of a reference contract.

GRAPHICAL REPRESENTATION

We can get a further look at this manager's attitudes toward risk by plotting the utilities of the various amounts of money we have measured. This is done in Figure 3-1 where we have also taken the liberty of passing a smooth curve through the points. It is now clear that the value of money for this man, as we have measured it, is not proportional to the amount of money. His utility function exhibits a diminishing marginal utility for money. That is, the more money he has, the less the utility of an additional dollar.

Now consider contract A which involves a profit of $200,000 with utility .90 (point a on the utility function) and a loss of $100,000 with utility .40 (point b). Now let q be the probability with which the profit of $200,000 is received. For any q we could compute the expected dollar return from contract A:

$$q(\$200,000) + (1-q)(-\$100,000)$$

and the expected utility for contract A:

$$q(.90) + (1-q)(.40)$$

The utility of the contract is, as we have shown, equal to its expected utility. We now plot the points whose coordinates are the expected dollar returns and the expected utilities for values of q from zero to one. These points will fall on a straight line between a and b. The reader who is not convinced of this should explore the matter through problem 3-2. The original value of q, which was .50, results in a point halfway between a and b, marked A. The coordinates of this point A are the expected dollar return for contract A, \$50,000, and its utility (or expected utility), .65. Contract B is represented in similar fashion by point B; and accepting neither contract, assuring a net gain of zero dollars, is represented by point C lying right on the utility function. Now the diagram shows what we have already discovered: The dollar expectation for A is greater than that for B, and both are greater than zero. The utility for A is less than the utility of C, while the utility of B is greater than that of C.

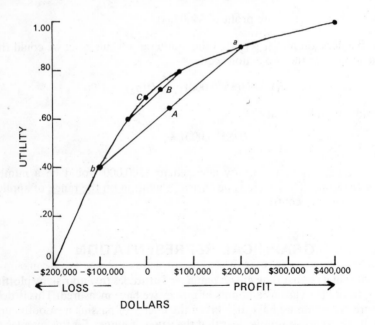

Figure 3-1.   The Manager's Utility Function

Notice also that if we consider prospects of the form:

a profit of K with probability .50
a loss of K with probability .50

these prospects have zero expected dollar return. As the value of K is increased from zero, the utility of the resulting prospect decreases. Notice also that as K increases the variance of the dollar return increases. Thus we could say that for a given expected dollar return, the manager would prefer the prospect with the smallest variance of the dollar return. This is another characteristic which is described by the term "risk aversion." This manager does not like to take chances if he can avoid it, and he seeks certainty in his undertakings.

OTHER TYPES OF ATTITUDES

Suppose the results of our utility measuring effort had been different. The utility function in Figure 3-2 describes the attitudes of a manager who does not feel that the amounts of loss involved in the contracts are such as to put his firm in serious difficulties; thus he is not averse to taking risks if the expected dollar return is positive. For this manager the utility of money is proportional to the amount, and the expected utility is proportional to the expected dollar

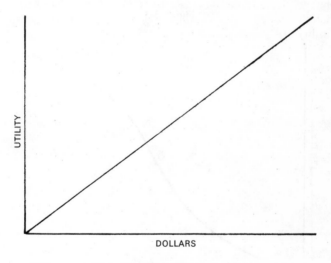

Figure 3-2

return. Such a man, if he acts consistently will want to choose so as to maximize expected dollar return. The analyst need not be concerned about establishing a utility scale, since it will differ from the dollar scale only by multiplication by a positive constant and addition of a constant.

The manager whose utility function appears in Figure 3-3 is a different man entirely. He very much wants to make large profits but is somewhat unconcerned about large losses. He welcomes opportunities to take risks, loves to gamble, and is willing to play long shots. Notice that a prospect promising a profit of D dollars certain, has a lower utility than a prospect having an expected dollar profit of D. For a given expected dollar return, this man prefers the prospect with the highest variance of dollar return.

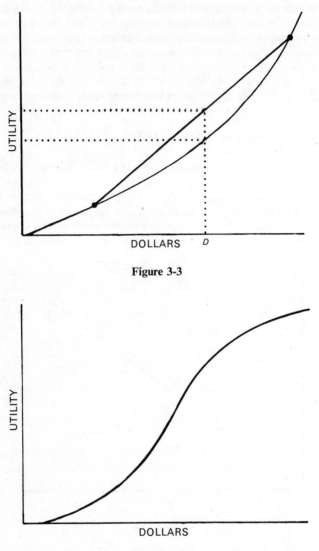

Figure 3-3

Figure 3-4

Finally, Figure 3-4 suggests a sort of utility function for which there is some experimental confirmation. This manager is willing to take gambles involving small amounts of money but not those involving large dollar amounts.

MISTAKES

The utility model we have outlined is subtle in its implications, and sometimes mistakes are made in using it. For example:

1. We do not want to fall into the habit of saying that P_1 is preferred to P_2 because $U(P_1) > U(P_2)$. Indeed, it is just the other way around: utilities represent and predict preferences; they do not cause them.
2. We cannot generally say that

$$U(P_1 \text{ and } P_2) = U(P_1) + U(P_2)$$

This will be true only if the utility function is linear. Note that in Figure 3-1

$$U(\$400,000) = 1.00$$

while

$$U(\$200,000) + U(\$200,000) = .90 + .90 = 1.80$$

3. We have so far considered the utility function for particular types of risky actions. We cannot be sure how far these results may be generalized. For example a given manager may be willing to accept contract *B* if it is a venture into the securities market but not if it represents a bet on a horse race.
4. Different people will be described by different utility functions, although we may be able to identify classes of people or firms that may be described by similarly shaped utility functions. We cannot, however, argue that if a gain of $1,000 increases one man's utility by .3 units, while a loss of $1,000 decreases another man's by .2 units, then society will be better off if we take this amount away from the second man and give it to the first. That is, we cannot make interpersonal comparisons of utility.
5. Utility is not an inherent characteristic of people nor of prospects. It is a model which the analyst uses to describe people's preferences or decisions among prospects.

UTILITY MEASUREMENT IN PRACTICE

The method of assigning utilities which has been outlined is useful for gaining understanding and insights into the decisions made by managers in the face of uncertainty. One can "explain" decision-making behavior in past decisions and predict consistent choices in future decisions. If the analyst and the manager have the same image or model of a decision and if the manager wishes to act consistently in the sense of the model of his preferences, then the predictions would presumably turn out to be correct. The manager would want to accept the analyst's recommendations. In this sense, the problem of the analyst in dealing with decisions under uncertainty would be "solved." He could provide the manager with consistent recommendations for action in complex decisions, thus relieving the manager for more troublesome problems.

If one could, within the limitations of time and effort imposed by the on-going affairs of business, measure the manager's utilities, one would clearly find it useful to do so. But what of the difficulties of dealing with an actual managerial situation in this way? Could this actually be done? At best it would appear difficult.

The axioms which lead to this method may be very roughly stated as follows:

1. The decision maker can make a complete and transitive ranking of the outcomes.
2. Any prospect or gamble involving equally desirable outcomes is just as desirable as either outcome by itself.
3. If outcomes A, B, and C are ranked so that A is preferred to B, B is preferred to C, and A is preferred to C, then a gamble exists involving A and C which is just as desirable as B.
4. If A and B are equally desirable then the gamble $pA + (1-p)C$ is just as desirable as the gamble $pB + (1-p)C$.

If these axioms hold, then the existence of the utility scale can be shown. The question of interest is whether these axioms do hold in the firm and whether the decision maker can answer questions of the sort indicated previously.

Would the manager be willing to answer the rather large number of questions one would have to ask? Could one put the questions in a meaningful way? Would the manager try to put the analyst off with casual responses, rather than serious consideration? Could he correct the intransitivities and other inconsistencies in his answers? Would his responses be reliable or would distractions lead to errors in the sense of different responses to the same question on different occasions?

Note also that, in presenting the method, we have assumed that the profit and loss aspect of the outcomes alone was relevant. Are there other aspects beside money which have value for him? We have not considered the problem of multiple goals which was raised earlier. If there are other aspects of the outcomes which concern him, then we would have to identify these in order to predict future choices.

Without prejudging whether it is possible to obtain a manager's utility to a useful degree of approximation with a reasonable expenditure of time and effort, we will suggest some "practical" approximations to this procedure. These approximations are in the form of principles of choice which are related to utility maximization in various ways, but which substitute the judgment of the analyst for the detailed construction of a utility function. These principles reflect practice in the sense that they describe the ways in which analysts often deal with decisions under uncertainty. Like utility maximization itself, they have two important uses. On the one hand they may be thought of as suggestions as to how one might proceed to make a decision under conditions of uncertainty. That is, each principle may be interpreted as a recommendation which a decision maker is invited to follow. On the other hand they may offer some assistance in explaining or understanding the decisions which we see people making around us.

DOMINANCE

The first step in making a decision under uncertainty is to eliminate from consideration any alternatives which are clearly not to be chosen no matter what principle of choice is used. The relation of dominance is useful in formulating our common sense in this respect. In the following simple decision, the profits for three alternatives and three possible futures are shown.

	p_1 S_1	p_2 S_2	p_3 S_3
a_1	$5	$1	$ 8
a_2	9	4	2
a_3	6	8	10

Inspection reveals immediately that no matter what possible future is considered, more profit is to be obtained from a_3 than from a_1. Thus a_1 would never be chosen in preference to a_3, and a_1 may be eliminated from further consideration. In such a case we say that a_3 dominates a_1, or that a_1 is dominated by a_3. To state the dominance relation more explicitly we might say, "If there are two alternatives a_g and a_h, such that

$$V(\theta_{gj}) \leqslant V(\theta_{hj}), \text{ for all } j$$

then a_g is dominated by a_h, and a_g may be eliminated from further consideration." Our first step is thus always to dispose of any dominated alternatives. If, after repeated applications of the principle of dominance, we are left with only one alternative, then it is clearly the preferred course of action. In general, this will not be the case, and other principles of choice may be brought to bear. All one needs to know to apply the relation of dominance is that the manager in this decision prefers more money to less of it. Dominance really requires only a ranking of the outcomes and is thus rather easy to discover. It is usually a more or less automatic simplification of the decision which is made in the preliminary stages of developing the model.

EXPECTED PROFIT

Possibly the most common principle of choice in practice suggests that the manager choose the action which maximizes expected profit or minimizes expected loss. We have already seen a case in which this was not satisfactory, but arguments can be given to justify its use in certain other situations. We assume for the present that the dollar consequences of outcomes are the only consequences of concern to the manager.

Suppose we are concerned with a routine decision under uncertainty in a large corporation. The maximum possible profit in the decision is $100 and the maximum possible loss is $50. We are thus interested in the manager's utility function for money in the range from a loss of $50 to a profit of $100. We hypothesize that whatever the shape of his utility function we will make only negligible errors if we approximate it by a straight line in this range. The smaller the range between minimum and maximum profits in a decision, the better will be a straight line approximation to the utility function. Thus it is argued that over a small range, maximizing expected profit will yield much the same decisions as maximizing utility or expected utility. For this reason, decisions involving moderate dollar consequences can be well understood by maximizing expected profit. As long as the analyst deals with such "small" decisions, he can deal with expected profits and be freed of the necessity for measuring the manager's utility function. The manager in turn is freed from small routine decisions, so that he may bring his judgment to bear on large important decisions. Just how to divide decisions into classes such that some may usefully be treated as expected profit maximizing problems while others require utilities, cannot be indicated precisely. The judgment and experience of the analyst together with the behavior of the manager must resolve this question in each business situation.

In future discussions we will generally assume that the term "expectation principle" refers to maximizing expected profits or minimizing expected losses. The symbol $E(a_i)$ will be used to refer to the expected profits or expected losses associated with the ith action.

Let us pause briefly to consider one of the arguments which sometimes arises in connection with any principle of choice which suggests that expectation maximizing is a reasonable guide for decision making. To be specific, consider a class of decisions in which dollar amounts are not large and the analyst suggests maximizing expected dollar return as a guide for behavior. Suppose a person had not arrived at this point by conceiving of it as an approximation to utility maximization as we have but simply encounters the suggestion that he "ought" to choose in decisions under uncertainty so as to maximize dollar expectation. He may well confront us with the basic objection that the expectation or average has empirical meaning only if a very large number of decisions are involved. If one or a small number of decisions are made, the actual or sample average of the outcomes may differ widely from the expectation as defined above. Thus, if we begin flipping a fair coin we know the expected number of heads is one half of the number of flips, but we would have to perform a very large number of flips to consistently observe this result. This notion is also familiar in the context of sampling. We know that the larger the sample we observe, the more likely it is that the sample average will be close to the population average. The best way to make this clear is to return to the statistician's definition of this property of the average, one form of which is called the weak law of large numbers.

The Weak Law of Large Numbers. Suppose x is a random variable with expected value $E(x)$ and that we observe successive values of x, say $x_1, x_2, x_3, ..., x_n$, where these values of x are independent. Then for every $e > 0$ as $n \to \infty$

$$\text{Probability}\left\{\left|\frac{x_1 + x_2 + x_3 + \cdots + x_n}{n} - E(x)\right| > e\right\} \to 0$$

In words, this says that the probability of the observed average differing from the expectation by any amount, e, approaches zero as the number of observations increases toward infinity. Notice that even this does not say the sample average will certainly be close to the expectation, but only that the probability of it being otherwise is very small for large n. Now this can be applied directly to a sequence of identical decisions whose outcomes are independent. Suppose on each of these decisions we choose a_i and that the value of the outcome of this choice is a random variable $V(\theta_{ij})$. The law would then say, for every $e > 0$ as $n \to \infty$

$$\text{Probability} \left\{ \left| \frac{V_1(\theta_{ij}) + V_2(\theta_{ij}) + \cdots + V_n(\theta_{ij})}{n} - E(a_i) \right| > e \right\} \to 0$$

where $V_1(\theta_{ij})$ is the value of the outcome of the first decision, $V_2(\theta_{ij})$ is the value of the outcome of the second, and so forth. Thus we could say that the average of the outcomes of our decisions on which we choose a_i is very likely to be close to $E(a_i)$ in the long run. Unfortunately this says nothing about what will happen in the short run if we make only one or a few decisions. Note also that the law applies, as we have given it, only to decisions whose outcomes are independent.

If a decision maker is making a large number of decisions or is willing to behave as though this were the case, then maximizing expectation has much appeal. Using the Weak Law of Large Numbers, we can establish the following result.

Law of Long-Run Success.   Consider a sequence of identical decisions whose outcomes are independent. Let S_n' be the sum of the values of the outcomes of the first n decisions when the principle of maximizing expectation is used, and let S_n be the sum of the values of the outcomes of the first n decisions when *any other* principle of choice is used. Then as $n \to \infty$

$$\text{Probability} \{S_n' > S_n\} \to 1$$

In words this means that the sum of the values of the outcomes of a series of decisions is greatest if we maximize expectation, with probability approaching one as the number of decisions increases. Clearly this is a very powerful result if one is confronted with a large number of decisions.

On the basis of these two results one can argue that maximizing expectation is clearly advantageous in the long run, but means nothing over the short run, or with one or a few decisions. To this common argument we might respond in the following ways:

1. In measuring the manager's attitude toward uncertainty we did not ask him how he would behave in the long run, but rather what his preferences were in one-time decisions under uncertainty. We were able to assign utilities so that his preferences were reflected by numbers which happened to be equal to expected utilities. All this was done with no reference whatsoever to long-run effects. Thus expected utility is a guide, an index, or an indicator which he will maximize if he acts in one-time decisions consistently with his own stated preferences. Insofar as we consider dollar expectation maximizing as an approximation to utility maximizing, the same statements hold. Dollar expectation is a guide to behavior, an index number, or indicator which he will want to maximize if he is to be consistent with himself.

2. When we report to a manager that he should choose a particular risky action and the expected dollar return associated with that action is $1,000, we should be careful to avoid having him get the impression that he will soon receive exactly $1,000. If the decision is to be repeated a large number of times, then he may, if he wishes, interpret the $1,000 as a

limit approached by the average profit per decision; but in the short run it is not necessarily the amount of any transaction which he will experience. For example, if we recommend to a manager that he undertake a risky action which promises a loss of $200 with probability .50 and a profit of $2,200 with probability of .50, then on no instance on which he takes such an action will he receive $1,000. Furthermore, it is important for the manager to understand that if he takes the recommended action once and loses $200, or even loses $200 several times in succession, this does not necessarily prove that our recommendation was "wrong." It may remain the action which is logically consistent with his own preferences.

3. If, however, a decision is to be repeated a large number of times, then the Law of Long-Run Success suggests that with probability approaching one his total profit will be greatest if he chooses so as to maximize expected profit. But this is equivalent to saying that in the long run there is increasingly little uncertainty associated with his total profit. Thus maximizing total profit by means of an expected profit principle will have the effect of maximizing the manager's utility. Thus we could argue that whether a decision is to be made once or whether it is to be made many times, *the consistent principle* is utility maximization. Further, in the long run maximizing expected profit results in maximizing utility.

THE MOST PROBABLE FUTURE PRINCIPLE

The utility maximizing principle provides a way of simplifying the complex elements of a decision under uncertainty to a single number for each alternative, the largest of which indicates the consistent choice. Maximizing dollar expectation is likewise a scheme for simplifying the complex fabric of real decision situations. The key, as we have said, to understanding management decision making is to understand what simplifications are involved. There are many other modes of simplification, three examples of which we shall illustrate. One response to a decision under uncertainty is, of course, to suppress the uncertainty entirely, transforming it into a decision under assumed certainty. Indeed it may be useful to think of this mode of simplification of uncertainty as the way (explicitly or implicitly) in which decisions under assumed certainty arise. In a decision under assumed certainty, we are not troubled about the nonlinearity of a manager's utility function. If the outcomes are expressed in dollars, maximizing dollars will have the same result as maximizing utility as long as the utility function has a nonnegative slope. This of course does not free us from the problems of multiple goals.

This principle suggests that, as the decision maker confronts the various possible futures, he simply overlooks all except the most probable one and behaves as though it were certain. More explicitly, find the S_j for which p_j is maximum, and for this possible future select the alternative i which will maximize $V(\theta_{ij})$. This principle is not very appealing if the analyst has already obtained estimates of the probabilities of a number of possible futures. It is usually more satisfactory in that case to use them all with the expectation principle, rather than throwing them out except for the largest and setting it equal to one. However, many decisions are based upon this principle since in fact only the most probable future is really studied. For example, many decisions to embark on new ventures are made only on the basis of what will happen if the venture succeeds, although there is almost always some nonzero probability that the venture will fail. Again, most decision makers would agree that there is some nonzero probability of a war in any given year, although they may make all their decisions as though peace were assured. In almost all decisions there are possible futures which we choose to neglect because they seem to have small probability. The most probable future principle clearly seems most appealing where there is some future whose probability far exceeds that of all the others, and where the outcomes of all possible futures are of roughly the same order of magnitude. In decisions where the possibility of catastrophe is present though with small probability, the order of magnitude of the loss might be so large that we could not neglect it. Thus, the firm may make such decisions to insure itself against fire.

On the other hand it may be used to explain a man's decision to drive to work in the morning. He knows that there is some nonzero probability that he will meet death in a fatal accident on the way, yet he does not consider this possibility every time he gets into his car. He considers only the most probable future, that he will make the trip safely. Thus he is freed from the anguish of considering the value of his own life and how the probabilities of preserving it depend on his driving habits and the like.

We hypothesize that much of the suppression of risk which occurs in decision making can be understood in terms of the most probable future principle. Sometimes we will deal with a variant of this principle which suggests that only the expected outcome or average outcome be considered and the decision again be treated as a decision under assumed certainty. For example, a manager planning production for the coming year might plan as though sales were going to be a single known quantity, perhaps equal to the expected value of past sales.

THE ASPIRATION LEVEL PRINCIPLE

The dollar expectation principle simplifies decisions by making a linear approximation to the manager's utility function. The most probable future principle suppresses the risk entirely. Now instead of making a linear approximation to the utility function, we might simplify it even further by representing it by a function which took on only two values. We might for example use the function

$$U(x) = K \qquad \text{for } x \geqslant A$$

$$U(x) = k \qquad \text{for } x < A$$

where x is the amount of a dollar profit or loss and $K > k$. The number A receives the name aspiration level. Since we have shown that we can do no harm by changing the zero point and unit point on our utility scale, we can let

$$K = 1 \qquad \text{and} \qquad k = 0$$

Now for any risky action which promises a value of $x \geqslant A$ with probability p and a value of $x < A$ with probability $1-p$, the utility (or expected utility) will be given by

$$p(1) + (1-p)(0) = p$$

and maximizing utility will become equivalent to maximizing the probability of achieving or exceeding the aspiration level A.

Just what value of A to use in any decision situation is a matter which can be answered only by attempting to learn about a manager's preferences. One might hypothesize, however, that in a wide variety of situations it would be far easier to get a manager to classify outcomes as "acceptable" or "not acceptable," than it would be to obtain his utility function. Psychologists exploring decision-making behavior have found the concept of aspiration level a very useful one. One proposal, which has had some confirmation, is that the aspiration level be taken to be the point of inflection on a utility function of the sort shown in Figure 3-4. The resulting approximation is suggested by Figure 3-5.

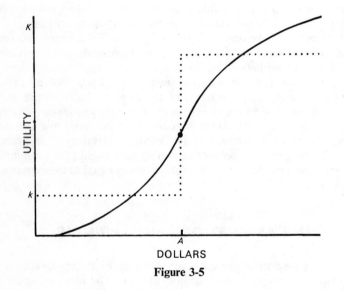

Figure 3-5

It is possibly true that some form of aspiration level principle is the most widely used of all principles in management decision making. An aspiration level is simply some level of profit which the decision maker desires to attain, or some level of cost which he desires not to exceed. The aspiration level may also be stated in terms of other criteria which are more or less related to cost or profit, as, for example, the firm which attempts to keep its facilities operating at a level of 70 percent capacity at least. For a decision under uncertainty, an aspiration level policy might be expressed as follows. For a given aspiration level, A, select the alternative which maximizes the probability that the outcome will be equal to or greater than A.

Many decisions which fall into the general class of control decisions utilize standards against which actual performance is judged. If the actual performance meets the standard, we decide not to take any action, but if not, some control action may be taken. In designing and operating the system which is thus controlled, one tries to select alternatives which will maximize the probability of having the system meet the standard. The whole idea of a standard which plays such an important part in these decisions is, of course, simply an aspiration level. Management uses standards for almost everything. Thus we have standard costs, standards for output, standards for quality, standards for personnel selection, standards for the performance of salesmen, and so forth. When the standard is met, we are satisfied; when it is not, we decide to take some sort of corrective action. This is the fundamental principle of management by exception.

There are several situations in which an aspiration level is appealing.

1. When it is costly or difficult to discover what the alternative courses of action are, we may wish to search for alternatives only until one is found which gives a reasonable probability of achieving the aspiration level. This may be more economical than an extensive search for the alternative which can be shown to maximize expectation, for example.
2. Sometimes it is difficult or impossible to evaluate the outcomes in a decision. It may be possible, however, to classify the outcomes into two groups, those which meet the aspiration level of the decision maker, and those which do not. Then the reasonable choice becomes the alternative which maximizes the probability of achieving the aspiration level. Thus, we may classify the outcomes of a decision into the categories "success" and "failure" and attempt to maximize the probability of success.
3. Sometimes the alternatives are of a transient nature and may not in fact be accumulated until one is ready to make a maximizing choice. Thus, when a person sells a house he may obtain a number of offers spread over a period of time, but each offer must be accepted within, say a 24-hour limit or it lapses. Here an aspiration level is almost essential. This problem is closely related to those presented later in the chapter on purchasing policy.

STOCHASTIC DOMINANCE

If some alternative, a_i is preferred using the aspiration level principle for all aspiration levels, then a_i is said to be stochastically dominant. This means that for any payoff one might specify, the probability of achieving that payoff at least, is greater for a_i than for any other alternative. Most people find stochastic dominance a very appealing principle once it is explained to them. It seems to occur surprisingly often.

An easy way to recognize stochastic dominance is to plot the complementary cumulative of the payoff distribution for each course of action in a decision situation. Figure 3-6 shows density functions and complementary cumulatives in a case where stochastic dominance occurs, and Figure 3-7 shows a case in which it does not. The reader may wish to explore the relationship of stochastic dominance to ordinary dominance by means of problem 3-46.

EXPECTATION-VARIANCE PRINCIPLES

We noticed earlier that for a decision maker whose utility function for money exhibited decreasing marginal utility (Figure 3-1) the utility of a prospect was related in part to the variance of profit. In particular, if one considered several prospects, all having the same expected profit, the utility would be greatest for the prospect having the smallest variance of profit. Thus, if one believed that a decision-maker's utility function for money did increase at a decreasing rate, one could make the following predictions without actually quantifying the utility function more precisely:

1. If two actions have the same expected profit, the one having the smaller variance of profit will be preferred.
2. If two actions have the same variance of profit, the one having the larger expected profit will be preferred.

We can generalize this notion in the following interesting way. Consider an action which will produce a profit x with probability $f(x)$. Let

$U(a)$ = the utility of this action

$E(a)$ = the expected profit associated with this action

$$= \int_x xf(x)\,dx$$

σ^2 = the variance of the profit

$$= \int_x [\{x - E(a)\}^2]f(x)\,dx$$

The utility function, $U(a)$ could be expanded as a Taylor series giving

$$U(a) = U(c) + (x-c)\frac{dU(c)}{dx} + \tfrac{1}{2}(x-c)^2\frac{d^2U(c)}{dx^2} + \cdots$$

where c is a constant. Now let $c = E(x)$ and take the expected value of both sides of the foregoing equation.

$U(a)$ = Expected utility of a

$$= U[E(x)] + \tfrac{1}{2}\sigma^2\frac{d^2U[E(x)]}{dx^2} + \cdots$$

This gives the utility of any probability distribution of money returns, in terms of the mean and variance of the distribution. If the phenomenon of diminishing marginal utility of money is present, then the second derivative of the utility function will be negative. Thus, for equal expectations, the firm would attempt to minimize the variance of the money return.

Now clearly one cannot compute $U(a)$ by this method unless the utility function is known to the extent that its second derivative at the point $E(x)$ can be estimated. However, the following expedients may be helpful. In decisions involving consequences of sufficient magnitude that the analyst does not wish

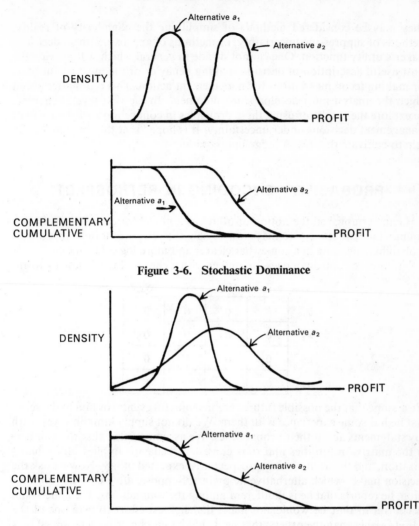

Figure 3-6. Stochastic Dominance

Figure 3-7. Absence of Stochastic Dominance

to base his recommendation on expected profit alone, the variance of profit might be computed. Perhaps some actions can be eliminated on the basis of two simple situations noted above. Beyond this, the computation and reporting of profit variances may serve to sharpen the insights of both the analyst and manager and provide another descriptive parameter of the actions on which judgment may be focussed.

CONCLUSION

These four principles, together with the dominance relation, suggest "practical" and expedient ways of dealing with decisions in the face of uncertainty.

They may be considered methods of simplifying the complexity of reality, methods of suppressing uncertainty, or methods of approximating a decision-maker's utility function. One cannot decide in general which will provide the most useful description of decision-making behavior or the most useful basic for making recommendations for management action. This is a matter about which the analyst must develop some judgment. In the next several chapters we explore the results of using these principles in connection with a variety of management decisions under uncertainty. It is hoped that these examples will help to cultivate the sort of judgment required.

PROBABILITY ENCODING IN RETROSPECT

Having established the notion of utility as a model for consistent behavior in uncertain situations, we may now review the reference lottery method of probability encoding in a somewhat clearer and more logical fashion.

Suppose we confront a decision maker with a choice of the following form:

	S_1	S_2	S_3	S_4
a_1	K	0	0	0
a_2	0	K	0	0
a_3	0	0	K	0
a_4	0	0	0	K

We assume that the possible futures are meaningful events for him in the sense that he has some experience with them. We do not supply him, however, with any statements about their probabilities. We assume further that the numbers in the matrix are utilities and thus consistent behavior implies utility maximization, and the utility of any prospect is its expected utility. Now we ask the decision maker which alternative he prefers. Suppose, after careful consideration, he reports that he is indifferent among the four actions. We understand this to mean that he would not make the slightest effort to take one of the actions rather than the others, that he would let his choice be determined by a chance device, or that he would delegate the decision with no concern as to what action was taken. Suppose further that we wish to explain his choice using the utility maximization model. We could say that his report is equivalent to the statement

$$U(a_1) = U(a_2) = U(a_3) = U(a_4)$$

This will be true if

$$p_j = .25 \quad \text{for all } j$$

since then

$$U(a_i) = (.25)(K) \quad \text{for all } i$$

We could then say that the decision maker acts as though he attached equal weights of .25 to each of the possible futures. These weights are then called subjective probabilities. Notice that these numbers are indicative of his attitudes toward risk in this decision and make no direct reference to relative frequencies.

The example is of the same form as a lottery with four tickets and a prize of utility K. As we saw in Chapter 2 we could imagine a lottery with a hundred tickets; and, if the decision maker was indifferent as to which ticket he held, we could then say that the drawing of any ticket was an event with which he associated the subjective probability .01. This lottery may be used as a measuring device in the following manner. To find the subjective probability he associates with the event "he will win a certain contract" we ask him, "How many tickets in the lottery would you find equivalent to the prospect of winning a prize of utility K in the event that you win the contract?" If he is able to answer this question, after due consideration, by saying that he would be indifferent between twenty tickets in the lottery and the prospect of winning the prize if he is awarded the contract, then we would call .20 his subjective probability of the event "he wins the contract." If we wished we could start with a lottery of 1000 tickets and perhaps learn that his subjective probability is .203.

FURTHER EXPLORATIONS OF PREFERENCE STRUCTURES

Up to this point we have looked primarily at the decision maker's preferences for outcomes which are characterized by two dimensions, uncertainty and dollar payoff. We turn next to the exploration of preference structures involving outcomes described by multiple dimensions, introducing this important topic here and returning to it in greater depth in Chapter 12.

We might get at our preference structure by asking what decisions we would make if we were confronted with various sets of alternative actions. We can thus simulate our decision-making behavior as a way of finding out what we want. This, of course, introduces an additional source of uncertainty so familiar to psychology. What is the relationship between what we think we would do in a hypothetical situation and what we would do in actuality? There is some evidence that tends to indicate that this is not an overly serious difficulty if we are well motivated to simulate our choices with deliberateness. Yet it is one we will want to keep in mind as we search for a better understanding of our goals.

The big payoff from developing a language which can be used to express our preferences comes if the language has some deductive possibilities. This is the property of a language which permits one to use logical manipulations to go from simple, intuitive, confident, and familiar expressions of preference, to complex and unfamiliar preference statements. If the complex, nonintuitive statements that we deduce turn out, upon careful examination, to be satisfactory expressions of our preferences, then the language may well be a significant aid in advancing our self-awareness. If we can use the language to proceed consistently from intuitive to nonintuitive preferences, then it can lead us to a greater understanding of our wants. As we set out to develop some illustrations, we should probably say once again, that these are not to be interpreted as recipes, prescriptions, or ideals to be imitated. They are far more productive if used as stimuli to the development of our own personal ways of expressing our objectives.

AN EXAMPLE

Let us begin with a problem involving various aspects of job opportunities. It is no small task to simply state those things about an opportunity which have some importance for us, and we do not wish to minimize this by assuming too easily that it has been accomplished. Yet we must begin somewhere. Suppose, for purposes which will shortly become clearer, we want to develop our rank ordering for the job attributes listed here.

Starting salary
Location
Possibilities for advancement
Job satisfaction
Responsibility
Job security

To simply introspect directly our rank ordering would be difficult for many of us. Suppose, instead of this, we try the following hypothesis: If constructing the rank ordering directly seems difficult, perhaps a pairwise comparison of the attributes will be significantly easier, more natural, and more intuitive. In this context "easier" means decidable with more confidence, more clarity, or more conviction. It may be relatively straightforward for us to say that starting salary is more important than location. We proceed in the same way with all possible pairs of attributes, indicating the preferred alternative in each decision by underlining. Suppose the result was:

<u>Starting salary</u>	Location
<u>Starting salary</u>	Advancement
<u>Starting salary</u>	Satisfaction
<u>Starting salary</u>	Responsibility
<u>Starting salary</u>	Security
Location	<u>Advancement</u>
Location	<u>Satisfaction</u>
Location	<u>Responsibility</u>
Location	<u>Security</u>
<u>Advancement</u>	Satisfaction
<u>Advancement</u>	Responsibility
<u>Advancement</u>	Security
<u>Satisfaction</u>	Responsibility
<u>Satisfaction</u>	Security
<u>Responsibility</u>	Security

The factor underlined five times, advancement, is preferred to all of the other factors, and thus ranks first. The factor underlined four times, satisfaction, ranks second, and so on. Thus we are able to proceed deductively from a set of simple preference statements to a more complex ranking using this property of paired comparisons. We could easily extend this to a much larger number of factors, should that be necessary. Further, this scheme has the very useful property of helping us to detect logical contradictions in our expressed preferences. If we should find two factors underlined three times, we would review the original expressions to find where we had said that A is more important than B, B is more important than C, but C is more important than A.

Having achieved this degree of clarity or uncertainty resolution about the factors we consider important in choosing a job, we might be moved to go even further. We will show shortly how these efforts might help us to come to an understanding of our preferences among jobs. It is likely that we may have feelings such as, "While possibilities for advancement are more important than job satisfaction, they are not very much more important. Both, however, are substantially more important than starting salary." We can perhaps use the language and format of a simple rating scale to make these feelings explicit. Suppose for example we list the ranked attributes of jobs and place next to the list a scale calibrated from 0 to 100. These are arbitrary units and most any scale would do as well.

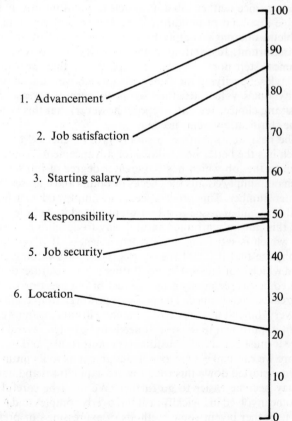

We draw a line from advancement to the 100 point on the scale, thus assigning it an arbitrary value of 100 units. We may now use the scale to express our relative evaluations of the other factors. These expressions may seem difficult, the scale may seem arbitrary, and the measurements on it far more precise than our uncertain feelings would warrant. It turns out, however, that in spite of these things, people find the use of such a technique helpful and the ultimate decisions which result from its application are found to be satisfying and reasonable ones.

We may feel that satisfaction, being almost important to us as advancement, might be put down as about ninety percent as important. We denote this by drawing a line from advancement to the ninety unit point on the value scale. This process continues to completion, at which point we should reflect carefully on what we have expressed, testing it as an expression of our real wishes.

ENRICHMENTS

Next we review a possible program of value clarification that one might undertake if he were confronted with the problem of choosing a job and if he were willing to attempt some deliberate uncertainty reduction. Suppose to begin with, that the choice is between two job opportunities. It is a difficult decision since neither job appears clearly and intuitively better. Rather than engage in a kind of nondirected, repetitive, suffering and struggling with the problem, one might simply begin by being explicit about the factors which are important. Just setting down the six factors as we have done is neither a common step nor a degree of explicitness that we can widely identify in our styles. Specifying the dimensions which we value may in itself sufficiently clarify one's value structure so as to permit a reasonably confident and satisfying choice. We will suppose, however, that this is not the case. Further value clarification seems needed.

The next step might be to simply give a "check," or a "point" to the job which has the better possibilities for advancement. Another check or point is given to the job which has the greater degree of job satisfaction, and so on. Then one simply counts the checks or points and chooses the job which has the greater number. This process seems so simple and so arbitrary that we might be almost embarrassed to admit we had used it. Yet there are those of us who find this not only a rather natural way to develop clearer preferences, but a way which is satisfying in its reasonableness. It is very important indeed to emphasize that it is not the overt process of awarding checks and counting them which is of greatest value. Rather it is the clarification of one's own mind that comes as seemingly a by-product of the overt process which is probably of greatest significance. The process, however simple minded it may seem, is not very difficult nor very costly in many instances, and we would perhaps find profit in putting it to the test. It needs to be tested several times, not just once, since it must begin to be customary, comfortable, and to some degree natural before we can make a reasonable judgment as to its ultimate usefulness.

Once started down this road toward explicitness and uncertainty reduction, it may become easier to go further. We must be careful at all times not to become involved in logically neat but overly complex and rationalistic schemes. Let us rather invent some methods of expressing our preferences which may suffer from certain elements of arbitrariness, but which are ours and require only an amount of effort commensurate with their effectiveness.

As a next step we might, as we have illustrated previously, rank the six job attributes, and use a point system to reflect this ranking. The job which has the greater possibilities for advancement gets six points, the job which seems to offer greater satisfaction get five points, and so on. This scoring method would then predict our preference for the job with the greatest total number of points. Again, we might want to test this method to see if it appears to produce reasonable and satisfying predictions that we can "live with." Again also, it is likely to be what we learn about ourselves through the process rather than the end product which is of most use to those who seek higher standards of reasonableness. Having gotten this far, it may be increasingly easy to continue.

The previous scheme may seem to fail as a reflection of our value structure in at least two ways. To give six, five, four, and so on, as the point scores for the factors fails to indicate that we find satisfaction almost as important as advancement, but both of these are considerably more important than the next ranked factor, starting salary. This immediately suggests the use of the rating process we have illustrated previously. We may also be concerned about the fact that the job with the greater possibilities for advancement gets six points while the other opportunity, which may indeed have almost as good possibilities, gets no points for this factor. This aspect becomes all the more troublesome if we consider a choice among more than two jobs. Here again we might introduce a rating device. Let the jobs be ranked according to possibilities for advancement, assign the highest ranked job 10 or 100 points, and then scale the others relative to it. This process could then be repeated for the other five factors. Each job would thus have a score for each factor, and each factor would have an important score. Perhaps we would then multiply each factor score by its importance score and sum these products for each job.

This version is beginning to be rather time consuming and produces a good deal of data to handle. It becomes problematical whether we should multiply and add as we have just suggested, or whether some other model should be used for processing the scores into an overall evaluation of a job. We may indeed have reached the point beyond which few of us would find it reasonable to go as unaided decision makers. If we reach this point, however, we will have learned rather a lot about our own preferences. If we invest the effort to try out such devices and to invent some of our own, the results may be rewarding.

There is in fact considerable evidence which suggests that these somewhat simple-minded and disturbingly arbitrary schemes have some very interesting properties. This evidence is based on schemes invented by others, not even by the subjects themselves. Decision makers tend to find these methods useful, interesting, and they tend to be pleased with the results. Even highly experienced professional persons operating in areas of their special competence have indicated their appreciation of the assistance such methods provide.

The best way to test these hypotheses and evaluate them in connection with one's own style is to try a simple exercise involving the choice among houses, or stocks, or summer vacations. While the results of other experiments may sensitize one to the effects that might be anticipated, the central problem is really what will happen when one attempts to invent and use languages and formats of his own.

EXPERIMENTAL EVIDENCE

Several experiments involving experienced decision makers have been reported. One, for example, involved high ranking military officers who had extensive backgrounds in their profession. They were asked to use the sort of methods just outlined to aid in making some rather realistic and tactical plans. The methods they used were suggested by the experimenter and were not created by the decision makers themselves. The officers were also asked, under appropriate experimental arrangements, to make the same plans using their personal, habitual, unaided methods. The results of this and similar studies suggest several interesting tendencies.

The experienced decision makers were able, though sometimes only with considerable effort, to make the judgments required. In some cases they found these expressions quite natural and intuitive. How much "weight" one places on a factor may be a fairly common way of approaching evaluation. The subjects tended to be satisfied generally and in some cases enthusiastic about both the process and the results. They appeared to welcome this sort of assistance with the difficult task of making their value systems operative. There was some indication that they might voluntarily elect such methods in certain situations where conflict was particularly troublesome. They were at least as satisfied with the results achieved using the decision aids as they were with the results of their own habitual methods of deciding.

There was a high correlation between the results achieved with and without the decision aiding formats. Thus one might conclude that the aids could be trusted not to lead one astray, nor to produce odd and unusual choices. Given that the results are generally trustworthy in this sense, the value of the process itself may be the chief benefit. There is, however, some evidence from a number of studies that subjects tend to disagree with themselves less frequently if such simple aids are used in moving toward increasing explicitness and uncertainty reduction. That is, repeated confrontation of similar decision situations tend to reveal that decision makers choose in inconsistent ways more frequently if they rely on implicit, unaided methods.

These kinds of efforts toward value clarification appeared to be especially appealing when one is confronted with two courses of action which are perceived as being very similar in their desirability. These efforts were indeed recognized and used by the subjects as conflict-reducing strategies. When the alternatives available contained one which was clearly preferred, little incentive existed to clarify one's objectives.

Those who have participated in such experiments seem to appreciate that they are in fact learning about their own preference structures and creating preferences which were not consciously available previously. There was some agreement that this advance in understanding one's goals was perhaps the most important consequence of such an undertaking.

It appears also that a first expression of preferences may be typically made more reasonable and more satisfying if some sort of feedback and revision occurs. This tends to make a person somewhat more relaxed about the initial expression of preferences since it is known that revision will later be possible, and such a condition probably enhances the amount of learning which occurs in the process. To have the opportunity to correct the inconsistencies in one's preferences and to revise them in the light of their unanticipated consequences leads to greater satisfaction with the ultimate results. The first time through, the results typically fell short of the subject's standards of reasonableness in some respects.

We will return in Chapter 12 to this difficult and important problem of multiple criteria decision making.

PROBLEMS

(*An asterisk following a problem number indicates that its solution appears in the Appendix.*)

3–1.* By using the utility assignment scheme described in the chapter, it is determined that for a given decision maker

$$U(-\$1,000) = .10 \qquad U(\$3,000) = .50$$

The decision maker reports that he is indifferent between the two alternatives shown below:

	$p_1 = .40$ S_1	$p_2 = .60$ S_2
a_1	$1,000	$1,000
a_2	-$1,000	$3,000

What is $U(\$1,000)$?

Suppose the utility scale had been set up so that $U(-\$1,000) = B$ and $U(\$3,000) = A$, where $1.00 \geqslant A > B \geqslant 0$. Show that this would make no difference in application.

3–2. Consider two points on a plane whose rectangular coordinates are x_1, y_1 and x_2, y_2. Let the coordinates of a third point be

$$x_3 = px_1 + (1-p)x_2$$
$$y_3 = py_1 + (1-p)y_2$$

where $0 \leqslant p \leqslant 1$. Show that the third point lies on a straight line joining the first two points.

3–3.* Consider the following decision under risk. The matrix values are dollar losses.

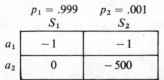

	$p_1 = .999$ S_1	$p_2 = .001$ S_2
a_1	-1	-1
a_2	0	-500

What could be said about the utility function of a subject who
  a) prefers a_1?
  b) prefers a_2?

3–4. Suppose you have just $20 in cash which you consider ample for an important social engagement scheduled for this evening. Would you be willing to bet your $20 on a flip of a fair coin?

Suppose again that you have just $20 in cash and want very much to leave immediately for a vacation. The bus fare is $35. Would you be willing to bet your $20 on a flip of a fair coin?

3–5.* What can be said about the shape of the utility function of a person who is willing to accept risky investments promising a chance of large gains in return for a chance of modest losses, even though the dollar expectation may be negative?

3–6.* Suppose a person refuses to insure his home using a commercial fire insurance policy. What can be said about the shape of his utility function?

3–7.* Psychologists have discovered that some persons have a utility function for money which first increases at an increasing rate and then at a decreasing rate. Suppose such a person shows increasing marginal utility from 0 up to $A and decreasing marginal utility from $A up to $B. Show graphically the region in which the expected utility of all fair bets involving outcomes between 0 and B dollars will fall. Show the region of the expected utility of all bets which a person would accept if he chose so as to maximize expected utility. A fair bet is defined here as one in which the expected payoff is equal to the amount wagered.

3–8. As a small business man (the net worth of your business is $100,000) you are offered the following contracts:
   a) Contract A promises a profit of $1,000 with probability $\frac{1}{2}$ and a loss of $500 with probability $\frac{1}{2}$.
   b) Contract B promises a profit of $200,000 with probability $\frac{1}{2}$ and a loss of $100,000 with probability $\frac{1}{2}$.
   Would you accept contract A? What about B? Explain your decisions in terms of
   a) Your utility function.
   b) The aspiration level principle.
   c) The expectation-variance principle.

3–9.* Suppose you offer a person a series of fair bets involving a .50 probability of winning *x* dollars and a .50 probability of losing *x* dollars. What can be said about a person's utility function if
   a) He is willing to bet for all values of *x*?
   b) He is not willing to bet for any value of *x* greater than zero?
   c) He is willing to bet for small values of *x* but not for large ones?

3–10. In her daily paper a mother reads probabilistic weather forecasts which say, "The chance of rain tomorrow is *x*." $(0 \leqslant x \leqslant 1.00)$ She asks you how to use the number *x* in deciding how to dress her children for school. How would you proceed?

3–11. Consider a manager who does insure his plant against fire. Assume the premium is $P, the loss if a fire occurs is $L, and the probability of a fire is *q*. Show graphically that this increases his utility and that of the insurance company as well.

3–12. A man is offered the chance to enroll in one or both of the following health insurance plans:
   Plan A pays all medical expenses up to a maximum of $1,000 for each illness.
   Plan B pays only those expenses in excess of $1,000 for each illness. How would you explain a decision to take both plans? To take only plan B?

3–13. A man is considering the purchase of collision insurance for his automobile. He wonders whether to buy "$50 deductible," "$100 deductible," or "$200 deductible." What advice could you give him?

3–14. A man has just sketched out his own utility function and that of his employer. He notes that if his income were increased by $1,000, his utility would increase by .100. If his employer's income were reduced by $1,000, it appears that the employer's utility would decrease by .010. Thus he asks his employer for a $1,000 raise, pointing out that this amount is 10 times more valuable to him than to the employer and that the utility of the community (or society) will be increased as a result. Comment on this. What advice would you give the employer?

3-15.* The manager whose utility function is shown in Figure 3-1 (see table below) must choose between contract B which promises a loss of $40,000 with probability .40 and a profit of $70,000 with probability .60, and a new contract called D. Contract D actually consists of two contracts, each of which promises a loss of $20,000 with probability .40 and a profit of $35,000 with probability .60. The outcomes of these two contracts making up D are independent. What choice would you recommend for the manager?

Utility Table
(Based on Figure 3-1)

Dollars	Utility
− 200,000	0
− 100,000	.40
− 50,000	.58
− 40,000	.60
− 25,000	.64
0	.70
15,000	.73
50,000	.78
70,000	.80
100,000	.83
200,000	.90
400,000	1.00

3-16.* Consider contract A of the example in the chapter, which promised a loss of $100,000 with probability .50 and a profit of $200,000 with a probability .50. Suppose four people, each with utility functions like that of Figure 3-1, decide to enter into this contract sharing equally in profits or losses. Suppose further they all use the above probabilities in considering the contract. Show that under these conditions each person's utility will increase. (See table, problem 3-15.)

3-17.* The manager whose utility function is pictured in Figure 3-1 feels that, although he would not choose contract A in the decision discussed in the chapter, if he had the opportunity to accept contract A many, many times, it might be more desirable. Show that the utility of taking contract A twice is greater than the utility of taking it once. (See table, problem 3-15.)

3-18.* Suppose we find that the following utility function reflects the attitudes toward uncertainty of a particular manager:

x	$U(x)$
0	0
$1000	.40
$2000	.70
$3000	.83
$4000	.90
$6000	1.00

a) What reference contract was used?

b) What is the maximum he would be willing to pay for an opportunity which promised the following:

$6000 with probability .15
$2000 with probability .70
$1000 with probability .15

c) How would he choose in the following decision:

a_1: $6000 with probability .50
$1000 with probability .50

a_2: $3000 with probability .50
$4000 with probability .50

d) How would you go about assigning a utility to $7254?

3–19. From your own experience suggest examples of decisions for which each of the four principles of choice seems appropriate. Suggest examples also to illustrate the conditions under which each of the principles seems to be unsatisfactory.

3–20.* Apply each of the principles of choice to the following decision. The values in the matrix are profits.

	$p_1 = .20$ S_1	$p_2 = .70$ S_2	$p_3 = .10$ S_3
a_1	$ 20	$100	$1,200
a_2	190	190	190
a_3	500	120	100

3–21. Select four actual business decisions with which you are familiar, either through reading or experience. What principle of choice best explains what was done in each case?

3–22. Two men, *A* and *B*, are offered tickets in a lottery in which the prize is an automobile worth some $4,000. The price of a ticket is $1.00, and they estimate that some 10,000 tickets will be sold. *A* buys a ticket but *B* refuses. What explanations can be offered for their behavior in terms of utility functions and the principles of choice discussed in the chapter?

3–23. Which alternative would you select in the decision below? The numbers in the matrix represent profits.

	p_1 S_1	p_2 S_2	p_3 S_3	p_4 S_4
a_1	2	12	0	19
a_2	5	17	11	16
a_3	10	18	12	21
a_4	9	8	9	6
a_5	3	13	4	20

3–24. Make up a principle of choice of your own. Show how it would be used in an example. What can be said for and against it?

3–25. A young man is attempting to choose between a career in management with a large corporation and going into business for himself. After considerable study he is able to estimate the probability distributions of the present worths of his future earnings for each alternative (figures are in thousands of dollars).

Corporation Management		Own Business	
Earnings	Probability	Earnings	Probability
200–250............ .60		50–100............ .50	
250–300............ .30		100–200............ .30	
300–350............ .10		200–400............ .15	
		400–600............ .05	

Discuss the application of the four principles of choice to this decision.

3–26. Large governmental organizations often carry no fire insurance; large firms often do not insure against small fire losses; but home owners are usually fully insured against fire. Can an explanation be offered which shows that all are acting reasonably?

3–27. What explanation could you suggest for the following observations?

a) During World War II a government faced the choice between two air raid shelter programs for a large city. One program involved many small shelters, while the other proposed a smaller number of large shelters. An analysis showed that the expected number of deaths per raid was smaller if a few large shelters were used, yet the government chose the other program.

b) Many people are far more disturbed by a single air crash involving say forty deaths than they are by a far greater number of deaths on the highways during a summer week end.

3–28. Would you advise a person to gamble in a commerical gambling house? Explain your advice. Suppose a person is known to be an occasional player of slot machines. How would you explain his decision to gamble in the terms of this chapter?

3–29. How would you analyze the decision to buy or not to buy a life insurance policy? What sort of a person buys such a policy?

3–30. What principle of choice might be used by management in selecting among alternative plant safety programs?

3–31.* Consider a $10,000, five-year term life insurance policy. For a person of age 25, the annual premium amounted to approximately $30. This policy promises to pay the beneficiary the face amount if the insured dies within the five-year period. It has no other benefits, no cash value, no value as paid-up insurance, and no value at the end of the term. A section of a current mortality table is shown below:

Age	Deaths per 1,000 Persons
25	1.53
26	1.55
27	1.59
28	1.64
29	1.71

Compute the expected return for such a policy. Is this a good basis for deciding whether or not to buy the polciy?

3–32*. A manufacturer of seasonal goods must produce in advance. His profit from the production of x units when the demand is D is given by

$$\text{Profit } (x) = (\$1.00)x \qquad \text{for } 0 \leqslant x \leqslant D$$
$$= (\$1.00)D - (\$.50)(x-D) \qquad \text{for } x > D$$

To simplify the problem suppose that only four values of D are possible: 1,000, 2,000, 3,000, and 6,000 units. Assume that each of these values had probability .25. The manufacturer wishes to choose among four production quantities also equal to 1,000, 2,000, 3,000, and 6,000 units. What would be his choice if
a) He chose to produce for the expected demand?
b) He chose so as to maximize expected profit?
c) He chose so as to minimize the probability of a loss?
d) He chose so as to maximize the probability of a profit of $3,000 or more?
e) He chose so as to minimize the variance of his profit?

3–33.* Consider the decision to propose or not to propose on a contract which is summarized below.

	p	$1-p$
Propose	$90,000	–$10,000
Do not propose	0	0

a) For what value of p would the expected dollar returns be equal for the two actions?
b) If the expected dollar returns were equal, which action would you recommend to a manager whose utility function was of the same general shape as that of Figure 3-1? Figure 3-2? Figure 3-3?
c) What action would you recommend on the basis of an aspiration level principle? Show your recommendation for various values of A.

3–34. What explanation could be given for each of the following decisions:
a) A public utility establishes its capacity so as to keep the probability of being unable to meet customer demand below a level p.
b) An airline designs its passenger terminal so that the probability of a passenger having to wait in line at the counter more than 20 minutes is less than or equal to q.
c) A trucking company advertises one-day service between two large cities and is satisfied if the proportion of shipments which take more than one day is kept below r.

3–35. It has been proposed that the problem of multiple goals could be explained and understood in terms of multiple aspiration levels rather than in terms of a single complex utility surface. Suggest an example of such an explanation.

3–36. Assuming the decisions involved to be decisions in the face of uncertainty, and using the principles of choice we have studied, explain *briefly* each of the following behaviors:
a) The board of directors which states that it is company policy *never* to run out of finished goods inventory. Aspiration Level
b) The plant manager in the same company who is more than satisfied if he runs out of finished goods inventory no more than once a week, on the average.
c) The steel user who is carrying no more than his usual steel inventories in spite of the talk about a possible steel strike.
d) The big company which conducts an elaborate market research program before launching a new product and their small competitor which does no formal market research at all before bringing out a new product.
e) The man who regularly bets two dollars a week on the horses but keeps his personal savings in government bonds.
f) The manager who assigns two groups of engineers to work separately and independently to solve the same important technical problem.

g) The big company which lets a computer decide whether or not a customer is a good credit risk, while a smaller company spends more money per customer to have an experienced credit manager make the same decision.

3–37. In an equipment selection problem, the following data are given for each of two machines:

Initial investment

$f_j(C)$ = probability distribution of operating costs during j^{th} year of operation

$g(S)$ = probability distribution of salvage value

Interest rate

Service life

Set up a model for comparing the two machines.

3–38. A study of trade association statistics on small business profits suggests that the rate of return on investment for drugstores is a normally distributed random variable with a mean of 16.1 per cent and a standard deviation of 4.2 percent. A similar study of gas stations shows that the return on investment is also normally distributed with mean equal to 11.8 per cent and standard deviation equal to 3.5 per cent. Discuss the question of which business is the preferred investment.

3–39*. A company is considering the installation of a plant to process one of its by-products from the main process into a marketable item. The major consideration is whether the plant is to be an automated, special-purpose installation, or whether it is to be made up of general-purpose equipment. In studying this decision the company finds that future profits will depend heavily on business conditions. It develops three views of the future which may be called boom-inflation (*BI*), recession (*R*), and stable-growth (*SG*). The plant is to be used for the next ten years in any case. The present worths of the future profits are given in the matrix below (in millions of dollars).

	BI	R	SG
Automated plant	$4	−$1	$2
General-purpose equipment.......	2	.5	1

The probability of *SG* is estimated to be .30. If the expectation principle is to be used, what must be the probability of *R* in order to make the automated plant the better choice? If both alternatives have equal expectations, what principle of choice would you suggest?

3–40. In explaining why the budget of the sales department has been cut and the budget of the industrial engineering department has been increased, a manager reports, "The chances of a successful cost reduction program are greater than the chances for a successful sales expansion program, for a given expenditure of money." How would you explain his decision in terms of the ideas of this chapter?

3–41.* You are invited to play the following gambling game. You flip a fair coin until a head appears. The payoff is 2^n cents if the first head occurs on the nth flip. The probability that the first head will occur on the nth flip is simply $(\frac{1}{2})^n$.

Show that your expected dollar return is infinite. How much would you be willing to pay in order to play? (The St. Petersburg Paradox).

Suppose the person who invites you to play is not infinitely wealthy, but has 2^{20} cents ($10,485.76). What is your expected dollar return?

3–42. The reliability of a weapons system is defined as the probability that it will successfully complete a mission. Given estimates of the cost and reliability of two weapons systems, how would you advise the Secretary of Defense on which to approve for production?

3-43.* Refer to the manager's utility function which is tabulated in problem 3-15*.

Suppose another analyst had studied this same manager using a reference contract of the form; "a profit of $200,000 with probability p, a loss of $100,000 with probability 1 − p". Suppose that the manager had given answers to the second analyst which are *consistent* with those tabulated in the text.

a) What utility would the second analyst assign to zero dollars?

b) What would the second analyst predict about the manager's preferences in the decision indicated below?

	.10	.40	.30	.20
a_1	$400,000	$200,000	0	− $100,000
a_2	$ 70,000	$ 70,000	0	0

c) The manager whose utility function is considered here is offered a fire insurance contract which (in its simplest form) insures him against a possible loss of $200,000 in return for the payment of a premium of **P** dollars.

   If the probability of the loss during the term of the contract is 3/35, what is the largest premium, **P**, the manager would be willing to pay?

d) Suppose the premium is actually smaller than the value found above and thus the manager does insure. Explain this choice in terms of

   i. the most probable future principle
   ii. the aspiration level principle
   iii. the expectation-variance principle

e) Suppose the tabulated utility function could be expressed by an equation of the form

$$U(x) = A + Bx - Cx^2 \quad \text{for} \quad -200,000 \leqslant x \leqslant 400,000$$

The manager is offered two business ventures. The profit from a_1 is a Normally distributed random variable with mean m_1 and variance v_1. The profit from a_2 is a Normally distributed random variable with mean m_2 and variance v_2. Show *symbolically* how you would predict his preference between the two.

3-44. Consider a manager whose utility function is given by

$$U(x) = a + bx - cx^2 \quad \text{for} \quad x \leqslant b/2c$$

Assume all quantities mentioned below lie in the range for which this function is defined.

What reference contract was used to obtain this utility function?

How would you compute the utility of a risky contract promising y dollars, where y is a uniformly distributed (continuous) random variable over the range

$$y_1 \leqslant y \leqslant y_2$$

Which of the following contracts would the manager prefer?

Contract A promises z dollars where z is a Normally distributed random variable with mean m_A and standard deviation s_A.

Contract B promises w dollars where w is a uniformly distributed (continuous) random variable with mean m_B and standard deviation s_B.

What must be the probability of winning in a double or nothing bet for k dollars if the manager is to be willing to flip?

3–45. The second derivative of the utility function is sometimes called "the coefficient of risk aversion." Explain very briefly why this name is appropriate?

3–46. Consider an uncertain decision in which there are two courses of action and two possible futures. If one action dominates the other, does it also stochastically dominate the other? If there is no ordinary dominance, is there any possible relationship among the payoffs and the probabilities which will yield a condition of stochastic dominance?

SUGGESTIONS FOR FURTHER STUDY

Beach, Lee Roy, and James A. Wise. "Subjective Probability Estimates and Confidence Ratings." *Journal of Experimental Psychology*, Vol. 78, No. 3 (1969), pp. 438–444.

DeFinetti, Bruno. "Logical Foundations and Measurement of Subjective Probability," *Acta Psychologica*, 34 (1970), pp. 129–145.

Peterson, C. R., and L. D. Phillips. "Revision of Continuous Subjective Probability Distributions." *IEEE Transactions on Human Factors in Electronics*, HEE-7, 1 (March 1966), pp. 19–22.

Raiffa, Howard. *Decision Analysis*. Reading, Massachusetts: Addison-Wesley, 1970.

Stael Von Holstein, Carl-Axel S. "Measurement of Subjective Probability." *Acta Psychologica*, 34 (1970), pp. 146–159.

Winkler, Robert L. "The Quantification of Judgment: Some Methodological Suggestions." *Journal of the American Statistical Association*, 62, 320 (December 1967), pp. 1105–1120.

Winkler, Robert L. "The Consensus of Subjective Probability Distributions." *Management Science*, 15 (October 1968), p. 2.

APPLICATIONS 4

To study a management decision we begin by making it explicit in the form of a model. The model is not the actual situation but simply a representation of it. The function of the model is to bring conceptual order out of the perceptual confusion with which experience comes to us. The model is an abstraction or simplification of reality. The creation of a useful model involves difficult compromises between complex models which reflect the rich detail of reality and thus give a more comprehensive basis for choice, and simple models which can be understood, readily manipulated, and require reasonable amounts of data and computation.

REPRESENTING DECISIONS BY MODELS

It is difficult, perhaps impossible, to give general directions as to how to create a model of a given decision situation which will turn out to be useful. Rather, the development of models must be regarded as an art. In the next few chapters we undertake one way of communicating this art; that is, to invite the reader to examine a number of examples of models of decisions under uncertainty. This art is learned by experience and experiment, and these examples attempt to begin this process. Let us begin with a typical decision problem and note the ways in which the model abstracts and simplifies.

A machinery manufacturer is concerned about the quality of a casting which goes into his machines. In particular, he asks an analyst to investigate the precautions which might be taken to prevent castings having certain types of internal defects from finding their way into finished machines. After considerable study he concludes that a choice must be made between three inspection policies:

a_1: Do not inspect the castings at all. Castings which fail in service will have to be replaced by a service representative sent out from a regional sales office.

a_2: Adopt an inspection device which detects the defects about 90 percent of the time if they are present. Use the device on every casting.

a_3: Adopt a more modern and foolproof inspection method which always detects the defects. Use this method on every casting.

At the expense of considerable effort he is able to obtain the following information upon which to base the choice. The cost of sending out a service representative to replace a casting which has failed in service is estimated to be $20 on the average. The cost of inspecting a casting using the device in a_2 is

40 cents. The inspection device contemplated in a_3 will cost an estimated $1.20 per casting inspected. Records of inspection for past lots of these castings indicate that it is rather consistently true that one casting in ten has these troublesome defects.

Now suppose we consider a particular casting which (unknown to us) has these internal defects. Under policy a_1 it will not be inspected but will eventually fail in service and cost the manufacturer $20 to replace it. Under policy a_2 the manufacturer incurs a cost of 40 cents for inspection, but there is a chance of 10 percent that the inspection will not detect the defects, and thus the casting will be used in a machine. It will later fail in service and an additional charge of $20 will be the result. Using policy a_3 the manufacturer spends $1.20 for inspection which invariably catches the defects. Consider, on the other hand, what happens when a perfectly good casting is encountered. Policy a_1 results in no expense; policy a_2 results in an inspection cost of 40 cents; and policy a_3, a cost of $1.20. If we add to this the idea that the probability of a defective casting is 10 cents, the choice may be summarized in the familiar notation:

S_1 = a defective casting detected by the inspection device of a_2
S_2 = a defective casting not detected by the inspection device of a_2
S_3 = a perfect casting
p_1 = (Probability of a defective casting) (Probability of detecting with a_2)
$\quad$ = (.10)(.90) = .09
p_2 = (Probability of a defective casting) (Probability of not detecting with a_2)
$\quad$ = (.10)(.10) = .01
p_3 = .90

	$p_1 = .09$ S_1	$p_2 = .01$ S_2	$p_3 = .90$ S_3
a_1	$20.00	$20.00	0
a_2	.40	20.40	$ .40
a_3	1.20	1.20	1.20

Now if we consider the amounts of money in this matrix small in terms of the resources of the manufacturer, we might reasonably recommend the action which minimizes the expected cost. This would be equivalent to approximating his utility function by a straight line in the region of interest in this decision. The result would be

$$E(a_1) = (.09)(\$20.00) + (.01)(\$20.00) + (.90)(0)$$

$$= \$2.00$$

Similarly

$$E(a_2) = \$ .60$$
$$E(a_3) = \$1.20$$

Thus policy a_2 would be recommended as the action which minimizes expected costs. Several comments might be made about this analysis of a decision under uncertainty.

1. The basic decision model may help to organize the data which is relevant to the decision and make it more readily understandable.
2. Somehow a conclusion has been reached to terminate the search for alternatives and consider only three. Others may have been briefly examined and discarded previously, perhaps on the basis of some rough aspiration level principle. When the analysis is completed, none of the three may be "acceptable" to the manager, and we may be asked to search further. If the actions studied do not lend themselves to satisfactory predictions or evaluations of outcomes, we may also decide to search further.
3. Uncertainty enters in two ways: by way of the probabilistic performance of the inspection device in a_2, and by way of the probabilistic occurrence of defective castings.
4. In dealing with the costs we suppressed uncertainty and used average values as, for example, in the case of the cost of sending out a service representative. If there is a possibility that this cost may on occasion be very large, our linear approximation to the manufacturer's utility function may be in danger.
5. We have exhibited money outcomes only, neglecting such other value considerations as the manufacturer's reputation for quality or the customers' ill will when failures occur. The difficulty of evaluating these outcomes leads typically to a situation in which an aspiration level principle is useful. For example, the analyst might recommend the action which minimizes the probability that a casting will fail in service.
6. If the probability of a defective casting had been much smaller, the decision might never have arisen, or it might have been treated with a most probable future principle.

These are but a few of the ways in which, by using a model to represent the decision, we simplify it and abstract from the complexity of reality. Whether it is a useful model is initially a matter of the analyst's judgment and finally a matter of the results observed when the manager undertakes some action. In the examples which follow, it will be left to the reader to raise such points as these in contexts of his own experience and interests. We will simply present a variety of examples of decisions under uncertainty, showing how the various principles of choice might be applied.

INSURANCE DECISIONS

A number of decisions are of the same general form as the decision to insure or not to insure against some loss. Many of these may be usefully treated as decisions under conditions of uncertainty. The general form of these decisions is roughly as follows. On payment of a premium, P, one will be insured against a loss of amount L. The loss L may itself be a random variable which depends on the nature of the catastrophe which generates the loss; however, we will treat it simply as a constant. The basic decision is then whether or not to insure against this loss. Let

$$a_1 = \text{insure}$$

$$a_2 = \text{do not insure}$$

$$S_1 = \text{the catastrophe occurs}$$

$$S_2 = \text{catastrophe does not occur}$$

Cost Matrix

	p_1 S_1	$1-p_1$ S_2
a_1	P	P
a_2	L	0

Examining this decision in the light of the expectation principle, it is clear that a_1 will be preferred if

$$E(a_1) = P < E(a_2) = p_1 L$$

The interesting thing about this decision is that in many applications the expectation principle does not lead to the decision to insure. If we are considering actual insurance decisions such as fire, accident, life, or health insurance, it would be reasonable to suppose that the insurance company wishes to make a profit, or at least cover its costs of operation. If the insurance company itself uses the expectation principle, as it well might, in fixing the premium, then to make a profit of average amount k on each policy it must be that

$$P = p_1 L + k$$

If this is the case then it follows that $E(a_1) > E(a_2)$ and the expectation principle will suggest that one not insure.

This type of decision seems clearly the place to apply some form of the aspiration level principle. Much of our thinking about insurance follows the line that we are willing to pay the premium and accept a small but certain loss in order to be protected against the possibility of a large loss. This might be expressed by suggesting that we have an aspiration level A which lies in the interval

$$P < A < L$$

and thus minimize the probability of having our loss exceed the level A by insuring.

In actuality this decision may be complicated by other factors. It might be that the probabilities used by the decision maker are different from those used by the insurance company. For example, the man whose family seems to incur more than the average amount of illness will consider health insurance a good buy. The family which has a history of less than the average amount of illness might decide not to insure. It may also be that the insurance company returns some of its investment profits to its policyholders and thus effectively reduces the premiums. Insurance statistics indicate that for a given type of industrial plant the probability of a fire in a one-year period is .003. Given that a fire occurs, the loss, y, is a random variable with an exponential distribution:

$$f(y) = .00001e^{-(.00001)y}$$

The expected loss L is

$$L = \int_y yf(y)\, dy = \frac{1}{.00001} = \$100,000$$

If a given plant is insured, the expected liability of the insurance company is simply the probability of a fire times the expected loss, given that there is a fire.

$$(.003)(100,000) = \$300$$

If the insurance company charges a premium of \$300 it will just break even in the long run. It must, however, cover its operating expenses and perhaps make a profit. Suppose it does this by increasing the premium by 10 percent to \$330 per year.

Now the manufacturer who wishes to buy fire insurance finds that, if he does insure, his expected cost is simply the premium of \$330, but if he does not insure, the expected cost is only \$300. In most cases, however, he will be willing to pay the premium as a guarantee against the large losses which might result from a fire. If he wishes to maximize the probability that his cost will be less than A, he will insure for any $A > \$330$.

Examples of other decisions of roughly the same form as this are indicated in the following list. It should be noted that in some of these the expectation principle will appear more reasonable than in others.

1. Equipping a fleet of trucks with spare tires
2. Investment in flood control structures
3. Installation of safety and fire prevention devices
4. Provision of spare machines
5. Provision of spare parts
6. Cross-training workers for critical jobs
7. Provision of safety banks of material along a production line

To apply the expectation principle to decisions having outcomes involving human life, such as safety programs, fire prevention, and flood control, requires the placing of a value on a human life. One usually tries to avoid this problem and reach some acceptable level of risk of loss of life.

MAINTENANCE POLICY

Decisions involving policy for preventive maintenance or replacement of machines and machine components are often treated as decisions under uncertainty. The source of uncertainty in this case is usually the difficulty of predicting exactly when a machine is going to break down or require maintenance. If one could predict exactly when the fuel pump of a truck was going to fail it would be easy to replace the pump just before failure. While this would be the best possible maintenance policy, it is not generally possible to make such predictions.

Let us take as a simple specific example of such a decision, the case of a large automatic transfer machine which contains a number of cutting tools. The decision involves the time at which these tools should be replaced. The basic values involved include the very high cost of having a tool fail during the production period, shutting down the machine and the entire production line of which it is a part, and replacing the tool as quickly as possible. Here the major costs are in terms of lost production and enforced idleness of the facilities. On the other hand, there is the possibility that all the tools might be replaced during some time when the machine is idle anyway in the hope that the new tools will reduce the incidence of failures during the production period. Since tools are expensive and the cost of installing them is not trivial, one does not wish to recklessly replace all the tools in a machine every day. The first decision is whether to replace tools only when they fail, or to adopt some policy of preventive replacement of all tools at periodic times. While this decision may itself be studied as one under conditions of uncertainty, let us assume that it has been decided that some preventive replacement policy will be used. The problem then is how often to perform this preventive replacement.

Let us further suppose that it is possible to describe the uncertainty involved by studying the lives of a large sample of such tools. To further simplify the problem assume that all tools behave in nearly the same way with respect to service life. Let

$p(t)$ = the probability that a new tool will fail after t periods of service

Assume further that time is to be measured in discrete intervals and that all failures and replacements may be thought of as occurring at the end of an interval. The problem might then be to choose a policy of the following form:

1. All tools which fail are replaced immediately.
2. After T periods, all tools, whether they have failed or not are removed and replaced. This is what is meant by preventive replacement.

The problem of choice is that of selecting the best value of T in the light of two costs:

C_1 = cost per tool of preventive replacement
C_2 = cost per tool of replacement when failure occurs during the production period

Now suppose under our policy we begin with N new tools installed. The first question to be answered is, "How many tools will fail in some period t?" It is simplest and perhaps most natural to answer this question in terms of the expected number of tools which will fail, and thus at the very outset we are led toward the use of an expectation principle. In period t, some tools will fail after having served successfully for the intervening periods. The expected number behaving in this way is

$$Np(t)$$

Some tools will also fail in some period x prior to t, they will be replaced, and their replacements will then fail in period t. The number of tools on the average behaving in this way will be

$$Np(x)p(t-x)$$

This can happen for any period x up to $x = t - 1$. Thus, the number of "second failures" in period t will be on the average

$$N \sum_{x=1}^{t-1} p(x)p(t-x)$$

There will be "third failures" and "fourth failures" and so on to be computed and summed to get the expected number of failures in period t. If we let $f(t)$ stand for this number, then

$$f(t) = N \left\{ p(t) + \sum_{x=1}^{t-1} p(x)p(t-x) + \sum_{y=2}^{t-1} \sum_{x=1}^{y-1} p(x)p(y-x)p(t-y) + \cdots \right\}$$

As an example, $f(3)$ would be computed as follows:

$$f(3) = N\{p(3) + p(1)p(2) + p(2)p(1) + p(1)p(1)p(1)\}$$

We are now in a position to apply the expectation principle to the choice of T. At the end of T periods we plan to replace all tools. The cost of doing this will be NC_1. Up to this time we will replace only the tools which fail. The expected cost of these replacements is given by

$$C_2 \sum_{t=1}^{T-1} f(t)$$

Using $T - 1$ for the upper limit of this summation corresponds to the assumption that failures which occur in period T are not replaced immediately (at cost C_2), but are replaced as a part of the preventive replacement program at the end of period T (at a cost C_1). If failures in period T are not replaced in this way, but must be taken care of immediately, then the upper limit of the summation should be T. Finally the expected cost for a given T is

$$E(T) = NC_1 + C_2 \sum_{t=1}^{T-1} f(t)$$

Since this is nondecreasing with T, we will actually wish to base the choice on the expected per-period cost, $E(T)/T$.

For T to minimize expected costs it must be that

$$\frac{E(T+1)}{T+1} - \frac{E(T)}{T} \geqslant 0$$

and

$$\frac{E(T-1)}{T-1} - \frac{E(T)}{T} \geqslant 0$$

The reader may verify that the results of applying these conditions are

$$C_2 f(T) \geqslant \frac{NC_1 + C_2 \sum\limits_{t=1}^{T-1} f(t)}{T}$$

$$C_2 f(T-1) \leqslant \frac{NC_1 + C_2 \sum\limits_{t=1}^{T-2} f(t)}{T-1}$$

The value of T which satisfies these relations will be that which yields a unique minimum as long as $f(t)$ behaves in an ordinary way, which need not concern us at the moment. These relations may be rewritten as

$$C_2 f(T) \geqslant \frac{E(T)}{T}$$

$$C_2 f(T-1) \leqslant \frac{E(T-1)}{T-1}$$

We may now make a familiar interpretation of the result. Preventive replacement should be made at the end of a period T for which the cost of replacing failures during the period is greater than the average per-period cost through the end of the period. As long as the marginal cost for the period is less than the average cost through the end of the period, then preventive replacement is not made. This latter statement follows directly from the second relation above.

As we have suggested previously, the nature of this decision leads quite naturally to treatment with the expectation principle. It is, however, possible to formulate other principles which have appeal. Especially if it is difficult to measure the cost coefficients which enter the expectations, one might wish to appeal to some sort of aspiration level principle. For example, we might decide to do preventive replacement at the end of some period T during which the expected number of failures first exceeds some predetermined level A. That is, perform preventive replacement as soon as $f(t) > A$. In considering such things as light bulbs, we might decide not to replace failures at all, but to replace all bulbs as soon as the number which have failed reaches some predetermined level.

To illustrate numerically the use of the expectation principle, suppose we start with 100 tools with known mortality distribution. From this we derive $f(t)$ with the following assumed results:

t	1	2	3	4	5	6	7	8	9	10
$f(t)$	3	8	14	15	15	14	12	18	15	17

In fact, we would have to be concerned with the behavior of $f(t)$ beyond ten periods, but to simplify the problem we will truncate the data at this point. Suppose it is also known that the cost of changing a tool when preventive replacement is undertaken is $10. The cost of replacing a tool and other resulting costs when failure occurs during the production period is $50. Table 4-1 indicates the usual method of solution. From this table it is evident that

Table 4-1

Col. 1	Col. 2	Col. 3	Col. 4	Col. 5
T	$C_2 f(T)$	$C_2 \sum_{t=1}^{T} f(t)$	$NC_1 + C_2 \sum_{t=1}^{T-1} f(t)$	Col. $4 \div T$
1............\$150	\$ 150	\$1,000	\$1,000
2............ 400	550	1,150	575
3............ 700	1,250	1,550	517
4............ 750	2,000	2,250	562
5............ 750	2,750	3,000	600
6............ 700	3,450	3,750	625
7............ 600	4,050	4,450	636
8............ 900	4,950	5,050	631
9............ 750	5,700	5,950	650
10............ 850	6,550	6,700	670

preventive replacement should be undertaken at the end of three periods. It may also be confirmed that the conditions for optimality derived previously are satisfied for both $T = 3$ and $T = 8$, although the absolute minimum occurs at $T = 3$.

RECTIFYING INSPECTION

One of the basic decisions in quality management is the decision to accept or reject a lot of a product received from a supplier. The decision hangs basically on the quality of the product in question, which we will suppose can be described simply in terms of good or bad, effective or defective. This decision is often handled by determining in advance an acceptance sampling plan which specifies the exact routine for making the choice. When a lot consisting of S units is submitted by the supplier, the purchaser takes a sample of N pieces at random from the lot. These pieces are classified by inspection as either effective or defective. In any given instance let the number of defective units discovered in the sample be x. The acceptance sampling plan contains a decision rule which states that if x is less than or equal to some acceptance number c, the lot is to be accepted, otherwise the lot is rejected. Uncertainty arises in this decision because the purchaser does not, in general, know in advance how many defectives are in a lot, and because the decision about the lot is based on inference from a sample rather than an examination of the entire lot.

The decision problem is usually treated as one of choosing an acceptance sampling plan. To make the analysis of this decision especially simple we add one additional assumption. Whenever a lot is rejected, it is then inspected 100 percent and all defective units are repaired or replaced. This process is called "rectifying inspection."

The basic expression of uncertainty in such a decision is the probability that a sampling plan will lead the purchaser to accept a lot which has some proportion of defectives p'. In general p' is unknown, but one may suppose a value for it and then calculate the probability of acceptance. The binomial distribution is often used to calculate this probability, Pa.

$$Pa = \sum_{x=0}^{c} \frac{N!}{x!(N-x)!}(p')^x(1-p')^{N-x}$$

In choosing a plan the relevant values often include the cost of performing the inspection and the cost associated with accepting a defective product. The more inspection done, the less bad product will be accepted on the average, and contrariwise. Here again expectations appear immediately as the most manageable and natural quantities with which to deal.

Any such acceptance sampling plan may be characterized simply by stating the sample size, N, and the acceptance number, c. The average amount of inspection per lot may be obtained as follows. Every lot will be sampled, and thus N items will be inspected. Whenever a lot is rejected, the remaining $S - N$ items will be inspected under our assumption of rectifying inspection. Thus the average number of items inspected per lot will be (average total inspection)

$$ATI = N + (1 - Pa)(S - N)$$

where $1 - Pa$ is the probability of rejecting a lot. Since Pa depends upon p', so does ATI.

The number of bad items accepted will be zero whenever a lot is rejected. However, when a lot is accepted there is the possibility of accepting some bad items in it. If the supplier furnishes a lot with a proportion of defectives p', the probability of acceptance may be computed as indicated previously. If the lot is accepted, $S - N$ items will not be inspected. These will contain an average of $p'(S - N)$ defective units. Thus the average number of defective units accepted per lot is

$$ADA = Pap'(S - N)$$

Now if we let C_1 be the unit cost of inspection and C_2 be the unit cost of accepting defectives, the expected cost per lot for a given sampling plan will be

$$E(N, c) = C_1\{N + (1 - Pa)(S - N)\} + C_2 Pap'(S - N)$$

This expectation depends on p', the proportion of defectives in the incoming lots. In most interesting decisions this quantity is not known in advance nor is a probabilistic prediction of it available. For purposes of illustration let us suppose that, although p' may not be known in advance, we are able to make a probabilistic prediction on the basis of past experience with the supplier in question. If this is the case, we will be able to select a sampling plan which will minimize expected costs. This is best suggested by way of a numerical example.

Let us suppose that our experience with the supplier suggests that when his process is operating satisfactorily the lots which he sends average about 1 percent defective. His process runs satisfactorily about 60 percent of the time. There are occasions when something goes wrong in his plant, and the fraction defective of the lots he sends rises to 2 percent. This happens about 30 percent of the time. Further, about 10 percent of the time his process goes seriously awry and the fraction defective jumps to an average of 4 percent. Thus, the decision will involve three possible futures which may be tabulated as follows:

$$S_1: p' = .01 \qquad p_1 = .60$$
$$S_2: p' = .02 \qquad p_2 = .30$$
$$S_3: p' = .04 \qquad p_3 = .10$$

Actually there are a very large number of possible sampling plans among which to choose, since any suitable sample size and acceptance number determine a plan. To make things simple, however, suppose we have somehow narrowed the choice down to three plans which now form the alternatives in the decision.

$$a_1: c = 1 \qquad N = 100$$
$$a_2: c = 1 \qquad N = 200$$
$$a_3: c = 3 \qquad N = 100$$

In going forward toward the computation of the expected costs for each alternative it is necessary first to obtain the probabilities of acceptance. These may be obtained by means of various statistical short cuts, with the following results:

PROBABILTY OF ACCEPTANCE

	S_1	S_2	S_3
a_1	.74	.42	.09
a_2	.42	.09	.003
a_3	.98	.85	.45

The reader should examine these to see if they agree with his intuitions about the problems.

Assuming that the product is shipped in lots of 1,000 units, the average amount of inspection per lot (ATI) and the average number of defectives accepted per lot (ADA) may be computed.

	S_1 ATI	S_1 ADA	S_2 ATI	S_2 ADA	S_3 ATI	S_3 ADA
a_1	334	6.7	622	7.6	919	3.2
a_2	664	3.3	928	1.6	998	.01
a_3	118	8.8	235	15.3	595	16.2

Again the reader should check these results against his intuition.

Now let us assume that the cost of inspection is $1.00 per unit and that the unit cost of accepting a defective item is $10.00. The expected costs for each of the alternative sampling plans under each of the possible lot fraction defectives are as follows:

	S_1	S_2	S_3
a_1	$401	$698	$951
a_2	697	944	999
a_3	206	388	999

Here there is little need to compute the expectations associated with each alternative since a_3 clearly minimizes expected cost. In general, however, it will be necessary to use the probabilities of the possible futures to actually compute the expected cost for each alternative. To show this suppose we alter the cost involved so that we now have

$$C_1 = \$.30 \qquad C_2 = \$10.00$$

The expected cost matrix then turns out as follows:

	$p_1 = .60$ S_1	$p_2 = .30$ S_2	$p_3 = .10$ S_2
a_1...............	\$167	\$163	\$308
a_2...............	232	294	300
a_3...............	123	223	340

Here the expectations must be computed.

$$E(a_1) = \$180 \qquad E(a_2) = \$257 \qquad E(a_3) = \$175$$

With this set of costs, a_3 is to be preferred if the expectation principle is used, although there is relatively little difference in the expected cost per lot between a_1 and a_3.

SETTING THE PROCESS AVERAGE

One of the interesting problems which arises in connection with decisions to control the quality of output of a production process is variation in the process which is taken to be economically and practically uncontrollable. If, for example, one is concerned with controlling the diameter of a cylinder turned on a lathe, it is common to find that even under reasonably careful conditions of control, some variation will be discovered in the diameters produced. Often this variation can be described in terms of a probability distribution. Thus, if x is the diameter, when the process is "under control" the variation in x can be satisfactorily described by some density function, $f(x)$. The density function forms the basis for a control chart which is a decision-making device for deciding whether or not the process is "under control." We wish to consider a different but related problem.

Let us suppose that the designer of the cylinder has placed tolerance limits on it. These specify the largest and smallest diameters which are acceptable from the viewpoint of the function of the final product. Let these tolerance limits be S_u and S_L, the upper and lower tolerance limits respectively. Pieces whose diameters fall outside these limits are scrap. If a piece has a diameter which falls above S_u, it may be reworked to acceptable size at a unit cost, C_u. If a piece falls below S_L, it must be scrapped completely, which results in a unit cost of C_L. In order to be specific, let us suppose that, when the process is "under control," $f(x)$ is given by a normal distribution with mean μ and standard deviation σ.

$$f(x) = \frac{1}{\sqrt{2\pi}\,\sigma} e^{-(x-\mu)^2/2\sigma^2}$$

Now in setting up the machine and controlling it, let us further assume that we can adjust the mean μ of the process but cannot further control it. Thus, for any given setting of the process mean we have a situation pictured in Figure 4-1.

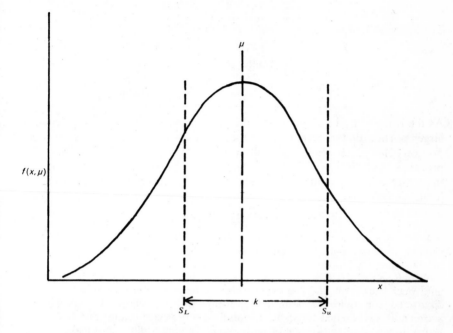

Figure 4-1. Setting the Process Average

The area under $f(x)$ above S_u represents the proportion of the output that is too large and can be reworked at a unit cost C_u. The area under $f(x)$ below S_L represents the proportion of the output which is too small and must be scrapped at a unit cost C_L. Thus, for any setting of the process mean we can compute the expected cost of the bad material produced.

$$E(\mu) = C_L \int_{-\infty}^{S_L} f(x, \mu)\, dx + C_u \int_{S_u}^{\infty} f(x, \mu)\, dx$$

The decision is that of choosing a process average which will minimize this expected cost. This is accomplished, of course, by taking the first derivative of the expected cost with respect to μ and setting it equal to zero. The result obtained is

$$\mu = S_L + \frac{S_u - S_L}{2} + \frac{\sigma^2}{S_u - S_L} \ln \frac{C_L}{C_u}$$

As one would suspect, the result depends on the ratio of C_L to C_u. The following example will give some feeling for the manner in which the process mean should be set. Let

$$S_u = S_L + k = S_L + 2\sigma$$

$\dfrac{C_L}{C_u}$	$ln\,\dfrac{C_L}{C_u}$	μ
1	0	$S_L + \sigma$
2	.6931	$S_L + 1.3465\sigma$
4	1.3863	$S_L + 1.6931\sigma$
.5	− .6931	$S_L + .6535\sigma$
.25	−1.3863	$S_L + .3069\sigma$

As the ratio of C_L to C_u increases, the process mean is moved up, placing a larger portion of the output above the upper tolerance limit, and a smaller portion below the lower tolerance limit. As the ratio of C_L to C_u decreases, the process average is moved down, placing a larger portion of the output below the lower tolerance limit and a smaller portion above the upper tolerance limit.

PROBLEMS

4-1.* A manufacturer of very heavy, custom-designed industrial equipment is planning the casting of a large housing. The housing is a part of a unique end item, for which no future orders can be expected. When the casting is poured, there is some probability p that it will be defective. The defects, however, would not be discovered until much later during the machining process. If he makes one casting and it is later discovered to be defective, he must then incur expensive delay and setup costs to make another. If he makes two at the outset he is protected against this, but is left with a useless casting if the first one is good. If both are bad, he must make a third casting. For simplicity, assume that the probability of the second casting being defective is p also, and that the probability of the third casting being defective is zero. The manufacturer wonders whether he should make one or two at the outset. Let C_1 be the cost of setting up to make either one or two, and C_2 be the other variable costs of producing a casting whether one or two are made.

  a) If $p = .50$ which plan will minimize expected cost?
  b) If $p = .10$ which plan will minimize expected cost?
  c) Under what conditions would you advise the manufacturer to do something other than minimize expected cost?
  d) How much would he be willing to pay for a nondestructive testing service which would tell him whether a casting was defective immediately after it was poured?

4-2.* Show that, in the search decision outlined below, the policy which maximizes the expected value of the present worth involves finding an aspiration level which is used in deciding whether to stop or continue search. A company is searching for investment opportunities. They have already found several, the best of which promises a present worth of future profits estimated at P_B. The company is willing to make decisions on the basis of the following assumptions:

  a) The cost of discovering each additional investment opportunity is a known constant C.
  b) The present worths of the profits for the population of all investment opportunities which exist (including those not yet discovered) can be represented by a probability density function, $f(P)$.

How should the company decide when to stop searching if they can invest in only one opportunity? (Note that investment opportunities are not transitory like stock or commodity prices. Once discovered, an opportunity remains available to the firm for a reasonable length of time.)

4-3. A small manufacturer hires a market research organization to do a test marketing of three versions of a new product. He receives a report which contains essentially three results:

Version	Est. Sales in One Year (Units)
A	300,000
B	310,000
C	400,000

The product has a market life of one year, with total profits given by

$$-\$100,000 + .40 \text{ (units sold)} \quad \text{for } A$$
$$-\ 150,000 + .55 \text{ (units sold)} \quad \text{for } B$$
$$-\ 160,000 + .50 \text{ (units sold)} \quad \text{for } C$$

The manufacturer is dissatisfied with the market research report, finding it of little assistance in choosing the version to market. What explanation might be offered for his dissatisfaction? What data would be helpful?

4-4.* By adjusting the size of the billet which goes into a rolling mill, the mean length of the bars rolled, m, may be controlled. The length of a bar, x, is a random variable with probability distribution $f(m, x)$. If there is a cost C_1 associated with a bar which falls below the lower specification limit L_1, and a cost C_2 associated with a bar which falls above the upper specification limit L_2, show how one might

a) Find m so as to minimize expected cost.

b) Find m so as to minimize the proportion of bars which fall outside the specification limits.

4-5*. If the probability distribution of bar lengths in problem 4-4 is uniform, obtain an expression for the optimal mean bar length. What principle of choice would you suggest if it were not possible to measure the costs involved?

4-6. During an especially cold winter a large metropolitan gas company was forced on two occasions to ask its large industrial customers to switch to alternate fuels for heating in order that sufficient gas could be assured for private homes. In the face of considerable public pressure the gas company argued that it did not need extra capacity and did in fact have adequate capacity for its demand. What sort of arguments could the gas company give to support its position?

4-7.* The designer of a three-stage electronic system wishes to improve the reliability of the system. The first design consists of three stages or components in series. The reliability of a component is defined as the probability that it will function successfully during a given mission or task. The system reliability, defined in a corresponding way, is taken to be the product of the stage reliabilities. He may improve reliability by placing components in parallel at any stage with a switching device which brings in the next component when one fails. The designer is limited in what he may do by a budget restriction which requires that the system cost less than $15,000. Also, space and weight restrictions limit the number of components in parallel at any stage to three. Using the following data, design a system which will have maximum reliability within these restrictions.

Stage	Number of Components in Parallel	Stage Reliability	Total Stage Cost
1	1	.80	$2,000
1	2	.90	4,000
1	3	.95	7,000
2	1	.70	2,000
2	2	.90	5,000
2	3	.92	9,000
3	1	.90	1,000
3	2	.98	3,000
3	3	.99	6,000

4–8. * Suppose you enter a gambling casino to play roulette with $700 and you wish to maximize the probability of leaving with a profit of $100. If you limit your alternatives to bets on red or black (see Chapter 1), what would be your betting strategy?

4–9. Is it reasonable for the federal government not to insure its buildings against fire?

4–10. In investigating fire insurance for its plant, a firm obtains the following facts:
Probability of a fire during a year = .003.
Given that a fire occurs, the density function of the dollar loss is given by

$$f(y) = me^{-my} \qquad \text{where } m = .0001$$

Annual premium = $40
The policy will cover 90 percent of the actual dollar value of any fire loss.
In terms of the principles of choice presented in Chapter 3, what explanations could be given for the firm's decision to insure? For a decision not to insure?

4–11. * A motor truck firm operates a fleet of 125 vehicles. The firm is considering two policies for handling tire failures.

a_1: Equip each vehicle with a spare tire. This will require a total of 140 spare tires because of the repair time. The annual cost for a tire is estimated to be $25. The cost of repairing a tire failure under this policy is $6.00.

a_2: Enter into service contracts with a number of garages along the routes traveled by the firm's vehicles. These contracts specify that the firm will supply the tires and the garage will handle all tire failures at a flat rate of $10 each. Under this policy the firm will need only 60 spare tires distributed among the garages.

The number of tire failures per 100,000 vehicle miles is a random variable having a Poisson distribution with a mean of 2. The trucks travel an average of 100,000 miles per year each. Which policy would you recommend?

4–12. * The probability of a fatal accident is 40 times greater if a person travels one mile by motorcycle than if he travels by automobile. If a person chooses to travel by motorcycle with a total cost of $.03 per mile instead of driving a car at a total cost of $.10 per mile, what can be said about the value which he places on his life?

4–13. * A manufacturing firm is considering the purchase of a spare machine for standby service at a crucial point in its production process. The machine will cost $18,000 and will have a salvage value of $3,000 after 15 years of standby service. The machine will be called into service whenever a breakdown occurs. The number of breakdowns per year is predicted on the basis of past experience to be a random variable having a Poisson distribution with a mean of 2. When a breakdown does occur, the costs which would result from lost production and enforced idleness would be a random variable y, if no standby equipment were available. It is estimated that y is equally likely to fall anywhere in the range from $300 up to $2,100. (Neglect interest.)

a) On the basis of the expectation principle, does the standby machine appear to be a good investment?

b) If the firm wishes to maximize the probability that the annual cost of dealing with breakdowns will be below some level A, show which alternative will be preferred as a function of A.

4-14.* A machine is designed and built to special order for a manufacturing firm. The machine builder offers to furnish a spare for a major part at the time the machine is built for an additional cost of $1,200. He also indicates that, if the spare is ordered later on, it will cost approximately $14,000 because of special setups and delays. Let the probability that a spare will be required during the life of the machine be p. The probability that more than one spare will be needed is so small that it may be neglected. For what value of p will the two alternatives be equally costly? Would you suggest an aspiration level principle for such a decision?

4-15.* A firm has purchased a large complex machine and is now offered a service contract by the manufacturer of the machine. The service contract guarantees all repairs and adjustments on the machine for a period of one year at a flat rate of $2,000. Two other alternatives are being considered. The firm might use its own technicians to service the machines. The incremental labor cost per breakdown is estimated to be $50 for this alternative. Parts must be purchased which are expected to average $240 per breakdown.

The firm may also call in the manufacturer's technicians as the breakdowns occur. The manufacturer will bill for labor costs at the flat rate of $75 per call, and for parts at a price 10 percent below that at which the firm could otherwise obtain them.

The number of breakdowns per year is a random variable having a Poisson distribution with a mean of 5. What policy will minimize expected costs? For each policy compute the probability that it will be best.

4-16.* A firm is considering the purchase of some major equipment from either supplier A or supplier B. It is felt that A is capable of delivering the equipment on time to meet a desired deadline. The price of A's equipment is, however, considerably higher than that of B. It was felt that B might deliver on time, but there was some possibility that B might deliver late. Further, it is suspected that B may never be able to deliver the equipment according to specifications. The firm feels that if it waited several months, much better information on B's capabilities would be available. Three alternative courses of action are under consideration:

a_1: Order from A. If it later becomes clear that B could deliver, this order can be canceled on payment of certain cancellation charges. Further delay would be encountered while B produces the equipment.

a_2: Order from B. If it later becomes clear that B cannot deliver, the order can be switched at a cost for cancellation and additional delay.

a_3: Wait until B's capabilities are known. This would involve delay in any case. The firm uses the present worths of profit over a six-year study period as a measure of value for each outcome. The results are shown in the following matrix:

	B Fails to Deliver	B Delivers Late	B Delivers on Time
a_1	100	100	100
a_2	40	50	250
a_3	80	120	180

Clearly, the probabilities of the possible futures can be obtained only on the basis of judgments. Construct a graph showing the values of p_1 and p_2 for which each alternative will be preferred using the expectation principle. Discuss the use of other principles of choice.

4–17.* The sales department of a large firm has a list of N prospects which it hopes to obtain as accounts. The sales manager wishes to establish a limit on the number of calls which will be made on a prospect in the attempt to obtain the account. On the basis of past sales activity he obtains the following data showing the probability that a prospect will be sold and the probability that he will be dropped as a function of the number of calls. These are simple probabilities, not conditional probabilities.

Call Number	Probability of Obtaining	Probability of Dropping
1	.06	.44
2	.04	.16
3	.03	.05
4	.01	.05
5	.004	.04
6	.002	.02

What policy with respect to the maximum number of calls will maximize the average number of accounts obtained per call? What other principles of choice might be appropriate for this decision?

4–18.* The intervals between ship arrivals at an unloading terminal are distributed according to the following probability distribution:

$$f(x) = me^{-mx}$$

where x is the interval between arrivals in days and m is .5.

It is desired to establish terminal unloading capacity sufficient to make the probability that a ship will have to wait to unload less than k. The terminal can handle only one ship at a time. Once the capacity has been established, the time required to unload a ship does not vary appreciably. Capacity is measured in unloading time.

Management is not quite sure how to select k and wishes to see a graph depicting capacity as a function of k for probabilities greater than .20. Plot such a graph.

4–19.* Military aircraft are sent to a certain maintenance depot in such a way that their arrivals appear to be random. The time to overhaul an aircraft is found to be random also. Under these conditions a study reveals that the probability distribution of the number of aircraft at the depot is given by

$$p(n) = \left\{1 - \frac{\lambda}{\mu}\right\} \left\{\frac{\lambda}{\mu}\right\}^n$$

The average time spent at the depot by an aircraft is

$$E(w) = \frac{1}{\mu - \lambda}$$

where

λ = the mean number of aircraft arriving per day
μ = the mean number of aircraft overhauled per day

The commander of the depot wishes to fix its capacity (measured by μ) at a level which will minimize the sum of the average daily costs defined as follows:

μC_1 = average daily operating cost for a depot with capacity μ
C_2 = cost of having an aircraft at the depot for one hour
C_3 = penalty cost for each hour the depot facilities are idle

What is the best capacity for the depot? What other principles of choice might be reasonable for the commander in this decision?

4-20. Write an expression for the utility of a capital investment opportunity when the operating costs and salvage value are viewed as random variables.

4-21. Suppose you were asked to predict your annual income for each of the next twenty years in the form of a random variable. What would typically happen to the variance of annual income as one considered years further and further into the future? What would be the corresponding effect on the utility of annual income as one went further into the future?

4-22. Suppose you wished to make a point estimate of a population mean on the basis of sampled data. The cost of an estimating error is proportional to the square of the difference between the estimate and the population mean. What estimate would minimize expected cost?

4-23. The performance of a statistical hypothesis test may be expressed in the form of its power function or its operating characteristic curve. Consider the problem of choosing between two hypothesis tests. Is this ordinarily regarded as a decision under assumed certainty, uncertainty? Explain briefly by showing a model for the decision.

4-24. Referring to the replacement policy model, let

$$q(t) = \frac{f(t)}{N}$$

Show that

$$q(t) = p(t) + p(1)q(t-1) + p(2)q(t-2) + \cdots + p(t-1)q(1)$$

$$= p(t) + \sum_{j=1}^{t-1} p(j)q(t-j)$$

4-25. The probability of failure for the lining of a tank used in a chemical process is given below as a function of age.

Age in months	1	2	3	4
Probability of failure	.05	.10	.40	.45

If the tank lining fails in service, the tank must be drained immediately, causing a variety of losses and interruptions in the production process. The costs associated with such a failure are estimated to be $10,000. On the other hand, the production schedule provides for emptying the tank at the end of each month and relining may be done at that time. If the tank is relined on schedule, the costs total about $2,000. In no case may the tank run more than four months without relining. Find the relining policy which will minimize expected costs. Assume that the firm operates a large number of such tanks. If a policy T is specified, it means that all tanks are relined when they fail as well as at the end of T months. A tank which fails during month T is repaired on schedule at the end of that month.

4-26.* A plant adopts a policy of replacing the fluorescent tubes over the production area whenever they fail. Failure data on 1,000 tubes indicate the following:

Time in months (t)	1	2	3	4	5	6	7
Number of failures $f(t)$	5	17	22	39	78	97	123

t	8	9	10	11	12	13	14	15
$f(t)$	131	138	140	141	143	149	150	151

The plant is considering a policy of simultaneously replacing all the tubes at the end of some period T. If this is done the replacement cost per tube is estimated to be $.67. Under present conditions the replacement of tubes individually costs about $2.20 each. Find the value of T which will minimize expected costs. Assume a tube failing in period T is replaced with the group at the end of the period.

4-27.* The probability that a certain aircraft component will last t hours is given by

t	100	200	300	400	500
$\dfrac{S(t)}{N}$	.90	.80	.60	.45	.15

If the component fails in flight, the aircraft must land for immediate repairs. The cost of such repairs is estimated to be $500 when all associated losses are included. Preventive replacement of the component costs approximately $50. Find the replacement policy which will minimize the total expected costs.

4-28. Derive the conditions for the optimum replacement interval.

4-29.* Given

$$N = 1,000$$
$$f(t) = 10 + 20t$$
$$C_1 = \$.20$$
$$C_2 = \$1.00$$

Find T.

4-30. In setting up a replacement policy for fuel pumps on taxicabs, what sort of a principle of choice would you suggest? What would you suggest for the tubes in your television set?

4-31.* A firm is considering two possible acceptance sampling plans to form the basis of a rectifying inspection scheme.

$$a_1: c = 2, \quad N = 50$$
$$a_2: c = 1, \quad N = 100$$

Lot size $= 1,000$

The possible futures and their probabilities are

$$S_1: p' = .01, \quad p_1 = .50$$
$$S_2: p' = .03, \quad p_2 = .50$$

If the cost of inspection is $1.00 per unit and the cost of accepting a defective item is $50, which plan would you suggest?

4-32. How can one estimate the probabilities of the possible futures in a problem such as 4-31? Would you expect this to be generally possible in actual situations? If these probabilities cannot be estimated, how can the decision be approached?

4–33. What principles of choice are ordinarily used by a firm in selecting an acceptance sampling plan?

4–34. Derive the expression for the optimum setting of the process mean.

4–35.* Find the best setting for the process mean given

$$S_u = 1.010 \qquad S_L = .990$$

$$f(x, \mu) = \text{normal with standard deviation } .004$$

$$C_L = \$1.25 \qquad C_u = \$.80$$

4–36. Using the data of problem 4–35, plot the optimum setting of the process mean as a function of the ratio of C_L to C_u.

4–37. If it were not possible to measure the costs in problem 4–35, what sort of a principle of choice would you suggest?

4–38.* A large computer manufacturer furnishes a program for capital equipment selection based on the following assumptions:

- Purchase prices known.
- Operating costs known functions of machine age.
- Salvage values known functions of service life.
- Interest rate known.
- Service lives predicted in the form of probability distributions.

a) Write a symbolic model for the expected equivalent annual cost of a machine.
b) Does a certainty equivalent exist?
c) Under what conditions might the expected equivalent annual cost be a poor basis for choice?

4–39.* A firm is developing plans for plant expansion over the next five years. The basis for this planning is a prediction of demand for the firm's product. Demand is viewed as a random variable with a normal probability distribution having a mean which is a function of time. For year t, the expected demand is given by

$$20,000 + 2,000t \text{ units}$$

and the standard deviation is

$$1,000 + 100t + 10t^2$$

where t takes the values $0, 1, 2, 3, 4$. Expansion is carried out through the purchase of machines, each of which will have an annual capacity of 1,500 units. Because of the cost of capital, the firm does not wish to expand any sooner than necessary.

a) Develop an expansion program if the firm is willing to run a risk of 50 percent of having the capacity of its plant at the beginning of any year fall short of the demand during that year.
b) Develop an expansion program if the acceptable risk is reduced to 25 percent.

4–40. In designing an airport it is important to fix the directions of the runways so that as often as possible there will be a runway in the direction of the wind. A study of detailed weather records for a proposed airport site indicate that the wind direction, x, may be described by a probability distribution $f(x)$. Here x is defined over the range 0 to 360 degrees. The designer wishes to place two runways so as to maximize the probability that there will be a runway having a direction within 20 degrees of that of the wind.
Write an expression for this probability and suggest how it might be maximized.

SUGGESTIONS FOR FURTHER STUDY

Clarke, T. E. "Decision-Making in Technologically Based Organizations: A Literature Survey of Present Practice." *IEEE Transactions on Engineering Management*, Vol. EM-21, No. 1 (February 1974), pp. 9–23.

Dyer, James S., William Farrell, and Paul Bradley. "Utility Functions for Test Performance." *Management Science*, Vol. 20, No. 4 (December 1973), pp. 507–520.

Edwards, Ward, et al. "Bayesian Statistical Inference for Psychological Research." *Psychological Review*, 70 (May 1963), pp. 193–242. Notes the difference between classical and Bayesian statistics.

——————. "Probabilistic Information Processing Systems: Design and Evaluation." *IEEE Transactions on Systems Science and Cybernetics*, Vol. SSC-4, No. 3 (September 1968), pp. 248–265.

North, D. Warner. "A Tutorial Introduction to Decision Theory." *IEEE Transactions on Systems Science and Cybernetics*, Vol. SSC-4, No. 3 (September 1968), pp. 200–210.

Raiffa, Howard. *Decision Analysis*. Reading, Massachusetts: Addison-Wesley, 1970.

Schlaiffer, Robert. *Analysis of Decisions Under Uncertainty*. New York: McGraw-Hill, Inc., 1969.

Spetzler, Carl S. "The Development of a Corporate Risk Policy for Capital Investment Decisions." *IEEE Transactions on Systems Science and Cybernetics*, Vol. SSC-4, No. 3 (September 1968), pp. 279–299.

Starr, Martin K. *Product Design and Decision Theory*. Englewood Cliffs, N.J.: Prentice-Hall, Inc., 1963.

INVENTORY POLICY 5

A very common field of management decision making, and one which is crucial in many businesses, is the area of inventory management. The decisions involved include those of deciding what stock levels to maintain, when to replenish stock, in what quantities to order, and so on. This is also a field in which analytical techniques for aiding these decisions are well developed and quite successful in practice. In many inventory situations, the primary factor in the decision to establish a stock level policy is the demand which is anticipated against the inventory. This problem of predicting future demand is often best solved by the methods of inferential statistics which will yield a prediction in the form of a probability distribution of demand. The decision then becomes an example of a decision under uncertainty, wherein several possible future demand quantities are recognized and their probabilities are estimated. A simple example of this type will serve to further illustrate the ideas of decision making under conditions of uncertainty.

AN EXAMPLE

To take a simple specific inventory decision, let us consider the problem of the small-boat builder who builds pleasure cruisers. He decides that it is economical for him to build a number of boats during the autumn and winter to have them ready for sale during the spring. This permits him to utilize his facilities during periods when he is not occupied with boats for which he has a definite order, and it permits him to reduce costs by building several at a time. His decision then is, "How many boats should be produced for stock?" One of the relevant considerations is the demand for boats which he can expect during the coming season. An analysis of sales over past years using appropriate statistical techniques reveals that there are no significant trends or other identifiable effects which influence sales. In fact, it is concluded that past sales could be described satisfactorily by a probability distribution. It is then decided that the best prediction of sales for the coming year is that they will be much like those in the past. The prediction is then made in the form of the probability distribution of demand. Using D to stand for number of boats sold and $p(D)$ for the probability distribution of demand, the results might be:

D	$p(D)$
1	.10
2	.20
3	.30
4	.20
5	.10
6	.10

These possible demands would correspond to the possible futures in our model for a decision under uncertainty. Let us suppose that the other considerations which enter into the decision are the loss which will be suffered if more boats are built than sold and the loss in profit which will be suffered if more orders come in than can be filled with the boats in stock. The first of these losses arises from such things as keeping money tied up in unsold boats for a long period, the necessity of lowering the price in order to move the boats, and so on. The second kind of loss arises when a customer orders a boat, but because the order cannot be filled from stock, the customer goes elsewhere and the profit that would have been realized on the sale is lost.

STRUCTURING THE DECISION

This decision problem may now be structured in terms of the matrix model for decisions in order to clarify it somewhat.

Alternatives	= number of boats to be built	$= I$
Possible futures	= number of boats demanded	$= D$
Probabilities	= density function of D	$= p(D)$
Outcomes	= number of boats in excess of demand (overage)	$= I - D$
	= demand in excess of stock (shortage)	$= D - I$
Evaluation of outcomes	= cost of overage at C_1 dollars per boat	$= C_1(I-D)$
	= cost of shortage at C_2 dollars per boat	$= C_2(D-I)$

We have assumed that the cost of being over by one boat can be measured and that overage costs are simply linear in the number of boats over. Like assumptions have been made for shortages. For the present let us assume that the expectation principle is to be used. Specifically, we wish to select the alternative which will minimize the total expected cost. Total expected cost will be the sum of the expected costs due to overages and the expected cost due to shortages. Computing the expectations in the usual way, we have for the total expected cost associated with the choice of a stock level I:

$E(I)$ = expected overage cost given I + expected shortage cost given I

If an overage occurs, its amount will be given by $I-D$, and the cost of such an outcome will be $C_1(I-D)$. The probability of this outcome is $p(D)$ for values of D which will yield an overage, namely $0 \leqslant D \leqslant I$. The expected overage cost would then be

$$\sum_{D=0}^{I} C_1(I-D)p(D)$$

By similar reasoning the expected shortage cost turns out to be

$$\sum_{D=I+1}^{\infty} C_2(D-I)p(D)$$

and the total expected cost then is

$$E(I) = \sum_{D=0}^{I} C_1(I-D)p(D) + \sum_{D=I+1}^{\infty} C_2(D-I)p(D)$$

The task of computing $E(I)$ for each possible value of I in order to discover the best choice, may be greatly shortened by appealing to mathematical techniques which will do this. If the function $E(I)$ were a continuous function, we would take its first derivative with respect to I, set it equal to zero, and the solution of the resulting equation could be shown to be the minimizing choice. Since the number of boats is in fact a discrete variable, as is demand, we must move from the infinitesimal calculus to the calculus of finite differences. The corresponding theorem there suggests that if we knew the optimal I, call it I_0, then if we were foolish enough to build $I_0 + 1$ boats, this would clearly increase (or at least not decrease) expected costs. Likewise, if we were foolish enough to stock $I_0 - 1$ boats, this would also increase (or at least not decrease) expected costs. Mathematically we could write this as

(1) $E(I_0 + 1) - E(I_0) \geqslant 0$

(2) $E(I_0 - 1) - E(I_0) \geqslant 0$

The inequations are called the first forward difference and the first backward difference, and they represent the conditions which must hold at the optimal choice of I namely I_0. The situation is pictured in Figure 5-1.

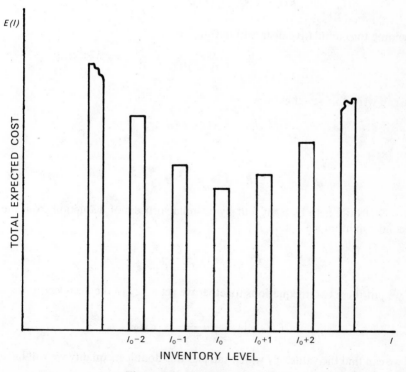

Figure 5-1 Total Expected Cost

COMPUTING THE OPTIMAL STOCK LEVEL

We can now use conditions (1) and (2) above to compute I_0. We first write $E(I_0 + 1)$ which will be required for use in condition (1).

$$E(I_0 + 1) = \sum_{D=0}^{I_0 + 1} C_1(I_0 + 1 - D)p(D) + \sum_{D=I_0 + 2}^{\infty} C_2(D - I_0 - 1)p(D)$$

$$= C_1 \sum_{D=0}^{I_0} (I_0 + 1 - D)p(D) + C_2 \sum_{D=I_0 + 1}^{\infty} (D - I_0 - 1)p(D)$$

$$= C_1 \sum_{D=0}^{I_0} (I_0 - D)p(D) + C_1 \sum_{D=0}^{I_0} p(D)$$

$$+ C_2 \sum_{D=I_0 + 1}^{\infty} (D - I_0)p(D) - C_2 \sum_{D=I_0 + 1}^{\infty} p(D)$$

Subtracting from this the quantity

$$E(I_0) = C_1 \sum_{D=0}^{I_0} (I_0 - D)p(D) + C_2 \sum_{D=I_0 + 1}^{\infty} (D - I_0)p(D)$$

we obtain

$$E(I_0 + 1) - E(I_0) = C_1 \sum_{D=0}^{I_0} p(D) - C_2 \sum_{D=I_0 + 1}^{\infty} p(D) \geqslant 0$$

Defining the cumulative distribution function as

$$\sum_{D=0}^{D_1} p(D) = P(D_1)$$

we can write this result as

$$C_1 P(I_0) - C_2 \{1 - P(I_0)\} \geqslant 0$$

or

$$P(I_0) \geqslant \frac{C_2}{C_1 + C_2}$$

This is of little help by itself, but by a similar process of deduction from the second condition we obtain

$$P(I_0 - 1) \leqslant \frac{C_2}{C_1 + C_2}$$

If we put these two inequations together we get a key to the best decision:

$$P(I_0 - 1) \leqslant \frac{C_2}{C_1 + C_2} \leqslant P(I_0)$$

If we can find the value of I which satisfies this double inequality we will have the optimal choice, I_0.

SOLUTION OF THE EXAMPLE

Returning to our original decision, suppose the cost of being over by one boat is $100 and the cost of being short by one boat is $300. Then

$$\frac{C_2}{C_1 + C_2} = \frac{300}{300 + 100} = .75$$

The cumulative distribution function for demand may be computed as

D	$p(D)$	$P(D)$
1	.10	.10
2	.20	.30
3	.30	.60
4	.20	.80
5	.10	.90
6	.10	1.00

Inspection reveals that the critical ratio .75 falls between $P(3) = .60$ and $P(4) = .80$. Thus

$$P(I_0 - 1 = 3) = .60 \leqslant .75 \leqslant P(I_0 = 4) = .80$$

The best choice is to produce four boats, and this choice has the property of minimizing total expected costs.

THE CONTINUOUS CASE

The continuous case for this type of decision differs not in principle but in mathematical procedure from the discrete case. Suppose that the alternatives are no longer restricted to integral values of I, and that demand is a continuous variable D, with probability distribution $p(D)$. Total expected costs would then be given by the function

$$E(I) = C_1 \int_{D=0}^{I} (I-D)p(D)\, dD + C_2 \int_{D=I}^{\infty} (D-I)p(D)\, dD$$

Here one may take the first derivative of $E(I)$, set it equal to zero, and solve for I_0. The result is

$$P(I_0) = \frac{C_2}{C_1 + C_2}$$

The theorem given in problem 5–26 is used in taking the derivative of this function.

Figure 5-2 shows the density function of demand and the notion that any choice I may be represented by a vertical line at the appropriate point of the D scale. The probabilities of being understocked and overstocked are represented by the areas to the right and left of this line respectively. Note also that the foregoing equation may be written in the form:

$$\frac{P(I_0)}{1 - P(I_0)} = \frac{C_2}{C_1}$$

This suggests the following decision rule: *To minimize expected costs, establish the inventory level at the point where the ratio of the probability of an overage to the probability of a shortage is equal to the ratio of shortage cost to overage cost.*

As an example of the continuous case, suppose we are to fix an inventory level of a commodity which is measured and stocked in quantities which can be treated as a continuous variable, such as liquid fuel. Suppose the demand

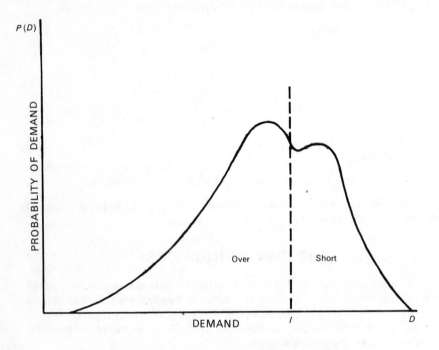

Figure 5-2   Inventory Level and Demand Distribution

distribution is given by the normal distribution with mean of 10,000 gallons per week and standard deviation of 500. Assuming that it is possible to quantify the costs of being understocked and overstocked, let us take

$$C_1 = \$.01 \text{ per gallon}$$

$$C_2 = \$.19 \text{ per gallon}$$

As was shown previously, I_0 must satisfy the relation

$$P(I_0) = \frac{C_2}{C_1 + C_2} = \frac{.19}{.01 + .19} = .95$$

If Z is a standard normal variable, we can read from a table of the normal distribution the value of Z such that $P(Z) = .95$. This value turns out to be

$Z = 1.645$. The relationship between Z and D is given by the transformation

$$Z = \frac{D - 10,000}{500}$$

Solving for D we obtain

$$D = 500(1.645) + 10,000 = I_0$$
$$I_0 = 10,822.5$$

OTHER PRINCIPLES OF CHOICE

In a variety of actual contexts the inventory decision has been based upon some sort of an aspiration level principle. This comes about in many situations because of the impossibility of actually measuring the values of C_1 and C_2 which are required for application of the expectation principle. Often the cost of a shortage must in fact reflect the loss of customer good will, the administrative difficulties, and a variety of other consequences not easily measured in dollar terms. In such situations it is common for management to use a principle such as: *Establish the inventory level so that the probability of a shortage is no greater than some specified value* p_a. This has great appeal when management is able to specify the risk it is willing to run of being short but is unable to determine the dollar costs of shortages and overages.

One may formulate other versions of the aspiration level principle for use in connection with the inventory decision. For example, we might wish to fix the inventory level so that the sum of the probability that $C_1(I - D) > A_1$ plus the probability that $C_2(D - I) > A_2$, is minimized. The sum of these probabilities may be expressed as

$$\int_0^{I - (A_1/C_1)} p(D)\, dD + \int_{I + (A_2/C_2)}^{\infty} p(D)\, dD$$

This sum will be minimized when

$$p\left(I - \frac{A_1}{C_1}\right) = p\left(I + \frac{A_2}{C_2}\right)$$

For example, in the continuous problem suggested previously suppose we take $A_1 = A_2 = \$20$. We then wish to fix I so that

$$p(I - 2,000) = p(I + 105)$$

Using the fact that the normal distribution is symmetric around the mean, we can see by inspection that $I = 10,947.5$.

It is also possible to compute the variance of the cost associated with any inventory level and to determine a level which will minimize some function of expected cost and variance of cost. The mathematics of such a principle is not especially simple and neat, however. By far the most widely used principles in this class of decision problems are the expectation principle and the aspiration level principle in the form first suggested.

ENRICHING THE DECISION

It is perfectly clear that the formulation of the inventory problem which we have just given is the simplest possible version of any interest at all. It is also clear that, in actuality, the general class of decisions about which we are speaking will be complicated by a wide variety of other considerations which we have not included. Many of these complications have been studied extensively and much is known about them. Several obvious enrichments are suggested in the following paragraphs.

1. It may be that the time between deciding on an inventory level and the realization of that level, the reorder time, is not zero as we have assumed, but is better described as a finite but variable period of time. The reorder time itself may be á random variable, thus adding an additional source of uncertainty.
2. The amount ordered to bring the inventory up to the desired level may differ from what is actually delivered. The actual amount received to replenish the inventory may be a random variable whose mean depends on the amount ordered, for example.
3. The amount ordered to replenish the inventory may be actually delivered in amounts which are to some extent random, at times which are also random.
4. The decision may be only the choice of the mean rate of input to the inventory in situations which prevent precise control of what is put into stock.
5. The amount ordered to replenish the inventory may itself influence costs. That is, we may have an economic order quantity problem in connection with an inventory level problem. Again, there may be price discounts for quantity buying which may influence the amount ordered.
6. The cost functions may be more complicated than we have suggested.
7. There may be a variety of ways of, say, responding to a shortage. The firm might hire additional workers, it might work the present force overtime, or it might simply back order. The real decision problem is thus more complex than simply that of fixing the inventory level.

All these and many other complications may be brought to bear upon the determination of inventory policy. Our point is not so much to achieve the rich detail of realistic analysis as to point out a decision-making principle which emerges here. There are a variety of decision problems which might be classed as decisions requiring the matching of a random output by means of a fixed input. The principle simply suggests that once we have decided that the output or demand is random, the best thing to do is pick a given input level and stick with it. "Best" here is used in the sense of minimizing expected costs. It is thus logically consistent to respond to a random demand prediction with a fixed inventory level. It does, of course, take courage to maintain a given inventory level when demand is fluctuating dramatically from period to period.

PROBLEMS

5-1.* A manufacturer stocks a certain spare part for one of his production machines. As soon as a breakdown occurs and one of the spares is used, another is immediately ordered. The lead time for the delivery of a spare part is fixed and known. The number of breakdowns per lead time is a random variable having a Poisson distribution. How many spares should be stocked to assure that the probability of not having enough spares is less than some value p?

5-2.* The monthly demand for an item is given by a Poisson distribution with a mean of 20 items per month. The item may be restocked only at the beginning of a month. The cost of stocking an item if it is not sold during a month is taken to be $1.50. The cost of being unable to supply a unit when one is required is assumed to be $8.50. What should be the stock level in order to minimize total expected costs?

5-3. Discuss the application of other principles of choice to the problem given in 5-2.

5-4. In problem 5-2, suppose the density function of demand were unknown, but you were willing to assume that demand would be at least 4 units per month and never more than 36. What inventory level would you suggest?

5-5. An electric utility firm has studied its past records and tabulated the frequency with which various peak demands occur. Peak demand is measured in megawatts and is tabulated for each day. The frequency of occurrence is expressed in terms of the expected number of days per month on which a given peak load will occur.

Peak Demand (Megawatts)	Expected No. of Days/Month
1,000	.10
1,050	1.12
1,100	2.25
1,150	3.80
1,200	4.50
1,250	6.46
1,300	4.50
1,350	3.80
1,400	2.25
1,450	1.12
1,500	.10

Generating equipment is available to the firm in 50 megawatt units. Management wishes to establish sufficient capacity so the expected number of days per month on which peak demand exceeds capacity is less than k. Plot a graph showing the required capacity as a function of k.

5-6.* The demand for a commodity over a fixed planning period is described by a normal distribution with a mean of 100 and a standard deviation of 10.

a) If $C_1 = \$5$ and $C_2 = \$40$, plot the optimal inventory level as a function of the standard deviation of the demand distribution.

b) Plot the optimal inventory level as a function of the ratio of C_1 to C_2.

5-7.* The number of units of a given item sold in a month by a retail store is a random variable with the following probability distribution:

$$p(D) = \frac{N!}{D!(N-D)!}(p)^D(1-p)^{N-D}$$

where $N = 10$ and $p = .10$. Plot the optimal inventory level as a function of C_2 if $C_1 = \$.20$. Assume the item can be stocked only at the beginning of a month.

5-8.* A gas station finds that its weekly sales of regular gas may be described by a random variable with a uniform distribution over the range 1,800 to 2,200 gallons. It is able to replenish its stock only once each week. It reckons the shortage cost at $.04 per gallon and the storage cost for gas unsold at the end of the week at $.005 per gallon. Find the optimal stock level.

5-9. Using the theorem given below, verify the result for the optimum inventory level to minimize expected costs in the continuous case.

Theorem: Let

$$g(y) = \int_{u_0(y)}^{u_1(y)} f(x, y)\, dx$$

then

$$\frac{dg(y)}{dy} = \int_{u_0(y)}^{u_1(y)} \frac{\partial f(x, y)}{\partial y}\, dx - f(u_0, y)\frac{du_0}{dy} + f(u_1, y)\frac{du_1}{dy}$$

5-10.* If the daily demand for an item is given by the probability distribution

$$p(d) = e^{-m}\frac{(m)^{d-d_0}}{(d-d_0)!} \quad \text{for} \quad d \geq d_0$$

then it follows that the probability distribution of demand for a period of t days is

$$e^{-mt}\frac{(mt)^{d-d_0}}{(d-d_0)!}$$

For fixed values of C_1 and C_2 show how the optimal inventory level varies as a function of the number of days between replenishments.

5-11.* The demand for a commodity is given by a uniform distribution with a range of 100 to 150 units per day. Replenishment is possible once each day. The storage cost for items not sold during a day is $.10. The shortage cost is $.20 per unit for shortages up to 10 units and $.25 per unit for shortages in excess of 10 units. Find the optimal inventory level.

5-12.* Find the inventory level which will maximize expected profit under the following conditions. The purchase price of each unit is C_0. Units not sold at the end of the inventory period are worthless. The revenue from the sale of each unit is R. There is a storage charge of C_1 per unit based on the number of units left over at the end of an inventory period. Demand is predicted in the form of a probability distribution. Assume inventory level and demand are continuous variables.

5-13.* Write an expression for the cumulative probability distribution of cost for the model developed in the chapter. Discuss the relevance of this distribution for management.

5-14.* Convert the model developed in the chapter to a profit model by adding the condition that there is a revenue of R per unit for each unit sold. For the continuous case find the inventory level which maximizes the expected profit.

5-15.* Write an expression for the probability that profit will be less than or equal to zero for the model developed in problem 5-14.

5–16*.   An inventory level may be chosen at the start of a period, but cannot be altered during the period. Demand is predicted in the form of a random variable. Two costs are considered:

$$C_1 = \text{cost per unit for the starting inventory}$$

$$C_2 = \text{cost per unit for shortages}$$

Assume the commodity is infinitely divisible.
 a) Find the policy which will minimize expected costs.
 b) Formulate and apply an aspiration level principle.
 c) Suggest an industrial or commercial situation in which each (a and b) would be appropriate.

5–17.*   Find the inventory level which will minimize expected costs in the following situation:

$$C_1 = \$100,000 \qquad C_2 = \$300,000$$

D	1	2	3	4	5	6
$f(D)$	.10	.20	.30	.20	.10	.10

What inventory level would maximize the probability that costs are less than or equal to $400,000?

5–18.*   The demand for a commodity is modeled by a normal probability distribution with mean $A + Bt$, and standard deviation $C + Dt$. An inventory must be established at the beginning of each month, t, to meet the demand throughout the month. If the cost of having inventory left over at the end of the month is C_1 and the cost of running short is C_2 (per unit), what is the best inventory level, as a function of t?

5–19.*   Using the data of problem 5–8 find
 a) An expression for the stock level which will meet the demand with probability p.
 b) An expression for the probability that cost will exceed a level A, as a function of the stock level.

5–20.*   Demand for a commodity in a given period is predicted in the form of a normally distributed random variable with a mean of 1,000 units and a standard deviation of 200 units. Plot the inventory level which will make the probability of a shortage equal to p for $.01 \leqslant p \leqslant .10$.

5–21.*   Demand for an item takes the values $0, 1, 2, 3,$ and 4 with equal probabilities. There is a storage cost of $100 per unit, based on the number remaining at the end of an inventory period, and a cost of $200 per unit for shortages. At the start of an inventory period management is advised of the number of units left on hand from the previous period. They may choose to continue with the number on hand or to make a production run in order to add more units to the inventory. If they decide to make a production run, there is a fixed setup cost of $50 which is independent of the number of units produced. Find a policy for deciding when to make a production run and how many to produce which will minimize expected costs.

5–22.*   Suppose the demand for an item is predicted in the form of a uniformly distributed discrete random variable over the range $1 \leqslant d \leqslant 6$. The cost of having units left over at the end of an inventory period is $1,000 per unit. The cost of being unable to meet a demand is $2,000 per unit.
 a) How many units should be stocked?

b) If careful study could produce a prediction that demand is equally likely to be *d*, *d* + 1, or *d* + 2 for values of *d* = 1, 2, 3, 4, how much would such information be worth?

c) How much would it be worth to know in advance the exact demand?

5-23.* Consider the inventory decision examined in this chapter, but suppose that the cost for any inventory level is proportional to the square of the difference between inventory and demand.

a) What inventory level would be consistent for a man with a linear utility function?

b) What inventory level would be chosen by a decision maker who wished to minimize the probability that the cost in any period will exceed A dollars?

c) What inventory level would be chosen by a risk-averse decision maker?

5-24.* If an inventory level exceeds demand, the utility associated with this condition is given by

$$-k(I-d)^2$$

and if the demand exceeds the inventory level, the utility of this condition is given by

$$-k(d-I)^2$$

The probability distribution of demand is Poisson with mean 100.

a) What inventory level maximizes utility?

b) What is the utility of the inventory level found in part *a*)?

5-25.* Find the optimum inventory level in the following situation.

$$C_1 = \$20 \qquad C_2 = \$20$$

Demand is Normally distributed with mean *m* and variance *v*. If *I* units are stocked some of them will be defective and cannot be sold. The number of defectives found in the *I* units is a normally distributed random variable with mean *pI* and variance $p(1-p)I$.

5-26. If a manager's utility function, $U(x)$, is known, write an expression for the utility of an inventory level *I*.

SUGGESTIONS FOR FURTHER STUDY

Arrow, K. J., S. Karlin, and H. Scarf. *Studies in the Mathematical Theory of Inventory and Production.* Stanford, Calif.: Stanford University Press, 1958.

Bedworth, David B. *Industrial Systems-Planning, Analysis, Control.* New York: The Ronald Press Company, 1973.

Naddor, E. *Inventory Systems.* New York: John Wiley and Sons, Inc., 1966.

Putnam, A. O., E. R. Barlow, and G. N. Stilian. *Unified Operations Management.* New York: McGraw-Hill Book Company, Inc., 1963.

Sasieni, M., A. Yaspan, and L. Friedman. *Operations Research: Methods and Problems.* New York: John Wiley & Sons, Inc., 1959.

Schmidt, J. W., and R. E. Taylor. *Simulation and Analysis of Industrial Systems.* Homewood, Ill.: Richard D. Irwin, Inc., 1970.

Schweyer, H. E. *Analytic Models for Managerial and Engineering Economics.* New York: Van Nostrand Reinhold Company, Inc., 1964.

Starr, Martin K., and D. W. Miller. *Inventory Control: Theory and Practice.* Englewood Cliffs, N.J.: Prentice-Hall, Inc., 1962.

Starr, M. K. *Production Management: Systems and Synthesis.* Englewood Cliffs, N.J.: Prentice-Hall, Inc., 1964.

Wagner, H. M. *Principles of Operations Research.* Englewood Cliffs, N.J.: Prentice-Hall, Inc., 1969.

BIDDING POLICY 6

Many business undertakings involve the submission of bids in the hope of being awarded a contract to carry out some activity. This is almost universally true of projects undertaken for governmental agencies. For many large projects, such as highway construction or missile manufacture, an elaborate structure of bids is necessary, involving a prime contractor and many sub-contractors.

THE BIDDING PROBLEM

An understanding of bidding policy as a guide to bidding decisions is thus of interest, not only because of its general application, but also because it may be studied as another example of decision making under uncertainty. While there are several schemes for obtaining bids and awarding contracts, we will be concerned with only the sealed bid competition where the award is made to the lowest bidder. The decision is simply what to bid for a given contract. Clearly, the considerations in making this decision would involve an estimate of the cost of performing the contract, the profit desired, the anticipated behavior of competing bidders, and perhaps how badly the firm wanted the contract. There are at least two sources of uncertainty in such a decision—the uncertainty associated with estimating the cost of performance, and the uncertainty associated with predicting the action of competitors. We will consider a situation in which the firm has been submitting bids in a specific field of activity for some time. Such a situation implies that the firm is in a position to keep records of past competitions as a basis for prediction, and that an expectation principle of choice might be a reasonable basis for policy.

ESTIMATING ABILITY

We begin by supposing that the firm is in a position to study its own ability to estimate the costs of performing the type of contract in question. Specifically, we assume that it has data on bids and actual performance costs for the contracts which it has had in the past. For each such contract we form the ratio

$$e = \frac{\text{our estimate}}{\text{actual cost}}$$

and we assume that e is a random variable with probability distribution $f(e)$. Now e may differ significantly for large and small contracts, among various types of projects, or as the firms estimating ability improves. We will assume that these effects have been studied and that $f(e)$ is appropriate for the size and type of project under consideration. Thus, it reflects the firm's current estimating ability. Recall from Chapter 2 that the mean of e is a measure of the accuracy of the estimate, and indicates whether or not they are good in the long run. If $\bar{e}$ is not equal to 1, there is a constant bias in the estimates for which one may correct. Let the corrected cost estimate be

$$c' = \frac{c}{\bar{e}} = \frac{\text{our estimate}}{\text{mean of } e}$$

The variance of e is a measure of the precision of our estimates and we would like to have it as small as possible. The only way to reduce this variance, however, is to strive continually to identify and reduce the sources of error in the estimating process. This is likely to be a long-term undertaking. The change in variance over time is a good measure of how the estimating process is being improved.

EXPECTED PROFIT

The alternatives in the decision are the various amounts, B, which might be bid for the contract. For a given bid B, if it turns out to be the winning bid, our best estimate of the profit from the contract would be $B - c'$. Supposing that we knew the probability that a bid of B would win, say $p(B)$, then the expected profit from such a bid would be

$$E(B) = (B - c')p(B)$$

We assume that if our bid does not win, then neither profit nor loss results. Clearly, if we could write out $p(B)$, it would be possible to find the bid which would maximize expected profit.

ESTIMATING THE PROBABILITY OF WINNING

Again we suppose that the firm has records of its own bids on past contracts, and has also kept records of bids submitted by competitors on these contracts. This information is often made public when the bids are opened. Let us first assume that the competition is among a number of firms who bid with some regularity for the contracts in question. Then, for a specific competitor, firm X, we could obtain data on the ratio of X's bid, b, to our cost estimate over past contracts. Let

$$x = \frac{b}{c}$$

$g(x) = $ the probability distribution of x

In a competition in which we were opposed only by X, the probability of our winning with a bid of B would then be

$$W(X) = \int_{x=(B/c)}^{\infty} g(x)\, dx$$

If we know that we are to be opposed by several competitors, X, Y, and Z, we would compute the probability of winning against Y and Z individually, as we have done for X. Let the resulting probabilities be $W(Y)$ and $W(Z)$. The probability of winning in a competition against all three will then be the product

$$W(X)\,W(Y)\,W(Z) = p(B)$$

Given $p(B)$, we could then find the bid which would maximize expected profit.

Another approach to estimating the probability of winning might be more appropriate if we were not so certain which or how many firms would be opposing us.

In such a situation one might simply choose to view the competitors as being essentially the same with respect to bidding behavior and use the concept of an average or stereotypic competitor. The bidding data on all competitors might then be pooled to obtain a description of an average competitor. This would be an alternative to attempting to identify specific competitors and quantify the individual bidding patterns.

Consider an average or stereotypic competitor, T, whose bidding behavior may be represented by the quantity t.

$$t = \frac{b}{c} = \text{the ratio of an average competitor's bid to our cost estimate}$$

$$g(t) = \text{density function of } t$$

The probability of a bid B winning against a single average competitor is given by

$$W(T) = \int_{t=(B/c)}^{\infty} g(t)\, dt$$

Given that we are opposed by k average bidders, the probability of winning the contract with a bid of B is $\{W(T)\}^k$. To complete the analysis we would need data on the number of bidders against whom we had competed in the past. This would permit the estimate of a density function for k, say $h(k)$. This would give the probability of being opposed by exactly k competitors. The expected profit from a bid of B is then

$$E(B) = \sum_{k=0}^{\infty} h(k)\{W(T)\}^k (B - c')$$

By taking the first derivative of expected profit with respect to B, we could find the bid which would maximize this quantity. The general nature of the problem is now somewhat clearer. As the amount of the bid is increased, the profit also increases, given that the bid wins. However, as the amount of the bid increases, the probability of winning decreases. Usually the expected return rises to a maximum and then declines as the bid is increased. The typical behavior is shown in Figure 6-1.

EXAMPLE

Consider a bidding problem in which the number of opposing bidders has the following probability distribution.

k	2	3	4
$h(k)$	$\frac{1}{6}$	$\frac{2}{3}$	$\frac{1}{6}$

These competitors are to be viewed as average competitors and their bidding behavior is described by the density function

$$f(t) = \text{uniform over the range } .95 \leqslant t \leqslant 1.35$$

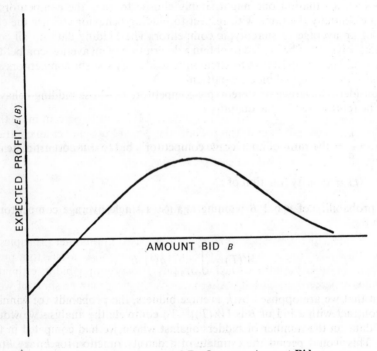

Figure 6-1 Expected Profit versus Amount Bid

Given a bid of B, the probability of winning against one average competitor is

$$W(T) = \frac{1.35-(B/c)}{.40}$$

and the expected profit in this case is

$$E(B) = (B-c')\left\{\frac{1}{6}\left(\frac{1.35-(B/c)}{.40}\right)^2 + \frac{2}{3}\left(\frac{1.35-(B/c)}{.40}\right)^3 + \frac{1}{6}\left(\frac{1.35-(B/c)}{.40}\right)^4\right\}$$

We will assume for simplicity that $c = c'$. The determination of the bid which will maximize expected profit is illustrated by Table 6-1. This table suggests

Table 6-1

B	$B-c'$	$W(t)$	$p(B)$	$E(B)$
1.05c'	.05c'	$\dfrac{1.35-1.05}{.40}$	.428	.0214c'
1.07c'	.07c'	$\dfrac{1.35-1.07}{.40}$	.350	.0245c'
1.10c'	.10c'	$\dfrac{1.35-1.10}{.40}$	.252	.0252c'
1.12c'	.12c'	$\dfrac{1.35-1.12}{.40}$	.200	.0240c'
1.15c'	.15c'	$\dfrac{1.35-1.15}{.40}$	.140	.0210c'
1.20c'	.20c'	$\dfrac{1.35-1.20}{.40}$	.062	.0124c'
1.25c'	.25c'	$\dfrac{1.35-1.25}{.40}$	.020	.0050c'

that the way to maximize expected profits is to bid about 10 percent more than the corrected cost estimate. If this is done, the average profit over all contracts bid on will be 2.52 percent of cost. The average profit for those contracts which are actually performed will, of course, be 10 percent.

OTHER PRINCIPLES OF CHOICE

The establishment of bidding policy is often based upon other principles of choice than expectation maximizing. The firm may simply aspire to a profit of x percent on any contract which it obtains. It may simply bid its estimated cost plus x percent on all bids. Alternatively, the firm may be short of work and willing to undertake contracts for any price which exceeds the variable cost of performance. This excess will then help to reduce the fixed cost loss which the company would suffer without the contract.

In formulating the bidding problem in this manner it has been assumed that the firm's bidding behavior does not directly influence that of its competitors. In other words, the bids of the competition are taken to be independent of the firm's bid. An alternative approach is suggested by the "Theory of Games," in Chapter 10, which would not require this assumption.

PROBLEMS

6–1.*   On the basis of a study of the performance of its estimating department, a firm concludes that the ratio of actual cost to estimated cost for past contracts is a random variable. It may reasonably be described by a normal distribution with mean 1.00 and standard deviation .03. It views its competitors as stereotypic bidders. The ratio of a competitor's bid to the firm's cost estimate is also a random variable.

It may be described by a normal distribution with mean of 1.00 and standard deviation .10. The number of competitors which have bid for past contracts is suggested by the following frequency distribution:

Number of Competitors	Relative Frequency
2	.10
3	.60
4	.30

Find the bidding policy (in terms of the firm's cost estimate) which will maximize expected profit.

6-2. Find the bid which will maximize expected profit in the following situation: The density function of the ratio of estimated to actual cost, based on the firm's experience, is taken to be normal with mean 1.05 and standard deviation .053. The competitors are viewed as stereotypic bidders. The ratio of a competitor's bid to the firm's cost estimate is normally distributed with mean 1.00 and standard deviation .04. The probability that the firm will be opposed by k other bidders is as follows:

k	0	2	3	4
Probability	.05	.20	.65	.10

Interpret your answer.

6-3. Given:

$$f(e) = \text{normal } (\mu = 1.00, \ \sigma = .10)$$
$$g(t) = \text{uniform } (.95 \leqslant t \leqslant 1.35)$$

k	2	3	4
$h(k)$	$\frac{1}{5}$	$\frac{3}{5}$	$\frac{1}{5}$

Find the bid which will maximize expected profit.

6-4. Discuss the application of principles of choice other than the expectation principle to the bidding policy decision. How may the current financial and workload status of the firm influence the principle of choice used?

6-5. What are the sources of uncertainty in the bidding policy decision? How might the decision be treated if it were not possible to express this risk in the form of probability distributions?

6-6.* A firm's estimating success is described by the density function:

$$f(e) = \text{normal } (\mu = 1.05, \ \sigma = .03)$$

In a certain contract competition it expects to be opposed by three familiar competitors, X, Y, and Z. From public bid openings in the past, evidence on the ratio of each of these competitors' bids to the firm's cost estimates has been obtained.

$$g(x) = \text{uniform } (.92 \leqslant x \leqslant 1.12)$$
$$g(y) = \text{uniform } (.99 \leqslant x \leqslant 1.21)$$
$$g(z) = \text{normal } (\mu = 1.02, \ \sigma = .04)$$

Find the bidding policy which will maximize expected profit on a job for which the firm's uncorrected cost estimate is $10,000.

6–7. How might one obtain the information necessary for an analysis such as that of problem 6–6? For an analysis such as that of problem 6–1?

6–8. Given

$$c = \$1850$$
$$f(e) = \text{uniform} (.95 \leqslant e \leqslant 1.05)$$
$$\text{Two competitors:} \ X; \ g(x) = \text{uniform} (1.03 \leqslant x \leqslant 1.23)$$
$$Y; \ g(y) = \text{uniform} (\ .88 \leqslant y \leqslant .98)$$

Find the bid which maximizes expected profit.

6–9. In what situations would you consider expected profit maximization a suitable basis for bidding policy? What arguments would you offer in its support? In what situations would some other principle be preferred? Explain

6–10.* Write the cumulative probability distribution of profit for the model developed in the chapter. How might this be useful in making recommendations to management?

6–11.* A company keeps records for some time of the *lowest competing* bid, X, in bidding competitions. It finds that the ratio of X to its own (uncorrected) cost estimate can be described by a random variable having a uniform density function over the range .95 to 1.35. It finds also that the ratio of its own cost estimates to actual costs is a normally distributed random variable with mean of 1.00 and standard deviation of .10. What should be the firm's bid if it wishes to maximize expected profit?

6–12. Develop a model for determining the bid which will maximize the decision maker's utility. Would a "risk averse" decision maker bid higher or lower than one with a linear utility function in the same situation?

SUGGESTIONS FOR FURTHER STUDY

Bedworth, David B. *Industrial Systems-Planning, Analysis, Control.* New York: The Ronald Press Company, 1973.

Hillier, F. S., and G. J. Lieberman. *Introduction to Operations Research.* San Francisco: Holden-Day, Inc., 1967.

Raiffa, Howard. *Decision Analysis.* Reading, Massachusetts: Addison-Wesley, 1970.

Schlaifer, Robert. *Analysis of Decisions Under Uncertainty.* New York: McGraw-Hill, Inc., 1969.

Wagner, H. M. *Principles of Operations Research.* Englewood Cliffs, N.J.: Prentice-Hall, Inc., 1969.

PURCHASING POLICY 7

The problem of purchasing a commodity on the open market involves uncertainty because of the movement of the market price which cannot be known with certainty in advance. The purchasing officer who purchases for his firm such commodities as leather, scrap iron, or grain must contend with this uncertainty in the formulation of buying strategy. The basic decision involves the determination of when and in what quantities to buy to satisfy the requirements of the firm in some "best" way. This is made difficult both by the fluctuations of the prices quoted by the market and by the transitory nature of any given price quotation. Once a price is known, a quick decision is required to take advantage of it. In this chapter some simple approaches to purchasing decisions under conditions of uncertainty will be discussed. The reader is invited to consider these not only because of the importance of the purchasing decisions themselves to many firms, but also because the analysis brings to light two important points. First, most decisions in the ongoing development of the firm appear as members of a sequence of decisions. In such a sequence, past decisions may have an important bearing on present decisions, and, in turn, future decisions may not be entirely independent of present decisions. Here we have an illustration of the sequential nature of decisions. Second, these purchasing decisions will provide an instance of choice where an aspiration level principle seems most appropriate, and the aspiration levels themselves can be chosen on the basis of a reasonable principle of choice.

It is interesting to note the similarity between the problems faced by the person who invests or speculates in securities and the purchasing agent who buys commodities for his firm. Successful trading for both depends upon the ability to predict future price movements and to formulate a strategy for taking advantage of the predicted movements. Here we will explore the logic of various market strategies under the assumption that the decision maker views future prices as random variables with predicted density functions. In the field of industrial purchasing such strategies as forward buying, "hand-to-mouth" buying, and speculation have been discussed. In the realm of the stock market, somewhat more complicated strategies have been used, going under the names of dollar cost averaging, formula planning, leverage, and so forth. For simplicity, what is being purchased will simply be referred to as "the commodity." Strategies which involve more than one market, such as hedging, and strategies which involve more than one commodity, such as leverage, will not be discussed. Rather, the problem of purchasing a single commodity in a single market will be examined.

SINGLE PROCUREMENT STRATEGY

Consider first the problem of purchasing a given amount of a commodity before a known future deadline. It will be assumed that the market can supply the required quantity, but at a price which is quoted periodically (daily). Each day a market price becomes known which is good for that day, but that day only. Market prices for future days are predicted, and these predictions are taken to be random variables. The purchaser has a variety of strategies open to him in making this procurement. He might decide in advance how much he will buy on each of the days which remain before the deadline. Alternatively, he may wait until the day's price has been quoted and then buy some quantity which might depend on the quoted price and the amount yet to be purchased. To begin the analysis we suppose that the purchaser has determined to obtain his requirements in a single procurement and seeks a good strategy for making this single procurement. The problem may be simplified by omitting several features of importance in actual purchasing problems. Thus it is assumed:

1. That the quantity required is determined.
2. That no costs or restrictions are associated with storing the commodity.
3. That there are no costs or brokerage fees for executing the procurement.

Because of the transitory nature of each day's market price, the purchaser can never make sure that he procures at the lowest possible price. Instead, he must consider each quotation as it is made and decide whether to buy or to wait in the hope of a better price at some future time. The core of the problem is to determine the critical price level, below which he buys, and above which he waits. Given probabilistic forecasts of future prices, these critical levels may be determined to minimize the expected price paid for the commodity. To show this, we define:

$$x = \text{a price quotation}$$
$$f_k(x) = \text{density function of price for day } k$$
$$N = \text{number of days available before the deadline}$$
$$X_k = \text{critical price level for day } k$$

The purchasing strategy may be expressed as:

$$\text{if on day } k, \ x \leqslant X_k, \text{ then buy}$$
$$x \geqslant X_k, \text{ then wait}$$

These critical price levels are, of course, aspiration levels and each day's choice is based upon an aspiration's level principle.

Using such a policy, the probability that the price on day k will be below (or equal to) X_k is

$$P_k = \int_0^{X_k} f_k(x) \, dx$$

and assuming no purchase has been made on days 1 through $k-1$, the expected price paid on day k is

$$e_k = \int_0^{X_k} x f_k(x) \, dx$$

Price is taken to be a continuous variable for the moment, although later it will be convenient to consider it as a discrete variable. The expected price paid on day k is (unconditionally):

$$E_k = \{e_k\} \prod_{i=1}^{k-1} (1 - P_i)$$

and the expected price paid over the period of N days available for procurement is

$$V = \sum_{k=1}^{N} E_k$$

The reader should examine these statements carefully to make sure he really agrees with them. It is helpful to keep in mind that the statements refer to prices paid as opposed to prices quoted. Since one does not always buy, the price paid may be zero when the price quoted on the market is above the critical price level. It may help also to examine the following simple example. Suppose we let

$$N = 3 \qquad f_k(x) = \frac{1}{b-a} \quad \text{for } a \leqslant x \leqslant b \text{ and}$$

$$\text{for all } k$$

$$X_k = \frac{a+b}{2} \quad \text{for } k = 1, 2$$

No critical price level for $k = 3$ since, if the purchase has not been made by that time, it must be made at whatever price is quoted.

Clearly, since the critical price levels for day 1 and day 2 lie at the mean of a uniform distribution, the probability that the quoted price will be below this level on either of these days is one half. This may be confirmed using the expression for P_k

$$P_k = \int_a^{(a+b)/2} \frac{1}{b-a} \, dx = \frac{(b-a)/2}{b-a} = \tfrac{1}{2}$$

For day 1 there is a probability of one half that we will not buy and thus pay a price of zero. There is also a probability of one half that we will buy. If we do, the expected price we pay will lie half way between a and $a + b \div 2$. Thus, the expected price paid is

$$\tfrac{1}{2}(0) + \tfrac{1}{2} \left\{ \frac{a+(a+b)/2}{2} \right\} = \frac{3a+b}{8}$$

This may be confirmed by use of the expression for e_k.

$$e_1 = \int_a^{(a+b)/2} \frac{x}{b-a} \, dx = \frac{x^2}{2(b-a)} \bigg|_a^{(a+b)/2} = \frac{3a+b}{8}$$

We now have

$$e_1 = \frac{3a+b}{8}$$

$$e_2 = \frac{3a+b}{8}$$

$$e_3 = \frac{a+b}{2}$$

It must be recalled that these are conditional expectations. They give the expected price paid on a particular day, given that the procurement has not been made previously. We may remove this condition simply by multiplying the expectations by the probability of the event upon which they are conditioned. The expected price paid on day 1 is unconditionally e_1 since we cannot buy prior to day 1.

$$E_1 = e_1$$

Note especially the way in which the limits on the product are interpreted in this case. The expectation for day 2 is conditional for not having purchased on day 1. The probability of not buying on day 1 is one half. This gives

$$E_2 = \tfrac{1}{2} \cdot e_2$$

Similarly

$$E_3 = \tfrac{1}{2} \cdot \tfrac{1}{2} \cdot e_3$$

We now need only note that what we pay on the average, over the three-day period, is the sum of the average amount paid on the individual days. Thus, from V we obtain the expected price paid for the three-day period as a whole. This expectation may be interpreted as the average price paid if the purchasing policy assumed is used for a very large number of three-day periods.

FINDING THE CRITICAL PRICE LEVELS

It is clear that the expected price paid, V, is a function of the critical price levels, X_k. Thus, one could go ahead to choose the X_k in such a way as to minimize the expected price paid. This gives us the interesting possibility of using the expectation principle to obtain aspiration levels which will actually be used in the execution of the policy. This is an example of one of the instances in which the aspiration levels can themselves be chosen in a best way.

For each k, the partial derivative of V with respect to X_k may be obtained and set equal to zero. It may easily be confirmed that the solutions of the resulting equations for the X_k will yield the set of critical price levels which will minimize V, the expected price paid. Thus, for $k \neq N$,

$$\frac{\partial V}{\partial X_k} = X_k f_k(X_k) \left\{ \prod_{i=1}^{k-1} (1 - P_i) \right\} + \sum_{j=k+1}^{N} e_j \left\{ \prod_{i=k}^{j-1} (1 - P_i) \right\} f_k(X_k)(-1) = 0$$

which yields

$$X_k = \sum_{j=k+1}^{N} e_j \left\{ \prod_{i \neq k+1}^{j-1} (1 - P_i) \right\}$$

It will be noted that the right hand side of this equation is simply the expected price paid over the days remaining before the deadline. Thus, the result has an interpretation which agrees with one's notions of strategy for the problem. Each day the purchaser compares the day's price quotation with the expected price he will pay if he waits and on each future day uses an optimal X_k. If the day's quotation is lower than his expected price using the optimal policy in the future, then he buys; if his expected price is lower, then he waits.

To illustrate the nature of the critical price levels obtained by this method, consider the following simple problem in which it is assumed that

1. $f_k(x) = f(x)$, for all k

2. $f(x) = \dfrac{1}{200}$, for $1{,}000 \leqslant x \leqslant 1{,}200$

For $k = N$, the purchaser has no choice, if he has not previously made the procurement. Because of the deadline he must buy at whatever price is quoted on day N. Thus,

$$e_N = 1{,}100$$

For $k = N-1$

$$X_{N-1} = 1{,}100$$
$$P_{N-1} = .50$$

$$e_{N-1} = \int_{1{,}000}^{1{,}100} \frac{x}{200}\, dx = 525$$

For $k = N-2$

$$X_{N-2} = 525 + (.50)(1{,}100) = 1{,}075$$
$$P_{N-2} = .375$$

$$e_{N-2} = \int_{1{,}000}^{1{,}075} \frac{x}{200}\, dx = 389$$

Similarly we obtain

$$X_{N-3} = 1{,}061$$
$$X_{N-4} = 1{,}052$$
$$X_{N-5} = 1{,}045$$
$$\dots\dots\dots\dots$$
$$\dots\dots\dots\dots$$

Figure 7-1 shows the critical buying levels for ten periods.

It is perhaps true that this result agrees with one's notions about the problem. If there is plenty of time before the procurement must be made, then one may hold out for a relatively low price. As the deadline for the procurement approaches, one is willing to accept a higher and higher price.

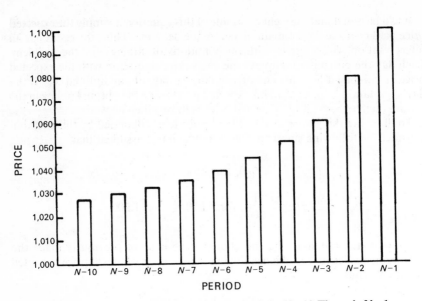

Figure 7-1   Critical Buying Levels for Periods $N-10$ Through $N-1$

GENERAL PROCUREMENT STRATEGY

It is sometimes argued, in connection with policy problems similar to that just discussed, that the purchaser would do better to distribute his purchases in some way over the time available before the deadline. Many such policies indicate that the amount purchased should depend on the quoted price, or more generally, on the price and the number of days remaining. While such policies may have appeal for purchasers who are unable to obtain predictions of future price movements, their value in the problem considered here is questionable. A little reflection on the foregoing analysis may serve to convince one that if the purchaser wishes to minimize expected cost of the procurement, then the single purchase strategy will do this. Nothing is to be gained by any strategy which involves multiple procurements. This important result may be more clearly established as follows. Suppose, as before, that Q units of the commodity must be purchased within N days, and that the basis for procurement is a function $q(x, k)$ which gives the quantity to be purchased. That is, on day k, if the quoted price is x, then the purchaser buys an amount $q(x, k)$. It is assumed that procurement ceases when Q units have been obtained.

It is convenient here to treat price as a discrete variable. Let the expected price quoted on day k be given by

$$A_k(x) = \sum_x x f_k(x)$$

and let

V_N = total expected cost of the procurement over N days

For $N = 1$, the purchaser can only buy all his requirements at the quoted price. Thus,

$$V_1 = QA_1(x)$$

For $N = 2$,

$$V_2 = \sum_x xq(x, 1) f_1(x) + \sum_x \{Q - q(x, 1)\} A_2(x) f_1(x)$$

The problem is thus to find the function $q(x, 1)$ which will minimize the expected cost V_2, subject to the restriction that

$$0 \leqslant q(x, 1) \leqslant Q, \quad \text{for all } x$$

This is a simple linear programming problem, the solution of which may be obtained by inspection. The expression for V_2 may be reduced to

$$V_2 = \sum_x \{x - A_2(x)\} q(x, 1) f_1(x) + QA_2(x)$$

It may be seen that this function will be minimized under the given restrictions by taking

$$q(x, 1) = 0, \quad \text{if} \quad x - A_2(x) > 0$$
$$q(x, 1) = Q, \quad \text{if} \quad x - A_2(x) < 0$$

This is precisely the same as saying, "If the quotation on day 1 is below the expected price on day 2, buy the entire amount required; otherwise buy nothing until day 2." This is simply the single procurement strategy already given. However, it is now seen that (for $N = 2$, at least) no policy involving more than a single purchase is desirable.

For $N = 3$

$$V_3 = \sum_x xq(x, 1) f_1(x) + \sum_x \{Q - q(x, 1)\} \frac{V_2}{Q} f_1(x)$$

$$= \sum_x \left\{ x - \frac{V_2}{Q} \right\} q(x, 1) f_1(x) + V_2$$

In general, if N days are available before the deadline, we have an N-stage process in the form of a dynamic programming problem. The expected cost is given by

$$V_N = \sum_x \left\{ x - \frac{V_{N-1}}{Q} \right\} q(x, 1) f_1(x) + V_{N-1}$$

or in the more usual form

$$V_N = \sum_x xq(x, 1) f_1(x) + V_{N-1} \left\{ 1 - \frac{1}{Q} \sum_x q(x, 1) f_1(x) \right\}$$

The solution is of the form obtained previously. Thus take

$$q(x, 1) = 0, \quad \text{if} \quad x - \frac{V_{N-1}}{Q} > 0$$

$$q(x, 1) = Q, \quad \text{if} \quad x - \frac{V_{N-1}}{Q} < 0$$

The optimal policy at any stage consists of computing the expected unit cost using optimal buying prices for all future stages and buying all requirements immediately if the current quotation is below this amount, otherwise buying nothing at present. This provides a demonstration of the optimal character of the single procurement strategy.

At this point certain complications may be easily introduced. If there are brokerage charges or other expenses which depend only on the number of procurements made, the single procurement strategy clearly minimizes these costs. Thus, no change in the policy will result. If known holding costs or storage charges are to be introduced, the price in any period may simply be increased by an amount equal to the unit cost of holding from that period until the deadline. For example, if a procurement were made in period $N-k$, and if holding costs were simply c dollars per unit per period, then the price in period $N-k$ may be taken as $x+ck$. While this will change the critical price levels, it does not detract from the optimality of the single procurement strategy.

DOLLAR AVERAGING

Although the optimality of the single procurement strategy has already been demonstrated under a particular set of assumptions, it is worthwhile to investigate certain other strategies which are in wide use. One form of purchasing policy in which the amount purchased is a function of price is called "dollar averaging" or "dollar cost averaging." This policy suggests that, at each purchasing opportunity, a fixed dollar amount should be expended, regardless of the price. Thus, for example, one is encouraged to invest $50 each month in a security without being concerned as to the price. The purpose of this policy is to free the purchaser from having to make a forecast of future price movements and to average down the mean price of the stock held, as more and more purchases are made. It accomplishes this latter result by leading to the purchase of relatively few units when the price is high, and relatively many units when the price is low. For the investor, this policy is supposed to increase the proportion of the time that his portfolio is "in the black," in the sense that the average price of units held is lower than the current quotation. Some of the properties of this policy may be illustrated in the following simple fashion.

Consider a series of purchasing opportunities which may occur daily, weekly, monthly, or according to the needs of the purchaser. We assume that a policy of spending exactly d dollars at each opportunity is to be used, and that the density function of price for the jth opportunity, $f_j(x)$, is given. Then the expected number of units purchased on the jth opportunity is

$$\int_x \frac{d}{x} f_j(x)\, dx$$

In N opportunities the expected total number of units purchased is

$$\sum_{j=1}^{N} \int_x \frac{d}{x} f_j(x)\, dx$$

The amount expended in N opportunities is Nd. Thus the expected unit cost after N opportunities is

$$E(c) = \frac{Nd}{\sum_{j=1}^{N} \int_x (d/x) f_j(x)\,dx} = \frac{N}{\sum_{j=1}^{N} \int_x (1/x) f_j(x)\,dx}$$

It is clear that the expected unit cost is independent of the fixed purchase expenditure d, but dependent upon the number of opportunities N.

For simplicity assume that $f_j(x) = f(x)$, for all j. In this case

$$E(c) = \frac{N}{N \int_x (1/x) f(x)\,dx} = \frac{1}{E(1/x)}$$

and the expected unit cost becomes independent of the number of opportunities as well. To show that the policy does, in fact, tend to reduce the expected unit cost of units purchased, assume further that

$$f(x) = \frac{1}{b-a}$$

To show that $E(c) < E(x)$, we simply compute, in Table 7-1, a few values of these expectations as function of b and a.

Table 7-1

b/a	$E(x)$	$E(c)$
1....................	a	a
2....................	$1.5a$	$1.44a$
3....................	$2.0a$	$1.82a$
4....................	$2.5a$	$2.16a$

In general, of course, dollar averaging cannot offer any special protection against portfolio losses in a declining market. Returning to the more general expression for $E(c)$

$$E(c) = \frac{N}{\sum_{j=1}^{N} E_j(1/x)}$$

it is of interest to note that $E(c)$ does not increase with N if

$$\frac{N-1}{\sum_{j=1}^{N-1} E_j(1/x)} - \frac{N}{\sum_{j=1}^{N} E_j(1/x)} \geq 0$$

which yields

$$E_N\left(\frac{1}{x}\right) - \frac{1}{N} \sum_{j=1}^{N} E_j\left(\frac{1}{x}\right) \geq 0$$

Thus, in a rising market, the value of $E(c)$ must rise also. If the rise is followed by a decline, then the portfolio may pass through an extended period "in the red." Table 7-2 illustrates a simple instance of this. Here it is assumed that the price quotation for opportunity j is given by

$$f_j(x) = \frac{1}{b_j - a_j}$$

where

$$b_j/a_j = 2, \quad \text{for all } j$$

Table 7-2

j	a	$E_j(x)$	$E(c)$
1 10		15.0	14.4
2 12		18.0	15.8
3 14		21.0	16.9
4 12		18.0	17.1
5 10		15.0	16.4
6 8		12.0	15.3
7 6		9.0	13.8
8 8		12.0	13.4
9 10		15.0	13.6

From the viewpoint of purchasing policy, dollar averaging cannot improve the purchaser's expectation beyond the single procurement strategy. However, it does have some appeal in situations where capital becomes available in regular amounts and at regular intervals. Perhaps its most appealing application is to the situation in which the purchaser does not wish, or is not able, to obtain a forecast of future price movements.

The fundamental idea of dollar averaging, increasing the number of units purchased as the prices declines, suggests immediately that the results might be improved by making the amount purchased even more sensitive to price. Thus, one might buy d/x^2 units on each opportunity, instead of simply d/x. Such a policy might be called "accelerated dollar averaging." It does in fact serve to reduce the expected unit cost of the units purchased. Returning to Table 7-1, it is easy to show that, under the conditions for which this table is valid, if one uses a d/x^2 policy, then for $b/a = 2$, $E(c) = 1.39a$. This represents an improvement over the results for the ordinary dollar averaging policy which yields $E(c) = 1.44a$. Extension of the idea of accelerated dollar averaging leads directly to the single purchase strategy discussed previously.

SPECULATION

While speculation is not a policy viewed with favor by many industrial enterprises, the simplest aspects of speculative buying and selling will be illustrated by way of contrast. Assume that a speculator wishes to maximize expected profit, and that he is confronted with a current price quotation, y, and a density function for the price on the next opportunity, $f(x)$. To maximize expectation, the speculator computes the expected price for the next opportunity $E(x)$ and applies the following rule:

> If $y - E(x) > 0$; sell as much as possible
> $y - E(x) < 0$; buy as much as possible

It follows directly that the expected unit profit is given by

$$|y - E(x)|$$

for each opportunity. If one assumes that the costs of making a transaction are small enough to be neglected, and that there is no problem of the speculator being ruined, then at every opportunity as much as possible should be bought or sold, according to the rule. If one takes $f(y) = f(x)$, then the expected unit of profit over a series of opportunities is

$$E\{|x - E(x)|\}$$

which is the average deviation of x. Thus, the greater the variability in the price of the commodity, the greater the expected profits from speculation.

In practice, many speculators modify this policy by not trading at every opportunity, and by restricting the amount bought or sold so as to limit the maximum possible losses. Of special interest is the problem of finding the probability that the speculator's wealth will fall below some given level within a certain number of opportunities.

The attempt has been made to give some insight into the nature of several purchasing policies by means of simple analysis. Perhaps the most typical procurement situation is that of obtaining a fixed amount of a commodity before a given deadline. If the market is characterized by probabilistic future price quotations, then it has been shown that the expectation minimizing policy is to make a single procurement. This procurement is made according to a set of buying price levels which determine whether a purchase is made, given a price quotation.

PROBLEMS

7–1.* A man has two days within which to sell his house. If it is not sold on the first day it must be sold on the second.

Let:

> $x =$ the highest offer received on the first day
> $f(x) =$ the probability distribution of x
> $y =$ the highest offer received on the second day
> $f(y) =$ the probability distribution of y

Offers are good only on the day received. The man desires to set an acceptance price for the first day, say A, such that

> if $x > A$ he sells at price x on the first day
> if $x < A$ he sells at price y on the second day

Find the acceptance price A which will maximize the expected price he obtains. Does this policy make sense from his point of view? Explain. Model this decision in the form of a tree.

7-2.* A firm wishes to buy 10,000 units of a commodity over the next five days. Its prediction of the price movements over this period takes the form of a probability distribution for the daily price, x.

$$f_k(x) = \text{uniform } (1{,}100 < x \leqslant 1{,}200)$$

Find the purchasing policy which will minimize the expected total cost of the procurement. Model this decision in the form of a tree.

7-3.* Given:

$$f_k(x) = \text{normal } (\mu = 1{,}000 + 50[k-1], \sigma = 100)$$
$$N = 6$$

Find the procurement policy for the purchase of 100 units which will minimize expected costs. Compute the minimum expected cost of the procurement. Interpret this quantity. Model this decision in the form of a tree.

7-4. What other principles of choice would you consider good possibilities for the purchasing policy problem which is defined in this chapter?

7-5. What relation between the expectation principle and the aspiration level principle is demonstrated by this decision? What can be said in support of computing aspiration levels in this way?

7-6. In what ways does the analysis of this chapter fail to agree with the formulation of industrial purchasing policy as you understand it? Is the analysis of this chapter typical of the way people buy stocks in the stock market?

7-7. How would you handle the problem of purchasing policy if the market price were not independent of the firm's purchase, and depended on the quantity bought?

7-8. Explain the meaning of the expression

$$E_k = \{e_k\} \prod_{i=1}^{k-1} (1 - P_i)$$

7-9. What happens to the purchasing problem if the time deadline is removed?

7-10.* You are invited to play the following game. You may draw a sample of one number from a population of numbers having a uniform distribution over the range -5 to 5. The numbers are restricted to integers. After each such draw you have two alternatives. You may accept a number of dollars from your opponent equal to the number drawn if it is positive, or pay your opponent an amount in dollars equal to the number if it is negative. Alternatively, you may discard the number and go on to another draw. At most you are allowed five draws, and when you decide to stop the payoff is the last number drawn. How should this game be played in order to maximize expectation?

7-11. Discuss the uses and advantages of dollar cost averaging. Design a plan for accelerated dollar cost averaging.

7-12. In what respects does the model of speculation suggested in the chapter fail to describe actual speculative behavior as you understand it? Is an expectation principle suitable for the ordinary speculator?

7-13. What are the values of analysis such as has been done here if exact quantification is not possible?

7–14.* A policy of accelerated dollar cost averaging might be based on the following rule: When the price is x, buy d/x^2 units where d is a positive constant. Write expressions for

    a) The average number of units bought on the jth opportunity
    b) The average total number of units bought in N opportunities
    c) The average amount spent on the jth opportunity
    d) The average amount spent over N opportunities
    e) The average unit cost for N opportunities
    f) The average unit cost for N opportunities if

$$f_j(x) = f(x) = \frac{1}{b-a}, \qquad \text{for all } j$$

    g) Compute the average unit cost from part *f*) for values of b/a of 2, 3, and 4.

7–15.* A firm has three days in which to buy 1000 tons of a commodity which it processes. It views the price on any day as a uniformly distributed continuous random variable over the range \$90.00 to \$110.00 per ton.

    a) Specify fully a procurement policy which will be best for a firm which has a linear utility function in the relevant region.
    b) Write (but do not compute) an expression for the expected total cost of the procurement program specified by your policy.
    c) The firm does not follow your policy, but instead buys all 1000 tons on the first day at a price of \$100 per ton. In terms of the *principles of choice we have considered* how could their behavior be explained?

7–16.* A man has two days in which to sell his house. If it is not sold on the first day, it must be sold on the second. He views the highest offer received on either day as a random variable x with pdf given by $f(x)$.

Offers are good only on the day received unless he elects to buy an option at price k. The effect of the option is to hold open an offer received on the first day so that he may, if he wishes, accept it on the second day.

Show explicitly his best policy if he has a linear utility function.

7–17.* A firm must buy a considerable quantity of a commodity within the next three days. The price is fluctuating at the present time and the firm is uncertain about future price movements. It is willing, however, to predict that the price on each of the next three days will be a uniformly distributed continuous random variable with the ranges shown below.

Day	Minimum Price	Maximum Price
1	\$8.50	\$14.50
2	9.00	15.00
3	9.50	15.50

What procurement policy would you recommend?

SUGGESTIONS FOR FURTHER STUDY

Bedworth, David B. *Industrial Systems-Planning, Analysis, Control.* New York: The Ronald Press Company, 1973.

Hillier, F. S., and G. J. Lieberman. *Introduction to Operations Research.* San Francisco: Holden-Day, Inc., 1967.

Raiffa, Howard. *Decision Analysis.* Reading, Massachusetts: Addison-Wesley, 1970.

Schlaifer, Robert. *Analysis of Decisions Under Uncertainty.* New York: McGraw-Hill, Inc., 1969.

Wagner, H. M. *Principles of Operations Research.* Englewood Cliffs, N.J.: Prentice-Hall, Inc., 1969.

DECISIONS WITHOUT PROBABILITIES

8

Consider a manufacturer using steel as a major input to his production process. The expiration of union contracts in the steel industry is approaching, and there is considerable public and private speculation concerning the possibility of a steel strike. Some steel users are buying extra quantities of steel as a protective inventory in the event of a strike. Our manufacturer raises the questions of whether he should provide such an additional inventory and what size it should be. Suppose we begin to make the decision explicit by considering the alternatives to be various amounts of extra steel inventory, the possible futures to be various durations of a steel strike, and the values of the outcomes to be the marginal costs resulting from the various inventory size–strike duration combinations. The remaining difficult question is what probabilities to associate with the possible futures.

Our first attempt might be the usual one of looking for available data on which to base these probabilities or trying to design some sort of experiment which will produce the data. Perhaps we find this difficult, even impossible. The obvious move of examining the history of past steel negotiations with a view toward finding some data which will lead to the required probabilities may be rejected because in our opinion the economic, political, profit, inventory, and union-strength situation is not sufficiently similar to past instances.

Our next step might be to confront management with our inability to proceed further by methods of data collection and analysis, asking for their judgments as to the likelihood of steel strikes of various durations. Perhaps we could transform these judgments into probabilities. Given these probabilities we would then be able to treat the decision as one under conditions of uncertainty by the methods we have previously suggested. We might point out to management that any recommendation we made would be a course of action consistent with management's own probabilities, rather than one consistent with probabilities based on data we have collected and explicitly analyzed.

Another similar possibility might be that of consulting some person or group believed to be expert in the field of labor relations in general or the steel situation in particular. We might decide to recommend to management a course of action consistent with the opinion obtained from such an expert. Again we might succeed in expressing the experts' judgment in terms of probabilities.

Instead of any of these responses we might finally take our conception of the decision-lacking probabilities and apply some principle of choice. In this chapter we will examine some principles of choice of this sort which do not require explicit probabilities.

To illustrate one such principle, suppose we confer with management asking them only to place an upper bound on the length of a steel strike which they consider possible. Presumably this is easier for them to judge than the likelihoods of strikes of various lengths. Suppose they agree that it is unlikely—indeed in their opinion virtually impossible—that a strike last more than four weeks. Of course this opinion may turn out to be wrong, but we will assume that they agree that policy for the firm is to be determined as though it were correct. That is, affairs will be managed in a fashion consistent with the opinion that it is impossible (probability zero) for a strike to last more than four weeks. With this in mind suppose we express the incremental costs involved in the matrix shown below.

One principle of choice proposed for processing data of this sort is the "minimax" principle. It suggests that one choose the alternative which would minimize the maximum cost. The maximum costs for the alternatives are listed to the right of the matrix. The minimum of these maxima is associated with the alternative, "Stock three weeks' supply of steel."

		\multicolumn{5}{c}{*Length of Strike* (*weeks*)}	*Maximum*
		0	1	2	3	4	*Cost*
	0	0	$20,000	$40,000	$60,000	$80,000	$80,000
	1	$10,000	1,000	20,000	40,000	60,000	60,000
Extra inventory	2	20,000	10,000	2,000	20,000	40,000	40,000
(*weeks' supply*)	3	30,000	20,000	10,000	3,000	20,000	30,000
	4	40,000	30,000	20,000	10,000	4,000	40,000

CONDITIONS LEADING TO DECISIONS WITHOUT PROBABILITIES

The analyst aims at making predictions of possible future events by means of an explicit prediction model and historical or experimental data, or by the encoding of expert opinion. When this cannot be done, then he may choose to conceptualize the decision as one without probabilities. Several futures are possible, but evidence is not available on which to base statements of their probabilities. This does not mean that complete ignorance prevails or that there is no relevant experience. The analyst, as a scientifically trained person, may not himself have experience with the situations in question, and if he had, he might be reluctant to inject his opinions into the analysis. Management, however, may have considerable relevant experience, or experts may be available whose experience may be called upon, but for various reasons indicated in Chapter 3, the encoding of this experience may be too difficult or too costly.

RESPONSES

Speaking generally, if, as an analyst, one conceives of a management decision as one without probabilities, then among the possible responses are

1. Get the data or do the experiment on which some probabilities may be explicitly based, thus transforming the decision into one under uncertainty by the addition of the ordinary sort of relative frequency probabilities. There are many cases in which this is simply impossible; and where it is possible, it involves the difficult questions of how much ought to be spent and how much data collected.
2. Obtain expert judgments or the judgments of managers themselves, expressing these in the form of probabilities.
3. Treat the decision using some principle of choice which does not require probabilities as part of its input data.

We are thus confronted with a series of difficult questions. Which of these responses will provide the best basis for understanding management decisions? Which will provide the best method of producing recommendations for management action? Once again, the answers to such questions cannot be given in general, and the analyst must develop experience and judgment of his own in the matter. In this chapter we will examine the problems and possibilities associated with these responses. We begin by examining a number of principles of choice which do not depend on the presence of probabilities in the analyst's conception of the decision and thus may be used directly.

PRINCIPLES OF CHOICE

As an example of such a decision, consider the following decision matrix. The numbers in the matrix are to be taken as profits or gains.

	S_1	S_2	S_3	S_4
a_1	4	4	0	2
a_2	2	2	2	2
a_3	0	8	0	0
a_4	2	6	0	0
a_5	0	1	1	0

As before, we will suggest several principles of choice which might be applied, and then discuss the considerations surrounding each of them.

Dominance.   If one of two alternatives is always preferred no matter what future occurs, this preferred alternative is said to dominate. The other alternative may then be discarded, since there is no further reason to consider it. In the example it is clear that, for any future, the profit from a_2 will be greater than the profit from a_5, and thus a_5 may be eliminated. The first step in approaching any decision under uncertainty is to eliminate any alternatives which are thus dominated. Formally stated, the principle of dominance suggests: *If there is a pair of alternatives a_i and a_k such that $V(\theta_{ij}) \geqslant V(\theta_{kj})$ for all j, a_i is* *said to dominate* a_k. *The alternative* a_k *may then be discarded from the decision problem.* This principle may not yield a unique alternative which would be recommended, but it may help to reduce the range of alternatives which must be further considered.

Laplace Principle (Principle of Insufficient Reason). There is a common tendency toward the assumption that all the futures will simply be considered equally likely. Having made this assumption, one may then maximize expectation. It is sometimes suggested that, in the absence of any evidence to the contrary, one might as well assume that the futures are equally likely. This argument, of highly questionable merit, has led to the name "principle of insufficient reason." To state the principle precisely: *Assume all possible futures are of equal probability, then select the alternative which maximizes expectation.* In the example, this leads to assuming

$$p_1 = p_2 = p_3 = p_4 = \tfrac{1}{4}$$

and the expected profits would be

$$E(a_1) = 2.5$$
$$E(a_2) = 2.0$$
$$E(a_3) = 2.0$$
$$E(a_4) = 2.0$$

The Laplace principle would lead them to the selection of a_1.

Maximin or Minimax Principle. A widely discussed principle suggests that we examine the minimum profit associated with each alternative, and then select the alternative which maximizes the minimum profit. This is clearly a conservative or pessimistic principle which directs attention to the worst outcome and makes the worst outcome as desirable as possible. It says: *Select the alternative, i, associated with* $\max_i \min_j V(\theta_{ij})$.

From this it derives the obvious name, maximin. If we were dealing with a decision in which costs instead of profits were given, the principle would be reinterpreted. It would suggest that we examine the maximum cost associated with each alternative, and then select the alternative which minimizes the maximum cost. In this form it is called the "minimax principle."

The obvious antithesis of the maximin principle might be called the "maximax principle." It suggests that we examine the maximum profit associated with each alternative, and then select the alternative which maximizes the maximum profit: *Select the alternative, i, associated with* $\max_i \max_j V(\theta_{ij})$.

The maximax principle is thus as optimistic and adventurous as the maximin principle is pessimistic and conservative. In the example, the minimum profits for a_1 through a_4 are 0, 2, 0, and 0, respectively. Thus, a_2 would be selected as the alternative which maximizes the minimum profit.

Hurwicz Principle. Most decision makers find their outlook somewhere between the extreme pessimism of the minimax principle and the equally extreme optimism of the maximax principle. A principle which accounts for all levels of moderation between these two extremes is called the Hurwicz principle. It suggests that the degree of optimism of the decision maker be measured on a scale from 0 to 1. If the decision maker is relatively pessimistic, this scale would supply an index, α, close to 0. If he is relatively optimistic, his α would be close to 1. Having obtained a measure of optimism, α, for the decision maker, we then multiply the maximum profit for each alternative by α, and the minimum profit for each alternative by $1-\alpha$. The sum of these products for each alternative is called the "Hurwicz criterion," and the alternative which maximizes this criterion is selected. The principle says explicitly: *Select an index of optimism α, such that $0 \leqslant \alpha \leqslant 1$. For each a_i compute $\alpha \{\max_j V(\theta_{ij})\} + (1-\alpha)\{\min_j V(\theta_{ij})\}$ and select the alternative which maximizes this quantity.*

Note that if the decision maker is optimistic in the extreme, $\alpha = 1$, and the Hurwicz principle becomes the maximax principle. The extreme of pessimism gives $\alpha = 0$, and we have the minimax principle. In the example we have

	$\max_i V(\theta_{ij})$	$\min_i V(\theta_{ij})$
a_1	4	0
a_2	2	2
a_3	8	0
a_4	6	0

In Figure 8-1 the value of the Hurwicz criterion has been plotted for each alternative over the entire range of α. From this diagram it may be seen that if $\alpha < .25$, a_2 is the preferred, but if $\alpha > .25$, then a_3 would be selected.

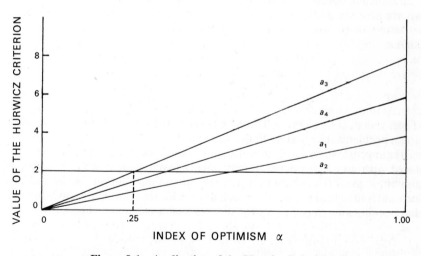

Figure 8-1   Application of the Hurwicz Principle

Savage Principle (Minimax Regret).   Still another principle has been proposed which has certain desirable features. This principle, proposed by L. J. Savage, suggests that a new matrix called a "regret matrix" be computed first. For each alternative-future combination, the difference should be computed between the profit that will result and the maximum profit that could be obtained for the future under consideration. This quantity is called "regret." In the example, the regret for a_1 and S_2 is found by subtracting the profit, 4, from the maximum profit that could be obtained given S_2, 8. The difference of 4 is the regret for the cell a_1, S_2. Having completed the regret matrix, the alternative is selected which minimizes the maximum regret. Regret is given by the relation

$$\text{Regret for } a_k \text{ and } S_j = \max_i V(\theta_{ij}) - V(\theta_{kj})$$

The regret matrix for the example is

	S_1	S_2	S_3	S_4	Maximum Regret
a_1	0	4	2	0	4
a_2	2	6	0	0	6
a_3	4	0	2	2	4
a_4	2	2	2	2	2

The alternative which minimizes the maximum regret is thus a_4. The intuitive appeal of the regret principle may be suggested by the following line of thought. If, after a course of action has been selected and carried out, we discover that some particular future, say S_2, actually turns out, then we might wish we had chosen a_3. The choice of a_3, from this hindsight position, would clearly have been the best. If we have in fact chosen some other alternative, say a_2, then we are disappointed or regretful about our choice. A measure of this disappointment or regret is the difference between the value of the best possible choice and our actual choice, given that a particular future has happened.

Note that in this example each of the four principles leads to a different choice.

Laplace........................a_1
Maximin........................a_2
Hurwicz ($\alpha > .25$)...............a_3
Savage.........................a_4

Thus, there is in general a difference between the four principles although in some problems they may yield the same results.

These principles may be understood in several ways. For example, a person faced with a complex decision may have a psychological need for a rule of thumb, a guide to behavior which simplifies the situation for him. These principles may be understood as such devices for simplifying the environment. In choosing among principles for this purpose a person would want to select one which reflected his feelings about the decision problem he faced. The principle would then be an aid to making his attitudes explicit. As analysts we might consider a principle to be a first, very simple hypothesis about management behavior. Testing the hypothesis with past decisions, or by means of direct questions to the manager, the analyst might select a principle as a model for predicting consistent management choices in future decisions. Thus, just as in the case of decisions under uncertainty, a recommendation based on a principle of choice could be considered a prediction of how the manager would choose if he were logically consistent.

Notice that these principles can be thought of as equivalent to expressing the attitudes of the decision maker in the form of subjective probabilities. The

Laplace principle is obviously equivalent to a uniform subjective probability distribution over the possible futures. The minimax principle is equivalent to the belief that the probabilities of the possible futures *depend on* which action is chosen and for any action the worst possible future will occur with probability one. Notice, however, that a manager who finds this principle useful may not hold this belief, but may simply be cautious and wish to protect himself against the worst that could happen. Similarly, in the Hurwicz and Savage cases, one may think of these as equivalent to subjective probabilities which are not independent of the action chosen.

THE LAPLACE PRINCIPLE

The very statement of this principle raises strong feelings of doubt. Its highly gratuitous character leaves little to be said for it, except that it is simple and gives definite selections among the alternatives. Its application is complicated by difficulties in obtaining statements of possible futures which form collectively exhaustive and mutually exclusive sets of futures. For example, in the decision to invest in a certain machine, it is generally no simple matter to decide on a way of listing the possible futures. Many listings might be given, and the choice may well depend simply on which list is used. For example, suppose we are deciding between a general-purpose machine and a special-purpose machine. Assume that we are negotiating for three contracts, any one of which would load the machine, and no more than one of which we would accept if negotiations are successful. There are two ways of listing the futures, which appear sensible among the several which might be used:

I. S_1 = we get no contract   II. S_1 = we get no contract
   S_2 = we get a contract S_2 = we get contract A
                                     S_3 = we get contract B
                                     S_4 = we get contract C

Assuming that under S_1 we might still have use for the general-purpose machine, the profit matrix might be

Using List I:

	S_1	S_2	$E(a_i)$
a_1 = special-purpose machine	−1	6	2.50
a_2 = general-purpose machine	1	5	3.00

Using List II:

	S_1	S_2	S_3	S_4	$E(a_i)$
a_1 = special-purpose machine	−1	6	6	6	4.25
a_2 = general-purpose machine	1	5	5	5	4.00

Thus the choice might depend simply on the way in which we decided to list the possible futures.

Now one may argue against this that the possible futures should be listed in such a way as to make them equally likely, but this presumes that we have some knowledge of the probabilities. This places the decision maker in that vague and difficult area where he is not willing to admit he is completely ignorant of the probabilities, but he finds it extremely difficult to make the precise statements about their values.

Another symptom of this same difficulty arises in the application of the Laplace principle to problems such as the following: Suppose an investment decision depends importantly on the salvage value of equipment at some future time. To say that we are "completely ignorant" of this salvage value is to say that it could be any number from negative infinity to positive infinity. This is clearly foolishness, and the decision maker must admit that he is not completely ignorant. In fact, what he may wish to do, is to say that a certain range of salvage values is possible, and that values outside this range are impossible. He may then assume that all values within the range are equally likely. As later examples will illustrate, the outcome of this process depends heavily on the range of possible values selected, and the Laplace criterion gives no guidance as to how this should be done.

THE MAXIMIN OR MINIMAX PRINCIPLE

The decision maker who chooses so as to maximize his minimum profit or minimize his maximum loss may certainly be described as conservative, pessimistic, security conscious, timid, and unadventurous. These principles have their most useful application in situations where conservatism and security are desired and seem appropriate to the decision maker. Life insurance is a typical example. Decisions made in many stable, "old line," conservative companies are characterized by these principles. There are other situations in which these ideas lead to such extreme conservatism as to be nonsensical and thus they are cast aside in favor of others. An extreme example of the kind of decision in which many feel ill at ease with the maximin principle is the following:

	S_1	S_2
a_1	$0	$1,000
a_2	1	1

Maximin clearly leads to a_2, while many feel that there is something intuitively more desirable about a_1. This is reinforced by the observation that the payoffs for a_2 could be reduced to one cent and the payoff for a_1, S_2 raised to a billion dollars without altering the choice indicated by the maximin principle. Another objection which might be raised against this principle is that it does not possess a property called "column linearity." This may be illustrated by the following example.

In the following matrix of profits, the maximin principle would clearly lead to the choice of a_1:

	S_1	S_2
a_1	$ 5	$8
a_2	10	2

Now suppose that it is stated that if S_2 is the possible future which is actually realized, the decision maker will receive an additional income of $4.00, no matter which alternative he has chosen. This simply has the effect of adding a constant to the column headed S_2. Many have argued that, since this constant depends only on which possible future is realized, and is in no way connected with which alternative is chosen, it should not change the decision maker's selection. However, this is not the case with the maximin principle, as an examination of the following modified matrix will reveal:

$$
\begin{array}{ccc}
 & S_1 & S_2 \\
a_1 & \$\ 5 & \$12 \\
a_2 & 10 & 6
\end{array}
$$

Now a_2 is chosen. To put it another way, it is argued that, since the additional $4.00 has exactly the same effect on both alternatives, it should not influence one's choice. The fact that the maximin principle does not have this property is taken by some to defract from its suitability as a useful principle of choice. It will be noted that the Laplace principle does have the property of column linearity.

THE HURWICZ PRINCIPLE

The Hurwicz principle was originated to avoid the extreme conservatism of minimax or the radicalism of a principle such as maximax. Thus, it allows various degrees of moderation according to the optimism or pessimism of the decision maker. The most obvious operational criticism of this principle centers around the method for determining the proper value of the index α. If this is simply left "to the judgment" of the decision maker, then the principle loses to some degree its objectivity. There is perhaps no other way of getting at the value of α; however, it has been suggested that such a judgment might be sharpened and made explicit. One way to do this might be to confront the decision maker with a choice problem of the following form:

$$
\begin{array}{c|c|c}
 & S_1 & S_2 \\
\hline
a_1 & 0 & 1 \\
\hline
a_2 & x & x \\
\end{array}
$$

Assuming the values in the matrix are profits, the decision maker is then asked to indicate for what value of x he would be indifferent as to which alternative he chose. For what value of x would the alternatives be equally desirable? If he can state a value of x, then the Hurwicz principle may be applied to quantify the equivalence of the alternatives.

$$
\alpha(1) + (1-\alpha)(0) = \alpha x + (1-\alpha)x
$$

The solution of this equation yields

$$
\alpha = x
$$

There are several difficulties with this process, which arise in many other places in the study of decision making. It may be difficult to find a sample choice problem which has enough meaning to elicit a reasonable response from the decision maker as to his value of x, or in turn, α. One must also assume that the α so determined is a general measure of his degree of optimism which can be applied to other decision problems. Clearly, also, a particular decision maker may be very sensitive to outside influences (such as the morning paper) and thus may change his attitude considerably over time. To clarify this process, consider the following simple example. A firm is about to undertake an engineering project, the success of which depends heavily on whether a large corporation decides to build a plant on the outskirts of town. Suppose analysis reduces the decision to the following profit matrix (in millions of dollars):

	Plant Built	Plant Not Built
Project	-1	5
No Project	0	0

Being unable to obtain any information about the probability that the corporation will build its plant in the area, the analyst decides to apply a maximin principle, which leads to the decision that the project should not be undertaken. Being dissatisfied with this, he decides to try the Hurwicz principle. To find α he confronts the decision maker with two wagers:

a_1: If the plant is built, the analyst will pay the decision maker \$10. If the plant is not built, the analyst will pay the decision maker nothing.

a_2: Whether or not the plant is built, the analyst will pay the decision maker x dollars.

The decision maker is then invited to state the value of x for which he would be willing to pay the same amount for either wager. This example has the same structure as was given previously, but possibly has the advantage of being somewhat interesting and realistic to the decision maker. One might be willing to assume that the α elicited in this way would be relevant to the actual decision under consideration.

Several other difficulties have been pointed out in connection with the Hurwicz principle. For many the principle leads to counterintuitive results in decisions of the following sort:

a_1	1	0	0	0	0	0	0	0	0	0
a_2	0	1	1	1	1	1	1	1	1	1

The Hurwicz principle suggests that these alternatives are equivalent to the decision maker. Many people find a strong preference for a_2 and thus find fault with the principle. Such a preference seems inevitably to involve some preconceived notion about the probabilities of the possible futures. One must assert that, if estimates of the probabilities can be made, they should be used.

Column linearity is also not a characteristic of the Hurwicz principle. To demonstrate this once more suppose we are given the following decision where the numbers in the matrix may be taken as profits:

1	4
3	3

For any $\alpha < \frac{2}{3}$, a_2 will be preferred, but if we add the constant 5 to the first column of the matrix, it will be seen that the choice is switched to a_1 for any $\alpha < \frac{1}{3}$.

"Convexity" is the name given to another property which is not possessed by the Hurwicz principle. Suppose for $\alpha = \frac{3}{4}$ we have the following decision:

a_1	0	1	0
a_2	1	0	0

The value of the Hurwicz criterion is $\frac{3}{4}$ for each alternative and the decision maker would be indifferent as to which he chose. It is then argued that if he is really indifferent there would be no harm in using a_1 some of the time and a_2 some of the time if the decision is to be made repeatedly. Thus, we could think of a third alternative which would be a combination of a_1 sometimes and a_2 at other times. Clearly this third alternative should be just as good as the previous two. To be specific, suppose the decision maker decides to use a third alternative which involves flipping a fair coin and using a_1 if heads comes up and a_2 otherwise. Call this a_3. The decision then looks as follows:

a_1	0	1	0
a_2	1	0	0
a_3	$\frac{1}{2}$	$\frac{1}{2}$	0

The Hurwicz criterion for a_3 turns out to have a value of $\frac{3}{8}$, indicating that a_3 is not as good as a_1 and a_2. This is called "lack of convexity." The property of convexity suggests that any combination (in the sense of the foregoing example) of equivalent alternatives, should also be equivalent.

THE SAVAGE OR MINIMAX REGRET PRINCIPLE

The Savage principle is intended to counter some of the ultraconservative results given by the minimax principle. For example, the problem used to illustrate the counterintuitive results sometimes given by the minimax principle was (maximin in this case)

	S_1	S_2
a_1	0	$1,000
a_2	$1	1

The regret matrix for this problem is

	S_1	S_2
a_1	$1	0
a_2	0	$999

and the principle thus leads to the selection of a_1 which is intuitively more satisfactory to many decision makers.

In many problems the regret matrix is simply equal to the loss matrix and both minimax and minimax regret have the very same results. This will be true in all problems for which the minimum in each and every column of the loss matrix is zero. More explicitly regret is simply the negative of loss if, and only if, $\max V(\theta_{ij}) = O$. This may be illustrated by the following decision:

LOSS MATRIX

	S_1	S_2	S_3
a_1	5	0	2
a_2	9	8	0
a_3	0	6	3

The minimax principle selects a_1. The regret matrix for the decision is

	S_1	S_2	S_3
a_1	5	0	2
a_2	9	8	0
a_3	0	6	3

yielding the same problem as before.

One of the logical difficulties associated with the regret principle is that it is not independent of the addition of irrelevant alternatives. Consider a decision maker who is confronted by the following problem:

PROFIT MATRIX

	S_1	S_2	S_3
a_1	1	6	4
a_2	5	3	6

The regret matrix is

4	0	2
0	3	0

leading to the selection of a_2. Now suppose a third alternative becomes available

a_3	4	8	1

The regret matrix of the new problem is

4	2	2
0	5	0
1	0	5

The distressing result is that a_3 is clearly not preferred by the decision maker, but its presence shifts his choice form a_2 to a_1. Thus, the appearance of a third alternative, which itself is of no interest to the decision maker, has the effect of changing his preferences among the original two alternatives.

This is distracting to many decision makers, but others try to point out that there are situations in which this sort of thing is not so unreasonable. Consider a manager who is deciding which of two machines to purchase. Both of the machines appear on the surface to be of the same capabilities, but prices differ markedly. Machine A is offered for \$12,000 and Machine B for \$10,000. The manager would like to buy *B*, but it is manufactured by a company which is little known and without reputation. He decides on *A*, which is made by a prominent manufacturer with an excellent reputation for quality and dependability. Just as the manager is about to authorize the purchase, the salesman from company *B* calls to point out that a precision thread grinding machine has been introduced by his company. The manager then says, "Thank you but I have no use for a thread grinder; however, we will place an order for your Machine *B*." The manager has reasoned, and perhaps rightly so, that if company *B* can put out a thread grinder, they are probably capable of making a good quality product, and thus their Machine *B* is a good buy.

CHOOSING A PRINCIPLE

The kind of arguments advanced against the various principles of choice for decisions under uncertainty clearly do not take the form of deductive proofs. They are based either on intuitions about the application of a principle in a specific decision problem, or upon the failure of a principle to exhibit some property which is taken to be desirable. We can do little about the variety of intuitions we have, except to agree where we can and disagree where we cannot. People have produced various lists of desirable properties which a principle should have, such as column linearity, convexity, and so on. It is often the case that none of the principles of choice we have discussed had all the properties on the list. One might go back one step further and argue about what properties should appear on such a list. It seems, however, more reasonable to simply conclude that the choice of a principle must remain a matter of reflecting a decision maker's attitude in a given decision-making context.

PROBLEMS

8–1. Suggest an example of a decision from your own experience which you feel is best treated as a decision without probabilities. What principle of choice would seem appropriate?

8–2. For each principle of choice suggest an example of a decision which illustrates its applicability.

8–3. Formulate a principle of choice of your own for decisions without probabilities. Show by an example how it would be used. What can be said for and against your principle?

8–4. Discuss the following ideas:
  a) We do not deal with "real" decisions but with our views or perceptions of decisions.
  b) How we view a decision may depend on accumulated experience, the evidence at hand, as well as a considerable amount of judgment.

8–5. What rough principles could be formulated to help one decide when to treat a decision as one without probabilities?

8–6. In formulating a view of a decision, how can we handle the feelings we have about probabilities which are not supported by objective relative frequency evidence? What is meant by "complete ignorance of the probabilities of the possible futures"?

8–7.* Apply the various principles of choice to the following matrix. The numbers in the matrix are costs.

18	18	10	14
14	14	14	14
5	26	10	10
14	22	10	10
10	12	12	10

Form a new matrix from the one above by taking each number, adding 2, and multiplying the result by 3. Again apply the principles of choice. What does this suggest with respect to value measurement?

8–8. What general description could you give of the appropriate circumstances for the use of each principle?

8–9. What difficulties would you expect to encounter in applying the Hurwicz principle in actual practice?

8–10. In your own terms, explain the reasoning behind the Savage or regret principle.

8–11. What is column linearity? Why is it to be desired in a principle of choice? Answer the same questions with respect to convexity.

8–12. Comment on the following argument: "Any principle of choice ought to select alternatives which would maximize expectation for *some* set of probabilities. If there is an alternative for which *there exists no* set of probabilities which would make it the expectation maximizing alternative, then no principle of choice should lead to its selection."

8–13.* Suppose a gambler were to confront the decision as to how to bet at roulette. Consider the alternatives RED, BLACK, and 0 AND 00. Suppose he knows the wheel to be biased but has no evidence as to how it is biased. How should he bet?

8–14. Consider an insurance policy which insures against a loss of amount L on payment of a premium P. Suppose no evidence is available to aid in estimating the probability of the loss. What principle of choice would you suggest for the decision to insure or not to insure?

8–15. Consider a gamble in which the probability of winning is unknown. An amount W may be won as the result of placing a bet B. What principle of choice would you suggest in deciding whether or not to bet?

8–16. An urn contains N balls. You are given N dollars and asked to decide how many black balls are in the urn. If your decision differs from the actual number, then a number of dollars equal to the amount of the difference will be taken away from you.

    a) What would be your decision if you were given no opportunity to obtain further information?

    b) What would be your decision if you were permitted to take a sample of three balls (with replacement) from the urn? Assume that N is very much greater than 3.

8-17.   A six-horse race is about to be run and you are determined to bet on one of the horses to win. How would you place your bet if:
a) You had no other information?
b) You could see the tote board?

8-18.   Regret has been called a measure of the loss which may be suffered as a result of imperfect information. Explain the sense of this interpretation.

8-19.   Suppose you know that the instructor in a certain course gives only the grades *A*, *B*, or *C*. He makes you the following offer: If you can guess the grade which he has already assigned you, he will raise it by one letter (except in the case of *A*); if you guess wrong, he will lower it by one letter; and if you choose not to guess at all, you will of course receive the assigned grade. Explain your choice.

8-20.*   Two bettors at a race track both believe in using the Laplace principle. They are considering a bet on a horse which carries the number 1 and wondering whether to bet $2 on this horse or not to bet on the race at all. If number 1 wins he is expected to pay $6, yielding a profit of $6 − $2 = $4. One bettor argues that there are two possible futures, the horse either wins or loses. The other bettor feels that there are six possible futures since one of the six horses in the race will win. What conclusions will they reach?

8-21.   A retailer is wondering how many units of a perishable item to stock. The demand for the item during a stocking period could, in his opinion, be 0, 1, 2, 3, or 4 units, but he does not feel able to estimate the probabilities. He will suffer a loss of $1 for each unit stocked but not sold, and make a profit of $10 on each unit sold. Would you advise a policy of minimizing the maximum loss?

SUGGESTIONS FOR FURTHER STUDY

Raiffa, Howard. *Decision Analysis*. Reading, Massachusetts: Addison-Wesley, 1971.
Raiffa, H., and R. Schlaifer. *Applied Statistical Decision Theory*. Boston, Mass.: Graduate School of Business, Harvard University, 1961.
Schlaifer, Robert. *Analysis of Decisions under Uncertainty*. New York: McGraw-Hill, Inc., 1969.
Shelly, Maynard W., and Glenn L. Bryan, (eds.). *Human Judgments and Optimality*. New York: Wiley, 1964.
Zadeh, Lofti A. "Outline of a New Approach to the Analysis of Complex Systems and Decision Processes," a chapter in Cochrane, J. L., and Zeleny, M. (eds.), *Multiple Criteria Decision Making*. Columbia, S.C.: University of South Carolina Press, 1973.

APPLICATIONS 9

In this chapter a number of examples will be discussed to illustrate the flavor of the analysis of decisions without probabilities. In many cases the application of several principles of choice will be discussed, without any particular attempt to resolve the question of which might best be used. It will be beneficial for the reader to check the results given by the various principles against his common sense, and to try to be explicit about the various decision-making contexts which might support the use of one principle as opposed to another.

OPERATOR SAFETY

To begin with a simple example, assume that a firm has purchased a new press and is offered an expensive safety device designed to protect the press operator from injury. Suppose that, because of the design of the press, the choice is between this safety device or none, and that if the operator is injured by the press the nature of the injury can be rather closely predicted. We will divide the actions of the operator into safe and unsafe classifications. Unsafe actions are those acts which will result in injury to the operator if the safety device is not in use. All other actions are classified, for purposes of this decision, as safe actions. It would be extremely useful in this decision to have some information on the probability that an operator would commit an unsafe action during some specified time interval, since this would suggest the possibility of analysis as a decision under uncertainty. We will suppose, however, that no such information is available. This is perhaps the most common situation. Assume that the cost of the safety device is $1,200 and that the alternatives are:

a_1 = install the safety device

a_2 = do not install the safety device unless an injury occurs, in which case the device will be immediately installed after the injury

Let:

S_1 = no unsafe action is committed by the operator during the useful life of the press

S_2 = at least one unsafe action is committed by the operator during the useful life of the machine

Then:

	S_1	S_2
a_1	$1,200	$1,200
a_2	0	V(injury and $1,200 expense)

We begin by applying the Laplace principle, which simply suggests that the probabilities of S_1 and S_2 each be taken equal to $\frac{1}{2}$. The expected costs would then be:

$$E(a_1) = \tfrac{1}{2}(\$1,200) + \tfrac{1}{2}(\$1,200) = \$1,200$$

$$E(a_2) = \tfrac{1}{2}(0) + \tfrac{1}{2}\{V(\text{injury and }\$1,200\text{ expenses})\}$$

Alternative a_1 will be preferred if $E(a_2) > E(a_1)$ which implies

$$\tfrac{1}{2}\{V(\text{injury and }\$1,200\text{ expense})\} > \$1,200$$

If we are willing to make the simplifying assumption about the decision maker's value system that:

$$V(\text{injury and }\$1,200\text{ expense}) = V(\text{injury}) + \$1,200$$

then it may be said that a_1 will be preferred if

$$V(\text{injury}) > \$1,200$$

Thus, if the firm attaches a cost to such an injury of more than $1,200, the safety device should be installed. Aside from its lack of logical appeal, the Laplace principle may be questioned here by the decision maker who feels that the probability of at least one unsafe act during the life of the machine is nowhere near one half. If this response is made, then the decision maker is not completely ignorant of the probabilities involved. It would perhaps be better to treat the decision as one under conditions of uncertainty, using the decision maker's judgments of the probabilities.

The minimax principle is easily seen to lead to the choice of a_1 as long as the injury has any value associated with it whatsoever. The maximum losses are:

for a_1: $1,200

for a_2: V(injury and $1,200)

Here it is seen that if the firm will install the safety device after an injury occurs it would clearly be wiser to install it immediately. This reflects the familiar principle which suggests the futility of closing the barn door after the horses have departed.

The Hurwicz criterion for a_1 is simply

$$\alpha(\$1,200) + (1-\alpha)(\$1,200) = \$1,200$$

and for a_2

$$\alpha(0) + (1-\alpha)\{V(\text{injury and }\$1,200)\}$$

or

$$(1-\alpha)V(\text{injury}) + (1-\alpha)(\$1,200)$$

Now a_1 will be preferred if

$$(1-\alpha)V(\text{injury}) + (1-\alpha)(\$1,200) > \$1,200$$

$$V(\text{injury}) > \frac{\alpha}{1-\alpha}(\$1,200)$$

If $\alpha = 1$, meaning the decision maker is ultimately optimistic, the safety device will be installed only if an infinite cost is associated with the injury. If $\alpha = 0$, meaning complete pessimism, this reduces to the minimax principle.

It will be noted that, in this decision problem, the selection of an α is logically equivalent to the selection of a probability distribution on the possible futures. This, however, is not the case in any problem where there are more than two possible futures. In spite of the equivalence in the foregoing case, it is worthwhile to maintain a distinction between measuring the level of optimism of a decision maker, and obtaining estimates of the probabilities, if only for purposes of discussion.

The Savage principle requires the computation of a regret matrix which will appear thus:

	S_1	S_2
a_1	\$1,200	0
a_2	0	$V(\text{injury})$

Minimizing the maximum regret leads to the selection of a_1 as long as $V(\text{injury}) > \$1,200$.

EQUIPMENT INVESTMENT

Consider the decision as to which of two production machines should be purchased for a given application. The requirement for a machine is expected to continue for either three or four years, but the probabilities of these events cannot be estimated. When the requirement no longer exists the machine will be disposed of. Neither of those under consideration are expected to have any net salvage value at any time. The following information is assumed to be known with certainty:

	Machine A	Machine B
Investment	\$10,000	\$12,000
Annual operating cost	4,000	3,200

Each of the machines contains a major component which will require a complete overhaul in either the third or fourth year of use. No data are available for either machine which permit the estimation of the probabilities that this overhaul will occur in the third year or the fourth year. Thus, for each machine we have two possible predicted patterns of maintenance expense:

	Machine A		Machine B	
	M_1	M_2	M_3	M_4
Year 1.........$	500	$ 500	$ 200	$ 200
2.........	500	500	300	300
3.........	1,500	500	2,800	300
4.........	500	1,500	200	2,800

A possible future in this problem may be specified by stating a maintenance prediction for each machine and a duration for the machine requirement. Evaluating the outcomes in terms of average annual cost and using the symbol L to stand for the duration of the machine requirement, the decision appears as:

	M_1 M_3 $L=3$	M_1 M_4 $L=3$	M_1 M_3 $L=4$	M_1 M_4 $L=4$	M_2 M_3 $L=3$	M_2 M_4 $L=3$	M_2 M_3 $L=4$	M_2 M_4 $L=4$
A	$8,167	$8,167	$7,250	$7,250	$7,833	$7,833	$7,250	$7,250
B	8,300	7,467	7,075	7,100	8,300	7,467	7,075	7,100

These machines are clearly rather closely matched. The numbers were chosen this way to show something of how the principles of choice behave under such conditions. The Laplace principle indicates that the probability of each of the possible futures should be taken to be $\frac{1}{8}$. The expected costs under this assumption are

$$E(a_1) = \$7,625 \qquad E(a_2) = \$7,485$$

Thus, machine B would be preferred by a very small margin.

The minimax principle leads to the selection of machine A with a maximum average annual cost of $8,167, as compared with $8,300 for machine B. The regret matrix is easily computed with the following result:

0	700	175	150	0	366	175	150
133	0	0	0	467	0	0	0

The maximum regret in each case is 700 for a_1 and 467 for a_2, indicating the selection of machine B.

The Hurwicz principle yields:

$$\text{for } a_1: (\alpha)(\$7,250) + (1-\alpha)(\$8,167)$$
$$\text{for } a_2: (\alpha)(\$7,075) + (1-\alpha)(\$8,300)$$

It may be confirmed that for any $\alpha < .432$, a_1 will be preferred, but again by a small margin.

It seems clear that these two machines are, from any viewpoint, very similar with respect to cost performances. Review of the results obtained from various principles of choice will show that slight variations in the cost performance could tip the balance in favor of one machine or another, depending upon which principle is used. As long as this is the case it seems fair to say that, in this application, none of the principles lead to a highly counterintuitive choice.

INVENTORY POLICY

In Chapter 5 we examined in some detail the problem of fixing an inventory level in the face of demand which was predicted in the form of a probability distribution. There we defined

C_1 = the unit cost of being overstocked

C_2 = the unit cost of being understocked

D = the number of units demanded during the period for which the inventory level is being established

$p(D)$ = the probability distribution of D
I = an inventory level

Using these variables and treating the decision as one under conditions of uncertainty, the expected cost associated with any inventory level I was expressed as

$$E(I) = C_1 \int_{D=0}^{I} (I-D)p(D)\,dD + C_2 \int_{D=I}^{\infty} (D-I)p(D)\,dD$$

The stock level choice, I_0, which minimizes expected cost was shown to be that stock level which satisfies the following equation:

$$\int_{0}^{I_0} p(D)\,dD = P(I_0) = \frac{C_2}{C_1+C_2}$$

This assumes that I is a continuous variable.

The application of this model may present various data collection difficulties, but the one of interest here concerns the density function of demand, $p(D)$. Clearly, in many situations it will be possible through the study of past demand, trends, and possible future contingencies, to form an estimate of the demand probability distribution. However, in some situations this may not be possible. For example, the commodity stocked may be a new one for which no demand data are available. It may be that (as so often happens) no records are available on past demand for a commodity, and thus no basis for prediction exists. Again, it may be that some of the factors which determine demand are believed to have altered to such an extent that predictions are not possible. The best move in such situations is, of course, to set in motion the process of collecting data upon which predictions may be based in the future. This, however, does not solve the problem of fixing a stock level for the present.

An immediate possibility is, of course, to treat the decision as one without probabilities. This presents a number of interesting insights, as the following analysis using various principles of choice will show. Before exaimning these principles, it is necessary to be somewhat more explicit about the analyst's "degree of ignorance" of the demand probability distribution. If he is literally "completely ignorant" of the demand distribution, this must mean that demand could be anywhere between minus infinity and plus infinity. Not much can be done in this case, but it is hardly a realistic situation. On the other hand, the analyst may be only "slightly ignorant" of the demand distribution, in the sense that he may have a rough idea of the mean and variance of the distribution, and possibly even some notion of its form. If this is the situation, then perhaps the best thing to do is to use these rough notions in the original model, or appeal to some limit theorem such as Tchebycheff's Inequality. The degree of ignorance presumed here lies between these two. It will be assumed that the analyst is able to predict a finite minimum and a finite maximum for demand, and nothing more. We assume, without loss of generality, that the minimum demand is taken to be zero and the maximum demand is taken to be $\bar{D}$ units.

The Laplace principle is easily applied in this decision for it simply suggests that the density function of demand be taken as a uniform density function. In this problem it would be taken to be uniform over the range O to $\bar{D}$. Thus

$$p(D) = \frac{1}{\bar{D}} \qquad P(D) = \frac{D}{\bar{D}}$$

Using the result obtained before

$$\int_0^{I_0} p(D)\, dD = P(I_0) = \frac{I_0}{\bar{D}} = \frac{C_2}{C_1 + C_2}$$

This yields

$$I_0 = \frac{C_2 \bar{D}}{C_1 + C_2}$$

Now in spite of the fact that little can be said about the merits of the Laplace principle, it does yield a definite answer to the problem of fixing an inventory level under uncertain demand. A little reflection will perhaps convince one that the answer is not highly unreasonable. It is important to note, however, that the answer is highly sensitive to the assumption one makes about the maximum possible demand.

The application of the minimax principle is best understood by referring to Figure 9-1. This figure shows a plot for any inventory level of the maximum cost due to overstock, $C_1(I-0)$, and the maximum cost due to understock, $C_2(\bar{D}-I)$. For a given level, I, the maximum cost due to overstock will occur when demand turns out to be zero. Similarly, the maximum cost due to understock will be suffered when demand turns out to be $\bar{D}$. For any inventory level the maximum cost will simply be the maximum of these two quantities, as is shown by the heavy line in Figure 9-1. It is easy to see that the inventory level, I_0, is the level which corresponds to the minimum point on the heavy line, or the intersection of the two maximum cost lines. This means that I_0 must satisfy the equation

$$C_1(I_0 - 0) = C_2(\bar{D} - I_0)$$

Solving this for I_0 we have;

$$I_0 = \frac{C_2 \bar{D}}{C_1 + C_2}$$

Interestingly enough, this is precisely the same result obtained with the Laplace principle.

The Hurwicz principle suggests that for each stock level one compute the maximum possible total cost, $TC(I)_{max}$, and the minimum possible total cost,

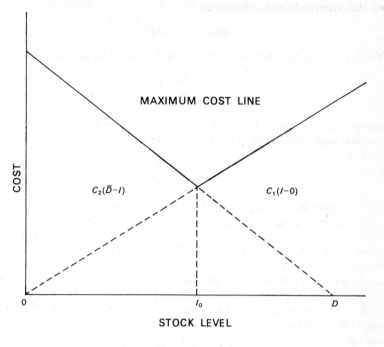

MAXIMUM COST LINE

COST

$C_2(\bar{D}-I)$ $C_1(I-0)$

0 I_0 D

STOCK LEVEL

Figure 9-1

$TC(I)_{min}$. Then the stock level should be selected which will minimize the function

$$\alpha TC(I)_{min} + (1-\alpha) TC(I)_{max}$$

Returning to Figure 9-1, it will be seen that for

$$I \leqslant \frac{C_2 \bar{D}}{C_1 + C_2} \; ; \; TC(I)_{max} = C_2(\bar{D}-I)$$

$$TC(I)_{min} = 0$$

The Hurwicz criterion takes the form

$$\alpha(0) + (1-\alpha) C_2(\bar{D}-I)$$

This function will be minimized, for any α, if I is made as close to D as possible. Here this means

$$I_0 = \frac{C_2 \bar{D}}{C_1 + C_2}$$

Now for

$$I \geqslant \frac{C_2 \bar{D}}{C_1 + C_2} \; ; \; TC(I)_{max} = C_1 I$$

$$TC(I)_{min} = 0$$

and the criterion function becomes

$$\alpha(0) + (1-\alpha)\,C_1\,I$$

Minimization is now achieved by making I as small as possible, thus

$$I_0 = \frac{C_2\,\bar{D}}{C_1+C_2}$$

Finally over the entire range of I and for any α whatsoever, the Hurwicz principle suggests that the stock level should be

$$I_0 = \frac{C_2\,\bar{D}}{C_1+C_2}$$

which is again the very same result obtained before.

Finally, the Savage or regret principle may be applied to the decision. It defines, for any stock level and any demand, the difference in cost between the minimum cost achievable had demand been known in advance and the cost resulting from the stock level in question, as the decision maker's regret. Thus, for any demand, if a stock level had been chosen equal to demand, cost would be 0, and the regret associated with any other I would be $C_1(I-D)$ or $C_2(D-I)$, depending on whether I was greater or less than D. Having computed the regret for each I and D combination, the principle suggests that one select the stock level which will minimize the maximum regret. Since, for any D, the minimum possible cost is 0, the maximum regret turns out to be equal to the maximum cost for any I. Thus, Figure 9-1 may be interpreted as a plot of maximum regret, and the minimizing value of I is the one previously found.

It is interesting to note, that whatever principle one selects, the suggested stock level is the same. It must be emphasized that this is not true of all decision problems. It is easy to construct or discover examples for which each principle yields a different result. No great significance can be attached to this fact in connection with the inventory problem, for it is the mathematical result of the problem formulation, rather than any subtle generality which has emerged. The result has, however, a certain practical value for situations in which inventory policy must be formulated without demand information. It gives a definite answer to the question of stock level, and the answer is the same when the question is approached from four points of view. Best of all, perhaps, the answer has certain demonstrable properties, such as minimizing the maximum cost, which are directly appealing to the decision maker.

EXAMPLES

In Chapter 5, an example was suggested involving the establishment of an inventory for a liquid fuel. The relevant costs were

$$C_1 = \$.01 \text{ per gallon}$$

$$C_2 = \$.19 \text{ per gallon}$$

Instead of assuming that demand is predicted as a random variable, let us now assume that it is estimated the demand will fall in the range of 8,000 to 12,000 gallons per week. Nothing, however, can be estimated about its probabilities within this range.

$$8,000 \leqslant D \leqslant 12,000$$

Clearly we will stock at least 8,000 gallons since, under our assumptions at least, we will always require this much or more. To simplify computations, define a new variable, d, to be the demand in excess of 8,000 gallons.

$$D = 8,000 + d \qquad 0 \leqslant d \leqslant 4,000$$

The Laplace principle leads to the assumption that the probability distribution of demand is uniform.

$$p(d) = \frac{1}{4,000 - 0} = \frac{1}{4,000}$$

$$\text{for } 0 \leqslant d \leqslant 4,000$$

The expression for the optimal stock level is now

$$I_0 = 8,000 + \frac{C_2 \bar{D}}{C_1 + C_2}$$

which gives

$$I_0 = 8,000 + \frac{(.19)(4,000)}{.20} = 11,800 \text{ gallons}$$

Here $\bar{D}$ is the upper limit of d.

In Chapter 5 it was shown that the condition for optimality was

$$P(I_0) = \frac{C_2}{C_1 + C_2}$$

To indicate that this gives the same result for this problem, we take

$$P(d) = P(I_0 - 8,000) = \frac{d}{4,000} = \frac{.19}{.01 + .19} = .95$$

$$d = (.95)(4,000) = 3,800$$

$$I_0 = 8,000 + d = 11,800 \text{ gallons}$$

For the other principles it is helpful to have a graph of the maximum and minimum costs associated with any inventory level. The minimum cost for any level is zero, and occurs when demand just equals the level. The maximum cost occurs when demand takes one or the other of its extreme values. For any inventory level I, the maximum cost is either an overstock cost for $d = 0$,

$$C_1 I = .01 I$$

or an understock cost for $\bar{D} = 4,000$

$$C_2(\bar{D} - I) = .19(4,000 - I)$$

Here we define I as the inventory in excess of 8,000 units.

The minimax principle leads to minimizing the maximum cost, which occurs at the intersection of the two lines on the graph. The value of I which is common to both lines may be found by equating their functions.

$$.01I = .19(4,000 - I)$$

This is easily solved to obtain

$$I = 3,800$$

As this has been defined as the inventory in excess of 8,000 units, the actual choice is

$$8,000 + 3,800 = 11,800$$

The reader may quickly satisfy himself that the regret principle and the Hurwicz principle, for any α whatsoever, will yield the same result.

It is interesting to look also at a discrete problem, such as the boat builder's decision introduced in Chapter 5. A discrete commodity was involved, the demand for which was predicted in the form of a probability distribution over the range $1 \leqslant D \leqslant 6$. The costs were

$$C_1 = \$100$$

$$C_2 = \$300$$

Assume that it is now felt that demand will fall in the range from one to six units, but that nothing can be said of the probabilities over this range. There are thus six possible futures in the decision, and our choice of an inventory level will more than likely be restricted to the same six alternatives.

		Demand					
		1	2	3	4	5	6
	1	0	300	600	900	1200	1500
	2	100	0	300	600	900	1200
	3	200	100	0	300	600	900
Inventory Level	4	300	200	100	0	300	600
	5	400	300	200	100	0	300
	6	500	400	300	200	100	0

Assuming that the probability of each possible future is $\frac{1}{6}$ and computing expectations we obtain

$$E(1) = \$750 \qquad E(4) = \$250$$

$$E(2) = \$517 \qquad E(5) = \$217$$

$$E(3) = \$350 \qquad E(6) = \$250$$

The Laplace principle thus leads to a choice of five units as the best inventory level. This corresponds to the result obtained if we use the relation

$$P(I_0 - 1) \leqslant \frac{C_2}{C_1 + C_2} \leqslant P(I_0)$$

$$P(I_0 - 1) = P(4) = .67 \leqslant \frac{300}{400} = .75 \leqslant P(I_0) = P(5) = .83$$

I	1	2	3	4	5	6
Maximum cost	$1,500	$1,200	$900	$600	$400	$500

The minimax principle thus reinforces the choice of five units as the best inventory level.

The Hurwicz principle requires the computation of the Hurwicz criterion for each alternative.

I	α(minimum cost) $+ (1-\alpha)$(maximum cost)
1	$\alpha(0) + (1-\alpha)(1,500)$
2	$\alpha(0) + (1-\alpha)(1,200)$
3	$\alpha(0) + (1-\alpha)(\ 900)$
4	$\alpha(0) + (1-\alpha)(\ 600)$
5	$\alpha(0) + (1-\alpha)(\ 400)$
6	$\alpha(0) + (1-\alpha)(\ 500)$

It may be seen that, whatever the value of α, the Hurwicz criterion will be maximized for an inventory of five units.

Since each column of the cost matrix contains as a minimum cost the value zero, the regret matrix will be identical to the cost matrix. Minimizing the maximum regret is thus equivalent to minimizing the maximum cost.

PRODUCTION PROCESSES

Suppose it is possible to produce a certain part on either an engine lathe or a turret lathe. The engine lathe is characterized by a small setup cost but a relatively high unit direct labor cost. The turret lathe has a higher setup cost but a lower unit direct labor cost. One of the machines is to be chosen for production, but it is not known in advance just what the size of the production run will be. Let

$a_1 =$ engine lathe

$a_2 =$ turret lathe

$D =$ size of the production run

$A_i =$ setup cost for alternative i

$B_i =$ unit direct labor cost for alternative i

$C(a_i, D) =$ total cost for alternative i if the production run is D units

Then

$$C(a_i, D) = A_i + B_i D$$

Assume that the total cost functions are as shown in Figure 9-2 and that it is possible to say that D will fall within the range

$$\underline{D} \leqslant D \leqslant \bar{D}$$

but nothing can be said about the probability of D in this range. It is easily shown that the various principles for decisions under uncertainty will yield the following results:

Laplace: Select the alternative which minimizes

$$E(a_i) = A_i + B_i \frac{\underline{D} + \bar{D}}{2}$$

Minimax: Select a_2.
Hurwicz: Select the alternative which minimizes

$$A_i + B_i\{\alpha\underline{D} + (1-\alpha)\bar{D}\}$$

Savage: Select a_1 if

$$A_1 + B_1\bar{D} - A_2 - B_2\bar{D} < A_2 + B_2\underline{D} - A_1 - B_1\underline{D}$$

otherwise select a_2.

A little reflection will suffice to show that this approach to the decision problem is to some extent incompatible with a common sense notion about this type of decision problem. For example, in the application of the minimax principle it is clear that the maximum cost for either alternative will occur

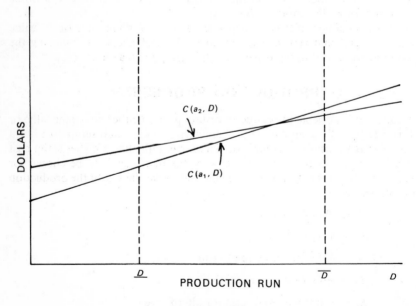

Figure 9-2

when $D = \bar{D}$, and that the selection of a_2 will minimize this maximum cost. However, it may well be that the most desirable event would be to have D take on its maximum value since this would mean that profit would be maximized. If we were really pessimistic our attention might be directed to what would happen if D takes its smallest value. Similarly, the Hurwicz principle is most naturally used to associate feelings of optimism with large production runs and pessimism with small production runs. Thus it might make more sense to assume a total revenue function in connection with such a problem and compute profits rather than cost. Suppose we take the total revenue function to be simply

$$TR(D) = PD$$

as is shown in Figure 9-3. Our principles of choice then yield somewhat more sensible results. The Laplace principle requires the maximization of

$$E(a_i) = (P - B_i)\left(\frac{D + \bar{D}}{2}\right) - A_i$$

which results in the same choice as before. The minimax principle is now interpreted as maximizing the minimum profit or minimizing the maximum loss. In this case the maximum loss for each alternative will occur when D is

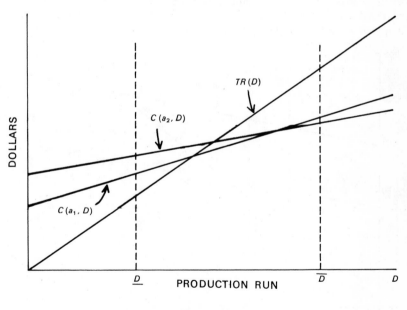

Figure 9-3

smallest. By inspection it may be seen that alternative a_1 will minimize the maximum loss. The Hurwicz principle leads to the selection of the alternative which maximizes

$$\alpha\{(P - B_i)\bar{D} - A_i\} + (1 - \alpha)\{(P - B_i)\underline{D} - A_i\}$$

The maximum profit will occur when the production run is as large as possible, and the minimum profit will occur when it is as small as possible. The Savage principle leads to the same choice as before.

EXAMPLE

Assume that for an engine lathe the cost to set up for a run of a particular part is

$$A_1 = \$26.00$$

and the unit production cost is

$$B_1 = .40$$

For a turret lathe which might be used for the same job the corresponding costs are

$$A_2 = \$200.00$$
$$B_2 = .10$$

The reader may verify that if the problem is stated simply in this form the results are as shown in Figure 9-4. Suppose it is possible to say that the size of the run which will be required lies in the range

$$300 \leqslant D \leqslant 800$$

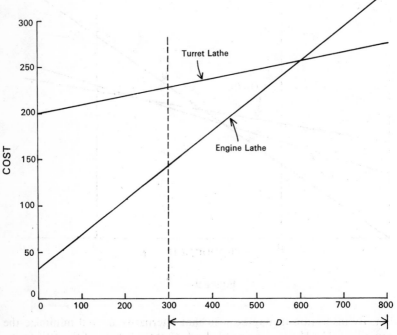

PRODUCTION VOLUME

Figure 9-4

Then

Laplace: $E(D) = 550$, select the engine lathe
Minimax: select the turret lathe
Hurwicz: for $\alpha \leqslant 11/25$ select the engine lathe
Regret: select the engine lathe

Now suppose that the decision can be looked at from the viewpoint of profit and that a total revenue function can be estimated.

$$TR = (.50)D$$

These functions are shown in Figure 9-5. Using the Laplace assumption the expected volume of production is 550 units. It is easily shown that, for volume less than 580 units, the engine lathe will have lower costs, while above this it

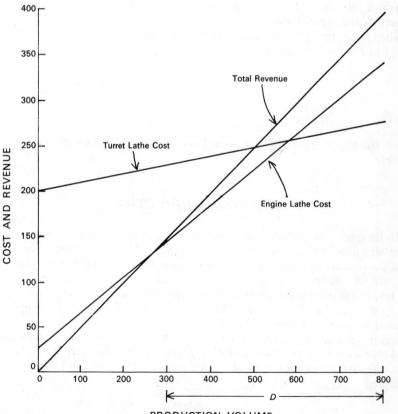

Figure 9-5

will be more economical to use the turret lathe. Thus the Laplace principle suggests the engine lathe.

The minimax principle is now applied so as to maximize the minimum profit. Examination of Figure 9-5 shows immediately that this will lead to the selection of the engine lathe.

For the Hurwicz criterion we have

$$\alpha(\text{maximum profit}) + (1-\alpha)(\text{minimum profit})$$

for each alternative. For the engine lathe this is

$$\alpha(400-346) + (1-\alpha)(150-146)$$

and for the turret lathe

$$\alpha(400-280) + (1-\alpha)(150-230)$$

It can be shown that the two machines yield the same value of the Hurwicz criterion for $\alpha = \frac{14}{25}$. For any value of α above this the turret lathe is chosen, otherwise the engine lathe.

The maximum regret will be experienced at one extreme or the other of the range of production volume.

	Regret	
	$D = 300$	$D = 800$
Engine lathe...............	0	$66
Turret lathe	$84	0

Thus, the engine lathe will be chosen if one wishes to minimize the maximum regret.

RECTIFYING INSPECTION

In Chapter 4 the problem of choosing an acceptance sampling inspection plan was treated as a decision under uncertainty. The assumption was made that the probability distribution of the fraction defective on the incoming lots of product was known. In many interesting quality control situations one has no way of knowing either the fraction defective of an incoming lot of product, or its probability distribution. Thus, the decision may be more properly treated as one without probabilities.

Let us compare the same three sampling plans as before, and once again make the assumption that when a lot is rejected it is then inspected 100 percent, the defective items are repaired or replaced, and the rectified lot is then accepted.

Plan	Sample Size (N)	Acceptance Number (c)
a_1 100		1
a_2 200		1
a_3 100		3

The product is shipped in lots of 1,000 units. Suppose it is possible to assert that the incoming lots will have a fraction defective in the range from 1 to 4 percent, but nothing can be said about the probability distribution within that range.

$$.01 \leqslant p' \leqslant .04$$

The unit cost of inspection is

$$C_1 = \$.30$$

and the cost of accepting a defective item is

$$C_2 = \$10.00$$

As before, we compute the average amount of inspection per lot

$$ATI = N + (1 - P_a)(S - N)$$

and the average number of defective items accepted per lot

$$ADA = P_a p'(S - N)$$

The total cost for any alternative, as a function of P_a and p' is

$$TC = C_1(ATI) + C_2(ADA)$$
$$= C_1\{N + (1 - P_a)(S - N)\} + C_2 P_a p'(S - N)$$

The probability of accepting a lot is

$$P_a = \sum_{x=0}^{c} \frac{N!}{x!(N-x)!}(p')^x(1 - p')^{N-x}$$

Carrying through computations in the usual way, we obtain the total cost for selected values of p' shown in the following table:

	.010	.015	.020	.025	.030	.035	.040
a_1	$167	$224	$263	$286	$300	$305	$307
a_2	232	275	294	298	300	300	300
a_3	123	175	223	266	296	319	340

These values have been plotted in Figure 9-6.

With no knowledge of the probability distribution of p', the lot fraction defective, we are forced to resort to one of our principles of choice. The Laplace principle suggests that one assume a uniform distribution for p'. To find the expectation for each alternative it would be necessary to integrate.

$$E(a_i) = \int_{p'=.01}^{.04} TC(a_i, p') f(p') \, dp'$$

Inspection for Figure 9-6 may, however, be sufficient to satisfy us that a_3 does in fact have the lowest expected cost under this assumption.

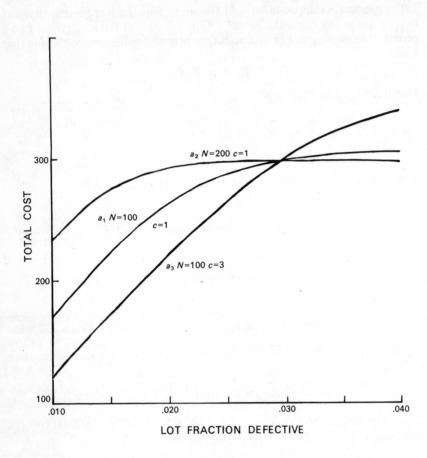

Figure 9-6

The minimax principle focuses attention on the maximum total costs associated with each alternative.

Maximum Total Cost

a_1.....................$307
a_2.................... 300
a_3.................... 340

Minimizing the maximum total cost suggests that we choose a_2. The Hurwicz criterion for each alternative may be written as shown:

Hurwicz Criterion

a_1...............$\alpha(167) + (1-\alpha)(307) = 307 - 140\alpha$
a_2...............$\alpha(232) + (1-\alpha)(300) = 300 - 68\alpha$
a_3...............$\alpha(123) + (1-\alpha)(340) = 340 - 217\alpha$

The reader may verify that for

$$0 \leqslant \alpha \leqslant .102 \qquad a_2 \text{ is preferred}$$

$$.102 \leqslant \alpha \leqslant .43 \qquad a_1 \text{ is preferred}$$

$$.43 \leqslant \alpha \leqslant 1 \qquad a_3 \text{ is preferred}$$

The regret principle is easily applied for it is clear that the maximum regret for any alternative will occur at one of the extremes in the range of p'.

	Regret	
	$p' = .01$	$p' = .04$
a_1	44	7
a_1	109	0
a_2	0	40

The choice under the regret principle falls upon a_3.

PROBLEMS

9–1.* A firm is considering the purchase of either an engine lathe or a turret lathe for the manufacture of a certain item. The production quantity x is unknown. Total production costs for the engine lathe are given by the function $A + Bx$ and for the turret lathe by the function $C + Dx$. Assume that $A < C$ and $B > D$. Which machine would you purchase?

9–2.* Your company, which requires a site for a new plant, is given a 48-hour option on a piece of land which is satisfactory for its purposes. The price is reasonable but not cheap, and the land is good but not outstanding. You must decide within the 48 hours whether to take up the option or let it go and look for another site. How would you treat this as a decision without probabilities?

9–3.* Kelvin's Law suggests that the cost of an electrical transmission cable may be expressed as follows:

$$\text{Total Cost} = \text{Investment Cost} + \text{Cost of Energy Loss}$$

or symbolically

$$TC(A) = C_1 K_1 A + \frac{C_2 K_2}{A}$$

where C_1 is the unit investment cost, C_2 is the unit cost of energy, and K_1 and K_2 are constants of proportionality. The decision variable is A, the area of the cable. Show how A might be chosen if

a) C_1, C_2, K_1 and K_2 are assumed to be certainly known.

b) C_1, C_2, and K_1 are assumed to be certainly known, but K_2 can be predicted only in the form of a probability distribution, say $f(K_2)$.

c) C_1, C_2, and K_1 are assumed to be certainly known and K_2 is assumed to fall in the range $K_{2L} \leqslant K_2 \leqslant K_{2U}$ with unknown probabilities.

9–4.* Treat problem 4–1 as a decision without probabilities assuming that the probability of a defective casting, p, will fall within some range whose limits are known, but that nothing further can be said about its probability distribution.

9–5.* Show how problem 4–2 might be considered as a decision without probabilities if the probability distribution of the present worth of future profits for the population of investment opportunities were not known.

9–6. Discuss problem 3–24 as a decision without probabilities.

9–7.* Refer to problem 4–10. How would you analyze the decision to insure or not to insure, if the probability of a fire were unknown?

9–8.* Refer to problem 4–14. What alternative would you suggest if the probability that a spare would be needed during the life of the machine could not be reasonably estimated?

9–9. After having formulated a decision as one without probabilities, one always has the choice of whether to select an alternative or to try to collect enough information so as to treat the decision as one under uncertainty. How would you make this choice? What principles could you formulate as guides?

9–10.* Refer to problem 4–15. Which alternative would you recommend if it were not possible to obtain data on the probability distribution of the number of breakdowns per year? Suppose it could reasonably be assumed that this number would lie in the range from 0 to 8.

9–11.* How would you treat problem 4–16 as a decision without probabilities?

9–12.* Refer to problem 4–27. Suppose no evidence were available to permit estimates of the probabilities of failure. Which alternative would be selected by each principle of choice? What would be your choice?

9–13. Formulate the problem of maintenance policy discussed in Chapter 4 as a problem of decision making without probabilities. What would be the effect of each principle of choice? Which would you advocate?

9–14.* Analyze problem 4–33 as a decision without probabilities using the assumption that the incoming fraction defective will fall in the range from 0 to .04, but its probability distribution is not known.

9–15. Given two single-sample, fraction defective sampling plans with known average outgoing quality curves. Assuming that average outgoing quality is taken to be a measure of effectiveness for a plan, what principle of choice would be most appropriate for choosing between the two?

9–16. Consider two quality control charts for process fraction defective, each having three standard deviation limits. Chart A uses a sample size of 9 and Chart B uses a sample size of 16. The process is to be brought into control with a process mean of .20. Assuming a sample is to be taken once each hour, which chart would you select on the basis of an hour's performance? The production rate is k units per hour, the inspection cost is C_1 per unit, and the cost for defective production is C_2 per unit.

9–17. Consider two single-sample, fraction defective sampling plans to be used for lots of size 5,000;

Plan A: sample size = 100; acceptance number = 2

Plan B: sample size = 500; acceptance number = 10

Using the assumption of 100 percent screening of rejected lots with replacement of defectives, which plan would you select? The cost of inspection is C_1 per unit, and the cost of passing bad product is C_2 per unit. The incoming fraction defective is unknown.

9–18.* Refer to problem 4–4. If the range of bar lengths is known to be from k units below the mean to k units above it, but the distribution of lengths is unknown, what would you suggest?

9–19.* Consider the problem of determining an economic purchase quantity. Suppose the total procurement cost associated with the purchase of a total of D units in lots of size L over a period of time T is given by

$$C(L) = C_1 \frac{D}{L} + C_2 \frac{LTP}{2}$$

Here C_1 is the fixed cost of making a procurement and C_2 is the cost of carrying inventory, based upon the average value of the inventory. The price paid is P, and the average number of units in stock is $L/2$. The number of unit-periods of inventory is $LT/2$, and the value per unit is taken to be P. Then C_2 is simply a fraction representing carrying costs as a proportion of inventory value.

Now suppose that it is known that the price paid will vary in the future. Clearly, the economic purchase quantity may be influenced by this variation. Assuming that it is not possible to obtain a probabilistic prediction of P, suppose it is only possible to estimate the upper and lower limits of P, say P_2 and P_1 respectively. It is necessary to fix the economic purchase quantity before the price is known any more precisely.

  a) Find the economic purchasing quantity if P is assumed to be known with certainty.

  b) Apply the Laplace, Hurwicz, and minimax principles.

  c) Apply the regret principle under the assumption that the alternatives are limited to those which are optimal for some possible future. That is, the alternatives considered fall in the interval $L_1 \geqslant L \geqslant L_2$ where

$$L_1 = \sqrt{\frac{2C_1 D}{C_2 TP_1}} \quad \text{and} \quad L_2 = \sqrt{\frac{2C_1 D}{C_2 TP_2}}$$

9–20.* Apply the analysis of problem 9–19 to the purchasing decision in which the following data are given:

$$C_1 = \$500$$
$$C_2 = .02$$
$$T = 12 \text{ months}$$
$$D = 60,000 \text{ units}$$
$$P_1 = \$4.50 \leqslant P \leqslant P_2 = \$5.50$$

9–21.* Management wishes to establish an appropriate inventory level in a situation where the cost of storing excess inventory is $5 per unit per month and the cost of a shortage is $10 per unit. The inventory level may be adjusted at the beginning of a month only. Demand for a month is essentially unknown; however, management is willing to state that in no case will it fall below 501 units nor above 1,500 units. Show the inventory level which would result from the application of each of the four principles of choice.

9–22.* Refer to problem 5–6. Suppose the probability distribution of demand were unknown but it seemed reasonable to assume that demand would fall in the range from 80 to 130 units. What inventory level would you suggest?

9–23.* Analyze problem 5–7 under the assumption that p is unknown. Show how your choice of inventory level would vary as a function of N.

9–24.* Suppose in problem 5–8 the density function of demand were not known, but the range was taken to be from 1,800 to 2,200 gallons. What inventory level would you suggest?

9–25.* On Sunday a man is informed that, before the market closes on the following Wednesday, he must buy 100 shares of a certain stock in order to cover a previous commitment. This man does not feel that he can predict the price movements of the stock in terms of probabilities, but he is willing to estimate the limits of the range within which he expects the price to move. Further, he is willing to plan his purchasing on the basis of the limits. His estimates are as follows:

		Day	
Price per Share:	Monday	Tuesday	Wednesday
Upper Limit	$24	$28	$30
Lower Limit	20	16	12

Treating the purchasing policy decision as one without probabilities, apply each of the four principles of choice. For simplicity assume that a single integer price quotation is made each day. Thus on Monday the price is $20, $21, ..., or $24.

9–26. Consider the purchasing policy decision presented in Chapter 7. Suppose that the density function of future prices is not known but that the range within which they will fall can reasonably be specified. Develop a formulation of the purchasing problem as a decision without probabilities. How would you compare this formulation of the problem with that given in Chapter 7?

9–27.* Refer to problem 7–1. Assume $f(x)$ and $f(y)$ are unknown but that the ranges of x and y may be stated. What policy would you suggest?

9–28. Formulate the bidding policy decision discussed in Chapter 6 as a decision without probabilities. Do you feel that this is a satisfactory formulation of the problem? Explain.

9–29.* A firm engaged in bidding finds that very limited historical data on the behavior of competitors is available. Management is willing to assume that the ratio of the lowest competing bid to their own cost estimate will be not less than .95 nor greater than 1.35. The evidence seems insufficient to say anything about the probabilities, however. They are willing to suppress the uncertainty associated with estimating errors in performance costs. Show how various principles of choice might be applied.

9–30. Consider problem 3–38 as a decision. What response would you make as a manager?

9–31. Show how each of the four principles of choice might be applied in the following situation. An inventory level must be chosen at the beginning of every month. The purchase price of each unit is C_0. Units not sold at the end of the month are worthless. There is a storage cost of C_1 per unit based on the number of units left over at the end of the month.

Assume demand and inventory level are continuous variables. Management believes demand will not be less than 0, nor greater than $\bar{D}$, but feels it can say nothing further about the probability distribution of demand.

SUGGESTIONS FOR FURTHER STUDY

Edwards, W., H. Lindman, and L. D. Phillips. "New Technologies for Making Decisions," in *New Directions in Psychology*. New York: Holt, Rinehart, and Winston, 1965.

Raiffa, Howard. *Decision Analysis*. Reading, Massachusetts: Addison-Wesley, 1970.

Raiffa, H. and R. Schlaifer. *Applied Statistical Decision Theory*. Boston: Graduate School of Business, Harvard University, 1961.

Schlaifer, Robert. *Analysis of Decisions Under Uncertainty*. New York: McGraw-Hill, Inc., 1969.

Shelly, Maynard W., and Glenn L. Bryan. (eds.), *Human Judgments and Optimality*. New York: Wiley, 1964.

COMPETITION AND CONFLICT 10

One very important class of decisions involve conflict or competition between two or more decision makers. These situations include such games as chess, competitive decisions made by businessmen, and decisions of military commanders in combat. They have been extensively studied, and a philosophy for understanding them has been produced called the "theory of games." The word "game" here is used in a special technical sense and in no way restricts the theory to the trivial analysis of parlor games. It should be emphasized that the following introduction to this elaborate theory is presented with the idea that, while the direct application of its consequences to decision making may be rather limited, it is rich in fundamental ideas of significance in the general understanding of decision problems.

COMPETITIVE DECISIONS

As an example, consider the following conflict situation which is a game in the ordinary sense of the word. Two decision makers are involved in the game of matching coins. One decision maker, called Red, has two alternatives. He may show heads or tails. Likewise, the other decision maker, called Blue, may show either heads or tails. Suppose the rules say that if Red's coin shows the same side as Blue's, Red wins Blue's coin; otherwise Red loses his coin to Blue. This may be represented in the usual matrix form:

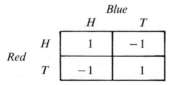

where the numbers in the matrix represent the profit or return to Red. The possible futures are controlled by Blue who is presumed to be both intelligent and in competition with Red. Thus, Blue may be expected to do his best to get Red's money. It is this feature which distinguishes competitive decisions from those studied so far. Previously we had assumed that the possible futures were not under the control of an intelligent competitor who was trying to do us in, but rather that they were events which were simply beyond the control of the decision maker.

GAME THEORY

The theory of games has certain very special suggestions to make in a decision of this sort. These suggestions may be accepted or rejected. It is our purpose here merely to explain them, and not necessarily to advocate their use. The theory approaches the decision as follows. Clearly, if the game is to be played only once it makes no difference what Red does; either alternative is as good as the other. The same is true of Blue. However, suppose the game is to be played repeatedly. Red might show heads consistently, but if he does Blue will soon discover this and respond by showing tails consistently, thus causing Red to lose. Similarly, Red might show tails consistently, but Blue will discover this and win from Red by responding with heads. The theory of games suggests what is almost obvious. The thing for Red to do is to show heads and tails at random, each with probability one half. This has two advantages. First, the randomness will make it impossible for Blue to predict from Red's behavior what he is going to do next. Secondly, it guarantees Red that, whatever Blue does, his expectation will be at least zero. That is, on the average he will at least break even. Taking Blue's point of view, the very same arguments hold, and it becomes clear that Blue should also randomize his choice between heads and tails with probability one half. It may then be added that if Blue does anything else, Red will eventually detect it, and take advantage of Blue, raising his expectation above the break-even point. Thus, the randomized choice has a third advantage for Red. It may further be seen that if both players use these recommendations, the expected outcome for each is zero. To demonstrate these points mathematically, assume that Blue shows heads with probability p, and tails with probability $1-p$. If Red shows heads with probability one half and tails with probability one half, his expected profit will be

$$\tfrac{1}{2}(p)(1) + \tfrac{1}{2}(1-p)(-1) + \tfrac{1}{2}(p)(-1) + \tfrac{1}{2}(1-p)(1) = 0$$

No matter what value Blue assigns to p, Red's expectation will be equal to zero. A similar equation can be written from Blue's point of view.

Now suppose Blue is ignorant of these arguments and decides to play heads with a probability .60, regardless of what Red does. Red may then take advantage of this mistake and play heads with probability 1.00. His expected profit will then be

$$(.60)(1) + (.40)(-1) = .20$$

In the long run such an error will ruin Blue. Note, however, that if Blue suddenly discovers what is happening, Red must immediately return to his original random mixture of heads and tails, each with probability one half.

TERMINOLOGY

The theory of games has technical names for many of the aspects of this situation. It is referred to as a "two-person, zero-sum, game," since there are two "players" and since the losses of one player exactly equal the gains of the other. This makes the sum of losses and gains always equal to zero. The alternatives are referred to as "pure strategies" and a randomized choice among the alternatives is called a "mixed strategy." The mixed strategy or pure strategy which has the properties described in the foregoing example is called an "optimal" strategy. The expected outcome when both players use their optimal strategies is called the "value" of the game. Games, such as the coin-matching game, which have values of zero are called "fair" games. A single episode is called a "play" of the game. Finding the optimal strategies and the value of a game is called "solving" the game. We shall always refer to the maximizing player as Red, and show his pure strategies along the left-hand side of the matrix, and to the minimizing player as Blue and exhibit his pure strategies along the top of the matrix. The theory of games is not limited to the study of zero-sum, two-person games, but this discussion will be so limited, since it purports only to be an introduction.

SOLUTION

In order to further explore the approach of the theory of games consider the following abstract game:

	Blue 1	2	3
1	4	1	0
2	3	2	3
3	0	1	4
4	2	1	0

Red labels rows.

The first step in attempting the solution of any game is to examine the pure strategies of each player for instances of dominance, and to cross out any strategies which are dominated. In this example Red 2 clearly dominates Red 4, and thus Red 4 may be dropped from consideration. Always assuming that neither player is able to cheat and discover in advance what his opponent will do, the theory of games suggests the following analysis. As Red looks at the game he must fear that, whatever he does, Blue will respond in such a way as to make his gain as small as possible. Red thus initially adopts a conservative viewpoint and looks for the strategy that will maximize his minimum profit. In this case Red 2 is the result, making his minimum profit 2. Blue uses exactly the same approach to find the pure strategy which will make Red's maximum profit as small as possible, fixing upon Blue 2. Now if both players adopt these pure strategies the gain to Red (and the loss to Blue) will be exactly 2 on every play of the game. This line of thinking might be called "first-order analysis."

The players, however, attempt to be more insightful than this, according to the theory. Red thinks, "I must assume that Blue is clever and follows the same reasoning that I have used. Blue will then discover that Blue 2 will minimize my maximum profit. Thus, if I expect Blue to play Blue 2, what would my best strategy be?" The answer is still Red 2. Thus Red's choice is the same on the basis of both first and second-order analysis. Blue, reasoning in the same way, concludes that second-order analysis leads him to Blue 2 as before. Thus we have a solution which has the property of being stable under the assumption that one's opponent is also acting according to the philosophy of the theory of games. This stability is characteristic of the optimal strategies which the theory suggests.

In this example the optimal strategies are pure strategies for each player, whereas in the previous example the optimal strategies were mixed. The easiest games to solve are those which lead to optimal strategies which are pure, and these games are characterized by what is called a "saddle point." If the minimum of the column maxima is equal to the maximum of the row minima, then the game has a saddle point. The optimal strategy for each player is then the pure strategy associated with the row or column of the saddle point, and the value of the game is the value of the payoff at the saddle point. Such a game is said to be strictly determined. In summary:

$$\text{Value} = \text{min of col max} = \text{max of row min}$$

Thus, the first step in solving a game is to test for dominance, and the second step is to look for a saddle point.

If the game does not have a saddle point then the optimal strategy of at least one player will be mixed. The discovery of optimal mixed strategies may be complicated, but certain cases can be handled easily. The simplest case is that in which each player has exactly two pure strategies, called a "two-by-two" game. Consider the example:

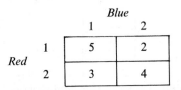

Examination will show neither dominance nor a saddle point. The following simple rule may then be used:

    a) For Red 1, find the absolute value of the difference in payoff between Blue 1 and Blue 2 (here we obtain $|5-2| = 3$), call this result A.

    b) For Red 2, do the same ($|4-3| = 1$), call this result B.

    c) The optimal mixed strategy for Red is then to play Red 1 with probability

$$\frac{B}{A+B}$$

and to play Red 2 with probability

$$\frac{A}{A+B}$$

In this example Red should play Red 1 with probability $\frac{1}{4}$ and Red 2 with probability $\frac{3}{4}$. It is common to express this mixed strategy as $(\frac{1}{4}, \frac{3}{4})$. Applying the same method to Blue will show that Blue's optimal strategy is $(\frac{1}{2}, \frac{1}{2})$. It is then easy to show that if Red uses $(\frac{1}{4}, \frac{3}{4})$ his expectation will be 3.5, no matter what Blue uses. Likewise, if Blue uses $(\frac{1}{2}, \frac{1}{2})$ his expectation will be -3.5, no matter what Red uses. Further, it will be seen that if Blue through ignorance or error fixes upon any other strategy, Red may take advantage of this to improve his expectation. For example, if Blue plays $(\frac{1}{3}, \frac{2}{3})$ then Red may play $(0, 1)$ and improve his expectation to 3.67.

Mathematically, if Blue uses any strategy $(p, 1-p)$ and Red uses his optimal strategy, Red will expect to gain:

$$\tfrac{1}{4}\{(p)(5) + (1-p)(2)\} + \tfrac{3}{4}\{(p)(3) + (1-p)(4)\} = 3.5$$

If Red uses any strategy $(q, 1-q)$ and Blue uses his optimal strategy, Blue will expect to lose:

$$\tfrac{1}{2}\{(q)(5) + (1-q)(3)\} + \tfrac{1}{2}\{(q)(2) + (1-q)(4)\} = 3.5$$

LARGER GAMES

For problems in which at least one of the players has more than two pure strategies, the foregoing rule does not apply. There are a variety of methods for solving such larger games, two of which will be presented. Consider first a game in which one of the players has exactly two pure strategies, but the other player has three or more. This is called a "2-by-n game." Such a game yields easily to a graphic method of solution. To illustrate we will use the example:

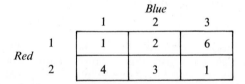

We begin by constructing a graph with an abscissa which represents the probability, x, with which Red plays his pure strategy Red 1. On the ordinate we represent the payoff to Red. Figure 10-1 illustrates such a graph. For each of Blue's pure strategies we now plot the payoff to Red for all values of x, the probability of Red 1. Thus, for pure strategy Blue 1, if Red plays Red 1 with probability x, his payoff is given by:

$$(x)(1) + (1-x)(4) = 4 - 3x$$

This function is then plotted on the graph. For Blue 2 and Blue 3 we obtain:

Blue 2 $(x)(2) + (1-x)(3) = 3 - x$

Blue 3 $(x)(6) + (1-x)(1) = 1 + 5x$

These functions are also shown in Figure 10-1. An examination of the graph reveals that if Blue were to play Blue 1, Red could respond with Red 2 ($x = 0$) and his payoff would be 4, and so on. Blue can minimize Red's maximum payoff by using the mixture of Blue 2 and Blue 3 which fixes Red's payoff at the ordinate value represented by the intersection of the payoff functions for these two pure strategies. That is, if Blue can find the right combination of Blue 2 and Blue 3, he can limit Red's payoff to no more than

$$3 - x = 1 + 5x$$

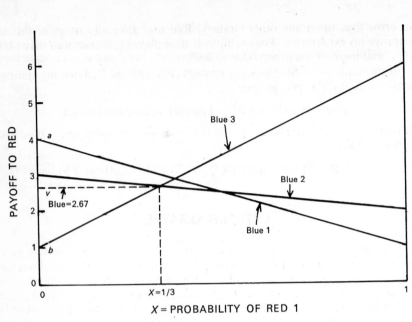

Figure 10-1   Graphical Solution

Red notices that this is true and decides to maximize his payoff by adopting the value of x which will satisfy this equation. Thus, either graphically or analytically, we discover that Red should play Red 1 with probability $\frac{1}{3}$, since $x = \frac{1}{3}$ satisfies this equation. This means obviously that Red 2 should be played with probability $\frac{2}{3}$.

Blue notices that Blue 1 is of no use to him, and that he must find the proper mixture of Blue 2 and Blue 3. Having thus eliminated Blue 1, there are three ways we might proceed.

1. With Blue 1 disposed of we have a 2-by-2 game which could be solved by the previous method.

The optimal strategy for Red is $(\frac{1}{3}, \frac{2}{3})$ as we have already shown, and for Blue $(\frac{5}{6}, \frac{1}{6})$. Returning to the original game, Blue's optimal strategy would be written $(0, \frac{5}{6}, \frac{1}{6})$.

2. From the graph we can see that if Red uses $(\frac{1}{3}, \frac{2}{3})$ then the value of the game will be

$$3 - \frac{1}{3} = 1 + 5(\frac{1}{3}) = \frac{8}{3}$$

Supposing that Blue's optimal strategy is $(0, y, 1-y)$, then it must be that

$$(y)(2) + (1-y)(6) = \frac{8}{3}$$

Solving this for y, yields $y = \frac{5}{6}$, and thus $1 - y = \frac{1}{6}$.

3. Still a third way of obtaining Blue's optimal strategy is from the graph itself. If we let av stand for the distance between point a and point v then

$$\text{Probability of Blue:} \quad \frac{bv}{ab} = \frac{5}{6}$$

$$\text{Probability of Blue:} \quad \frac{av}{ab} = \frac{1}{6}$$

This method is satisfactory for any 2-by-n game, and if one wishes to draw three dimensional graphs, it may be used for a 3-by-n game. Notice that it makes no difference which of the players has the 2 strategies and which has the n.

A special case of a 2-by-n game is represented by the following example:

		Blue		
		1	2	3
Red	1	1	2	6
	2	4	2	1

The graph of this game shown in Figure 10-2 indicates that the optimal strategy for Blue is $(0, 1, 0)$, a pure strategy. For Red, any value of x in the range $x = \frac{1}{5}$ to $x = \frac{2}{3}$ will be optimal. Thus Blue has an optimal pure strategy and Red has an infinity of optimal mixed strategies.

N-BY-N GAMES

Rather than embark upon the mathematics, we will simply illustrate an approximate method of estimating the solution of larger games, where each player may have $n > 2$ pure strategies. The method is called the "method of fictitious play," and is of some interest in its own right.

This method involves playing the game using a special set of rules for the behavior of each player. A record is kept of the play and from this record the optimal strategies and value may be estimated. The rules are:

1. On the first play, Red plays Red 1 and Blue plays Blue 1.
2. On any succeeding play, each player uses the pure strategy which is best from hindsight. Each player looks back on the plays of his opponent and selects the pure strategy which would have been best. He then uses this pure strategy on the next play.
3. In case two pure strategies appear equally good, the one with the lowest number attached to it will be used. (Any such rule is satisfactory for breaking ties, as long as it is consistently applied.) To illustrate this simulated or fictitious play, we will use the following example:

		Blue		
		1	2	3
	1	1	2	3
Red	2	4	0	1
	3	2	3	0

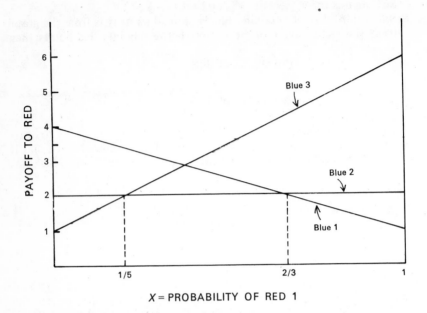

Figure 10-2 Graphical Solution

On the first play of the game each player uses his number 1 strategy. Red then notices that Blue has played Blue 1 and thus his payoff would have been 1 if he had played Red 1, 4 if Red 2, and 2 if Red 3. From hindsight Red 2 is best, and he plays this on the next play. Blue applies similar reasoning and decides to play Blue 1 on the next play.

When the second play is over Red sees that his total payoff over both plays, given Blue's choices, would have been 2 if he had used Red 1, 8 if he had used Red 2, and 4 if Red 3. On this basis Red 2 looks best and is selected for the third play. Blue's similar reasoning leads him to Blue 2 for the third play. Several plays are shown below.

			Red's Hindsight			Blue's Hindsight		
Play	Red Plays	Blue Plays	Red 1	Red 2	Red 3	Blue 1	Blue 2	Blue 3
1 1	1	1	4	2	1	2	3
2 2	1	2	8	4	5	2	4
3 2	2	4	8	7	9	2	5
4 2	2	6	8	10	13	2	6
5 3	2	8	8	13	15	5	6
6 3	2	10	8	16	17	8	6
7 3	3	13	9	16	19	11	6
8 3	3	16	10	16	21	14	6
9 1	3	19	11	16	22	16	9
10 1	3	22	12	16	23	18	12

This represents only a small sample of plays and thus will give only crude results. Precision requires that much larger samples be obtained. The optimal strategies of each player may be estimated by simply computing the relative frequencies with which the pure strategies have been used in the fictitious play. On the basis of these first ten plays the estimates would be

Red $(3/10, 3/10, 4/10)$ Blue $(2/10, 4/10, 4/10)$

To estimate the value of the game define

v_i = minimum of Blue's hindsight values on play i

v_i' = maximum of Red's hindsight values on play i

It is then true that the value of the game lies in the range

$$\frac{v_i}{i} \leqslant \text{value} \leqslant \frac{v_i'}{i}$$

These quantities for the first ten plays are

Play	v_i/i	v_i'/i
1	1	4
2	1	4
3	$\frac{2}{3}$	$2\frac{2}{3}$
4	$\frac{1}{2}$	$2\frac{1}{2}$
5	1	$2\frac{3}{5}$
6	1	$2\frac{2}{3}$
7	$\frac{6}{7}$	$2\frac{2}{7}$
8	$\frac{6}{8}$	2
9	1	$2\frac{1}{9}$
10	$1\frac{2}{10}$	$2\frac{2}{10}$

It then follows that the value must lie between the maximum of the v_i/i and the minimum of the v_i'/i. We could then estimate that the value must be in the range

$$1.20 \leqslant \text{value} \leqslant 2.00$$

If this simulated play is carried on for additional trials the results are:

	Red's Optimal Strategy	Blue's Optimal Strategy	Value
After 20 plays . . .	$(13/20, 3/20, 4/20)$	$(6/20, 4/20, 10/20)$	$1.81 \leqslant \text{value} \leqslant 2.00$
After 30 plays . . .	$(17/30, 9/30, 4/30)$	$(13/30, 7/30, 10/30)$	$1.81 \leqslant \text{value} \leqslant 2.00$

It can be shown that this method will converge upon the solution of the game.

APPLICATIONS

The part of game theory which has been discussed, the theory of zero-sum, two-person games, is too simple to find direct application in a wide range of competitive decisions faced by a firm. It is useful, however, to suggest a few hypothetical examples of its use. Most of the direct conflict or competition engaged in by a firm is represented by decisions concerning advertising, sales effort, pricing policy, new product development, and so on. Thus, most applications which have been studied are from these areas.

1. Suppose two firms are competing for a given market. For simplicity assume that each firm has a fixed advertising budget and must devote its entire budget to one promotional medium, or not advertise at all. If the market research department of Red could figure out the net gain in revenue for all possible contingencies, a matrix such as the following might be developed:

		Blue			
		Radio	*TV*	*Magazines*	*No Advertising*
Red	Radio	0	−4	−1	4
	TV	4	0	6	5
	Magazines	1	−6	0	3
	No advertizing	−4	−5	−3	0

In this game TV is clearly the dominant strategy for both firms, and the game has a saddle point with value 0. Thus each firm will use a TV campaign but end up with the same result as would have been obtained if they had not advertised at all. Neither firm, however, dares not to advertise.

2. Now suppose that the firms, having decided on television promotion, find two networks which offer them programs, ABS and DBC. Again we suppose that skillful market research can predict the results. DBC is the more effective network, as long as only one of the firms uses it. If both firms use the same network, then their efforts tend to cancel each other.

		Blue	
		ABS	*DBC*
Red	ABS	0	$-k$
	DBC	k	0

Both firms will use DBC and the result will be a sort of a draw.

3. Suppose in the previous examples that Red's advertising agency produces promotion messages which are not as effective as those used by Blue. It is predicted that if Red can get on one network by itself it will have some success, but if Blue uses the same network Red will fall behind.

		Blue	
		ABS	*DBC*
Red	ABS	$-k$	K
	DBC	K	$-k$

The game suggests a mixed strategy of $(\frac{1}{2}, \frac{1}{2})$ for each player. One is tempted to interpret this as saying that Red should spend half of its money on each network. A better interpretation is probably that, for any given period, Red should use only one network but should randomize between the networks from period to period.

4. Two firms are competing for a market which is divided into two sales districts. Each firm has a promotional budget which it must allocate between the two territories. Let

s_1 = sales potential of territory 1

s_2 = sales potential of territory 2 $(s_1 + s_2 = S)$

R = Red's promotional budget

B = Blue's promotional budget

r_1, r_2 = amounts spent by Red in territories 1 and 2, respectively

b_1, b_2 = amounts spent by Blue in territories 1 and 2, respectively

Now suppose it can be predicted that the difference between Red's sales and Blue's sales in territory 1 is given by the function

$$\frac{r_1 - b_1}{r_1 + b_1} s_1$$

An identical function is applicable to territory 2. In this game a pure strategy for Red is represented by a choice of r_1 and r_2, subject to the restriction that $r_1 + r_2 = R$. Red thus has an infinity of pure strategies and the game is called a continuous game. The same is true for Blue. It has been shown that the solution of this game requires that each firm allocate its funds in proportion to the sales potential of the territory.

$$r_1 = \frac{Rs_1}{S} \qquad r_2 = \frac{Rs_2}{S}$$

$$b_1 = \frac{Bs_1}{S} \qquad b_2 = \frac{Bs_2}{S}$$

If this is done, the value of the game is

$$\frac{R - B}{R + B} S$$

This example is interesting because it tends to confirm the decision rules actually used in many promotional programs.

USES OF GAME THEORY

It requires some stretch of the imagination to see much realism in the foregoing examples, and this seems to be generally true of attempts to apply the theory of zero-sum, two-person games to business situations. It is perhaps true that the more complex aspects of game theory, which deal with nonzero-sum games with several players will be more fruitful. Nevertheless, the difficulties of prediction and computation appear to be formidable. Knowledge of the theory is not by any means useless, however. It suggests a philosophy for approaching decisions involving competition or conflict. It provides a framework for attempts to make such decisions explicit. It also introduces the very important notion of a mixed strategy as a means of countering competitive pressures. Its most important function is to give insight to decision makers who face conflict situations, rather than to yield exact computations of optimal strategies.

PROBLEMS

Solve the following games:

10–1.* a)
4	7
5	3

b)
4	7
3	5

c)
4	7
3	9

10–2.* a)
22	12	32
36	1	15

b)
13	14	13
11	38	10

10–3.* a)
5	6	5
4	10	6

b)
−10	6	2	40
10	10	8	12
−8	−4	0	−10

10–4.* a)
1	−7
−1	2

b)
8	6	7
5	9	4

10–5.* a)
5	0
1	6
4	4

b)
1	8	2
6	2	8
5	1	6

10–6.* a)
3	4	12
8	6	3

b)
1	3	10
6	3	1

10–7.* a)
1	0	0
0	1	0
0	0	1

b)
3	2	3	1	6
4	4	0	4	3
1	5	3	6	4
3	2	4	3	2

10–8.* Two auto manufacturers, Red and Blue, are competing for a fixed market. If both manufacturers make major model changes in a given year, their respective shares of the market remain constant. Likewise, if both do not make major model changes, their shares of the market also remain constant. If Red makes a major model change and Blue does not, Red is able to take an amount x of the market away from Blue. If Blue makes a major model change and Red does not, Blue is able to take an amount y of the market away from Red.

10–9.* Refer to the fourth item in the list in the *Applications* section, this chapter. Let

$$s_1 = \$1,000,000 \qquad\qquad s_2 = \$200,000$$
$$R = \$6,000 \qquad\qquad\quad B = \$4,000$$

By testing several strategies for each player, show that the game has a saddle point. Find the value of the game.

10–10. Consider a 2-by-2 game in which the optimal strategy for each player is mixed. Suppose we plot the payoff to Red as a function of the probability with which Red plays Red 1 as in Figure 10–3.

a) Show that the payoff to Red resulting from a mixed strategy used by Blue can be represented by a straight line such as the line AB.

b) Why does the line CD represent the optimal mixed strategy for Blue?

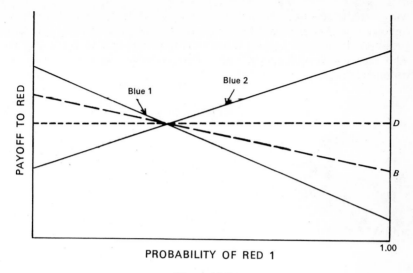

PROBABILITY OF RED 1

1.00

Figure 10-3

10–11.* Find the optimal strategies and the value of the following game. Red and Blue both show coins simultaneously. If both are heads, Red wins $1; if both are tails, Red wins nothing; and if one head and one tail are shown, Red loses $.50.

10–12.* Two partners own a business which has a net worth of C. Each owns half of the business and in addition has a personal bank account in amount N. After a long and bitter argument, they decide that one will buy the other's share of the business, according to the following plan: Each partner submits a *sealed* bid B. ($0 \leqslant B \leqslant N$) The partner making the highest bid pays the amount bid to his associate in return for full ownership of the business. If the bids are equal, the business is assigned to one by flipping a coin and without any payment. Find the optimal strategies and the value of the game.

10–13. It is sometimes suggested that the reasoning of game theory does not reasonably apply to competitive situations which are not encountered repeatedly. How would you answer this argument in view of the discussion of Chapter 3?

10–14. What difficulties would you expect to encounter in attempting to apply the theory of zero-sum, two-person games to union-management conflict over wages, hours, and working conditions?

10–15. Make up a game matrix which illustrates the following remark: "If two or more numbers exist which satisfy the saddle-point rule, each is a saddle point and each is a solution to the game."

10–16. One of the difficulties in applying zero-sum, two-person game theory to conflicts between nations is that the value of an outcome to one nation is not simply the negative of the value of that outcome to the other nation. Give an example of this.

SUGGESTIONS FOR FURTHER STUDY

McKinsey, J. C. C. *Introduction to the Theory of Games.* New York: McGraw-Hill Book Co., 1952.
Williams, J. D. *The Compleat Strategyst.* New York: McGraw-Hill Book Co., 1954.

THE ECONOMICS OF UNCERTAINTY REDUCTION

The traditional uses of statistics have been the drawing of inferences from samples in the form of point estimates, interval estimates, the testing of hypotheses, and the relationship among variables. For some scientific purposes such inferences are a sufficient end in themselves. In management decisions, however, inferences are of interest because they form the basis for action. Modern developments in statistics have led to a much closer integration of the process of inference and the processes of decision and action, thus leading to the notion of statistical decision. A statistical decision differs from the decisions studied so far only in that the process of collecting the data, drawing inferences from it, and determining the decision are included in a single body of theory. Thus, this is not really a new type of decision. It simply includes such features as the cost of collecting information about the possible futures and the costs of the outcomes which result from errors of inference.

This does, however, represent an important difference in viewpoint from ordinary approaches to statistical inference. For example, it is usual in selecting estimators to look for such properties as unbiasedness, or for maximum likelihood estimators. The new notion recognizes that the estimate is to be used in the decision process and, if the estimate is wrong, the result will be a cost to the decision maker. Thus, if we knew the costs of being wrong by various amounts, we might be able to form an estimate which would minimize the maximum cost to the decision maker. This estimate, of course, would be selected in reference to a particular decision problem, considering the alternatives, outcomes, and the value system involved. Again, in hypothesis testing it has become general practice to consider two types of errors of inference: the rejection of a hypothesis when in fact it is true (type 1 error), and the acceptance of a hypothesis when in fact it is false (type 2 error). The selection of hypothesis testing methods has been roughly based on the following criterion: *For a given probability of a type 1 error, select the test which minimizes the probability of a type 2 error.* The statistical decision approach suggests the consideration of the costs of these two errors in terms of a particular situation. It also includes directly the cost of sampling, thus permitting a balancing of sampling costs against the reduction in error cost which will result from taking larger samples.

STATISTICAL DECISIONS

Suppose we are confronted with a decision having several possible futures, the probabilities of which are given. Suppose further that we have an opportunity to make some sort of observations which will yield information about these probabilities and thus increase our knowledge of them. The original probabilities are referred to as *prior* probabilities, and those obtained as a result of the observations are called *posterior* probabilities. We will neglect, for the present, the cost of making these observations and simply show how they become an integral part of the decision process.

To take a specific example, let us suppose a foundry has poured ten lots of castings from ten heats of iron during a day. Under normal process operating conditions, the product averages about 2 percent defective. After the day's production has been completed, it is discovered that an important additive was omitted from the metal on one of the heats. When this happens, past experience has shown that the castings will average about 12 percent defective. To make the problem interesting, let us assume that because of administrative errors it is no longer possible to tell just which lot of castings was made with this bad metal. Thus there are ten lots, one of which is from a process which averages 12 percent defective, and the others from a process which averages 2 percent defective. Suppose it is necessary to ship one lot of castings immediately and that, if the bad lot is shipped, a penalty cost of $1,000 is incurred by the company. If the good lot is shipped, no penalty cost arises.

Under these conditions it is reasonable to say that, if any one of the ten lots is selected at random, the probability that it will be the bad lot is .10, and the expected penalty cost if it is shipped is

$$(.10)(\$1,000) = \$100$$

If there is no possibility of further investigation, then it makes little difference which lot is chosen for shipment.

Suppose, however, it is possible to take a sample of two castings from any one lot and inspect them. The inspection of a casting will result in its classification as either good or bad. The decision to be made after the sample has been obtained is whether to ship the lot sampled from or to ship any other lot. Let

a_1 = ship the lot sampled

a_2 = ship any other lot

S_1 = the lot sampled comes from a process with a fraction defective of 2 percent

S_2 = the lot sampled comes from a process with a fraction defective of 12 percent

p_1 = the prior probability of S_1 = .90

p_2 = the prior probability of S_2 = .10

In a sample of two castings there are three possible sets of observations which will be symbolized as follows:

x_1 = both castings good

x_2 = one casting good and one bad

x_3 = both castings bad

Having obtained one of these observations, we wish to compute the posterior probabilities of the possible futures. In general, for decisions under uncertainty, these may be computed from Bayes' theorem which states that the posterior probability of S_j given an observation x is

$$P(S_j|x) = \frac{p_j P(x|S_j)}{\sum_j p_j P(x|S_j)}$$

It is first necessary to compute the conditional probabilities $P(x|S_j)$. Assuming that S_1 is the case, the probability of observing x_1 in the sample is

$$P(x_1|S_1) = \frac{2!}{2!}(.98)^2 = .9604$$

This is the familiar binomial distribution. Similarly, the conditional probability of observing x_1 given S_2 is

$$P(x_1|S_2) = \frac{2!}{2!}(.88)^2 = .7744$$

The additional probabilities required are

$$P(x_2|S_1) = .0392 \qquad P(x_2|S_2) = .2112$$

$$P(x_3|S_1) = .0004 \qquad P(x_3|S_2) = .0144$$

These results are now used together with Bayes' theorem to compute the posterior probabilities of the possible futures. If x_1 is observed then

$$P(S_1|x_1) = \frac{(.90)(.9604)}{(.90)(.9604)+(.10)(.7744)} = .9178$$

and similarly

$$P(S_2|x_1) = \frac{(.10)(.7744)}{(.90)(.9604)+(.10)(.7744)} = .0822$$

If x_2 is observed the posterior probabilities are

$$P(S_1|x_2) = .6255 \qquad P(S_2|x_2) = .3745$$

and if x_3 is observed

$$P(S_1|x_3) = .2000 \qquad P(S_2|x_3) = .8000$$

The problem of choice is again one under conditions of uncertainty, with the probabilities being the posterior probabilities, thus:

	$P(S_1|x)$ S_1	$P(S_2|x)$ S_2
a_1	0	\$1,000
a_2	$\frac{1}{9}(\$1,000)$	0

dependent upon what has been observed in the sample. If x_1 has been observed, the expectations are

$$E(a_1) = (.0818)(1,000) = \$81.80$$

$$E(a_2) = (.9178)\left\{\frac{1,000}{9}\right\} = \$101.98$$

Thus a_1 would be preferred. If x_2 has been observed we have

$$E(a_1) = \$374.50$$

$$E(a_2) = \$\ 69.50$$

leading to the choice of a_2. Finally, if x_3 is observed

$$E(a_1) = \$800.00$$

$$E(a_2) = \$\ 22.22$$

which suggests a preference for a_2.

Clearly, expected cost can be reduced by the sampling process if the optimal choice is made in the above manner. If the cost of taking the samples is small compared to the possible losses involved, then it would be clearly beneficial. If, however, the cost of inspection is large, then some doubt may exist as to whether the samples should be taken at all. To explore this question, we begin by asking, "Before the samples are taken, what is the expected cost of the optimal decision given the results of sampling?"

If the samples are taken and the result is x_1, then the choice will be a_1. The probability that x_1 will be observed, based upon the a priori probabilities is

$$P(x_1) = P(x_1 \mid S_1)p_1 + P(x_1 \mid S_2)p_2$$

$$= (.9604)(.90) + (.7744)(.10)$$

$$= .9418$$

In the same manner we obtain

$$P(x_2) = .0564 \qquad P(x_3) = .0018$$

We may now formulate a new decision as to whether or not the samples should be taken. Let

A_1 = do not sample—ship a lot selected at random

A_2 = take the samples—select the alternative which minimizes expected cost based on the posterior probabilities

This decision may be arrayed in the following form:

	$P(x_1) = .9418$ x_1 is observed	$P(x_2) = .0564$ x_2 is observed	$P(x_3) = .0018$ x_3 is observed
A_1	\$100	\$100	\$100
A_2	$E(a_1) = \$81.80$ $+ C$	$E(a_2) = \$69.50$ $+ C$	$E(a_2) = \$22.22$ $+ C$

where C is the cost of taking the samples.
In this decision the expectations are

$$E(A_1) = \$100.00$$

$$E(A_2) = \$\ 81.01 + C$$

Thus, if C, the cost of sampling, is less than or equal to $18.99, it would pay to go ahead and take the samples. Otherwise it would be better to choose a lot for shipment at random, without the benefit of the information to be obtained from the sample.

At this point it is natural to ask about the efficacy of a sample of two castings. Might it not be better to take a sample of one, or three, or n castings? We could answer this question before taking any samples, by analysis similar to the foregoing. However, it may turn out that if we decide to inspect ten castings, and the first eight examined turn out to be bad, then there is little to be gained by inspecting the remaining two. Thus, the decision about sample size might better be revised continually as sampling progresses. This suggests the idea of a sequential sampling plan. Such a plan involves a series of decisions which begins with the choice of either selecting an alternative immediately on the basis of the prior probabilities, or of taking a sample of at least one casting. If it is decided to do the latter, then a sample of one is taken and the posterior probabilities are computed. It is then necessary to decide between the immediate selection of an alternative, and taking a sample of at least one more casting. This series goes on until the decision is finally made to stop sampling and select a course of action. At each stage the choice is based upon an examination of the expected return from the best alternative, computed on the basis of the posterior probabilities at that stage, and the expected return if the sampling process is continued and optimum decisions are made at each future stage. The computation of these expectations may be extremely difficult, but the principle on which sequential sampling is based is of universal importance. It suggests that in any information collection process one should continually balance the expected cost of making the decision, using the information available, against the cost of collecting at least one more increment of information and then making the best decision.

DECISIONS WITHOUT PROBABILITIES

The reader with any familiarity in the application of techniques of statistical inference will recognize that the prior probabilities may not be economically available in some problems. To illustrate, let us modify the previous example slightly. Let the alternatives be

$$a_1 = \text{ship the lot sampled}$$

$$a_2 = \text{scrap the lot sampled}$$

If a_2 is chosen, we will not be particularly concerned with which lot is shipped, but presumably the sampling process would have to be carried out on the other lots until one is selected for shipment. Using the possible futures as previously defined the decision now appears as follows:

	S_1	S_2
a_1	0	$1,000
a_2	$500	0

We have included a new assumption, namely that the scrapping of a good lot results in a cost of $500. The decision might arise in this form if it were discovered that several heats were made without the essential additive, but the number and identification of the bad lots are both unknown.

Statistical decision theory now suggests that we formulate all possible decision rules, where a decision rule simply specifies what alternative will be selected for each possible observation.

In our problem there are three possible observations and two possible alternatives. This results in $2^3 = 8$ possible ways of associating alternatives with observations, each of which is a particular decision rule. The following table indicates all eight rules. The symbol R_k is used to designate the kth decision rule.

Rule		Observation	
	x_1	x_2	x_3
R_1...........	a_1	a_1	a_1
R_2...........	a_1	a_1	a_2
R_3...........	a_1	a_2	a_1
R_4...........	a_1	a_2	a_2
R_5...........	a_2	a_1	a_1
R_6...........	a_2	a_1	a_2
R_7...........	a_2	a_2	a_1
R_8...........	a_2	a_2	a_2

The decision is then viewed as a choice among these eight rules. In order to make this choice it is necessary to compute the expected cost associated with each rule, for each possible future. This is done in several steps. We have already obtained the conditional probability of an observation, x, given a future S_j, symbolized by $P(x|S_j)$. This, together with the above table, will permit the computation of the probability that any alternative will be selected, given a rule R_k and a future S_j. Let this be $P(a_i|S_j, R_k)$. Since the cost for any selection a_i and any future S_j is known, we may then obtain the expected cost for a rule R_k given a future S_j.

For rule 1, the probabilities of selection for the alternatives are simple.

$$P(a_1|S_1, R_1) = P(x_1|S_1) + P(x_2|S_1) + P(x_3|S_1) = 1$$
$$P(a_2|S_1, R_1) = 0$$
$$P(a_1|S_2, R_1) = 1$$
$$P(a_2|S_2, R_1) = 0$$

For rule 2 we have

$$P(a_1|S_1, R_2) = P(x_1|S_1) + P(x_2|S_1) = .9996$$
$$P(a_2|S_1, R_2) = P(x_3|S_1) = .0004$$

and so on. The complete set of such probabilities are tabulated in Matrix 1.

Matrix 1

		S_1	S_2			S_1	S_2
R_1	a_1	1.00	1.00	R_5	a_1	.0396	.2256
	a_2	0	0		a_2	.9604	.7744
R_2	a_1	.9996	.9856	R_6	a_1	.0392	.2112
	a_2	.0004	.0144		a_2	.9608	.7888
R_3	a_1	.9608	.7888	R_7	a_1	.0004	.0144
	a_2	.0392	.2112		a_2	.9996	.9856
R_4	a_1	.9604	.7744	R_8	a_1	0	0
	a_2	.0396	.2256		a_2	1.00	1.00

It is now possible to compute the expected cost for each rule under each possible future. The expected cost for R_1 and S_1 is

$$V(R_1, S_1) = P(a_1 | S_1, R_1)V(\theta_{11}) + P(a_2 | S_1, R_1)V(\theta_{21})$$
$$= (1.00)(0) + (0)(\$500) = 0$$

For R_1 and S_2

$$V(R_1, S_2) = P(a_1 | S_2, R_1)V(\theta_{12}) + P(a_2 | S_2, R_1)V(\theta_{22})$$
$$= (1.00)(\$1,000) + (0)(0) = \$1,000$$

and so on. The final decision matrix for the choice between rules is given in Matrix 2.

Matrix 2

	S_1	S_2
R_1	0	1000.00
R_2	.20	985.60
R_3	19.60	788.80
R_4	19.80	774.40
R_5	480.20	225.60
R_6	480.40	211.20
R_7	499.80	14.40
R_8	500.00	0

Now any of the principles of choice which have been suggested for decision without probabilities might be applied. This would lead to the selection of a rule which would associate a course of action in the original decision with every possible outcome of the program of observation. Within the context of statistical decision theory it has been customary to suggest that the decision should be viewed as a game. That is, one might imagine the possible futures as being the pure strategies of nature. The decision maker then assumes that it is important to protect himself as best he can against the worst possible "play" by nature, where nature is thought of as having the intelligence and aims of an opponent in the game theory sense. Thus, the decision maker may sometimes be led to the use of a mixed strategy, that is, a randomized mixture of the decision rules. For the foregoing example, the game theoretic solution is carried out graphically in Figure 11-1. The optimal strategy for the decision maker is mixed. It suggests that R_4 should be used with probability .399, and that R_8 should be used with probability .601. Nature's optimal strategy is (.617, .383). The value of the game is $308.50.

As will be recalled, the optimal strategy for the decision maker has the property that, if used, the decision maker's expectation will be just the value of the game, no matter what nature does. Thus, viewing the decision as a game has the advantage that the expected cost after sampling can be computed and compared with the expected cost before sampling to see if the sampling process will be economic. If no sampling is done, we have a game of the form

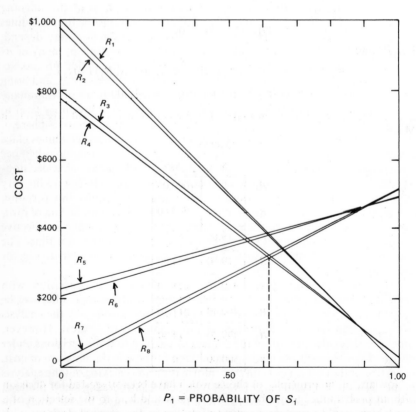

Figure 11-1 Graphical Solution as a Game

The optimal strategy for the decision maker is to select a_1 with probability $\frac{1}{3}$, and a_2 with probability $\frac{2}{3}$. The value of this game is then $333.33. If the cost of sampling is greater than $333.33 - 308.50 = $24.83, then it will not be economic to perform the inspection.

There has been considerable discussion as to whether it is useful to view nature as an intelligent competitor and as to whether mixed strategies have a place in decisions of this sort. Few will argue that nature is in any real sense an opponent who plays against the decision maker in the style recommended by game theory; however, some feel that this is a useful and conservative assumption to make. Having made this assumption, then the use of mixed strategies follows logically, even though it may be difficult to think of nature as responding to the decision maker's choices in such a way as to require the secrecy obtained by mixing these choices.

DECISIONS UNDER PRESSURE

Deadlines are an ever-present and troublesome feature of the ongoing operations of any firm. There are target dates to be met, production schedules to be satisfied, delivery dates on which customer satisfaction may depend, and so on. The firm is continually under the pressure of time in many of its activities. It must bring together all the inputs to the production process according to some coordinated time schedule, get the production out, and bring its product into the market with timeliness. This inevitably means that many of the decisions, such as which machine to purchase, what inventory level to hold, or when to buy its raw materials, cannot be made in an atmosphere of leisurely investigation and reflection. The pressure which these deadlines place on the decision process constitutes perhaps the most striking difference encountered in going from an academic discussion of management decisions into the world of action. Admittedly at present there seems to be nothing very subtle to be said about how decisions should be made under this pressure, but its existence must be clearly recognized. There is a certain feeling of disillusionment which comes to the analyst who is equipped to make an effective analysis, say of replacement policy, but discovers there just is not time. The decision is quickly made instead on the basis of hunches, experience, or intuition.

The chief effect of time pressures is to force one into making decisions with something less than the amount of information which would otherwise be desired. Time pressure is in fact one of the principal reasons why the analysis of decisions in the face of incomplete information is of interest. However, other pressures also act within the context of the firm to force decisions under meager knowledge of the consequences. One of these is the pressure of cost, in particular the cost of collecting the information and carrying out the analysis of the decision. Every manager knows that, before introducing a new product, it would be very useful to have the results of a thorough market study, including test marketing, consumer panels, and so on. This, however, is too expensive for many firms. It is also well known that, before buying a machine, a great many alternatives might be carefully investigated if funds were available to carry out such an investigation. Indeed, some information cannot be obtained at any cost, such as information about the future or perhaps information about a competitor's financial position.

Time and cost then act, sometimes together and sometimes individually, to exert pressures on the decision process, the chief consequence of which is to force decisions to be made with incomplete information. One might characterize the scientist who works undisturbed in his laboratory supported by a grant for pure research, as a man who has little concern for deadlines in his information-gathering and decision-making activities. In fact, scientists seldom, if ever, feel that they have enough information on which to base a scientific decision. The executive in his decision-making activities is at the other extreme. He is conscious of the deadline imposed upon him by the progress of the firm, thoroughly accustomed to making decisions on the basis of very little information, and has confidence in his hunches and judgments. Somewhere in between is the analyst, who is engaged in the application of scientific results to decisions under the pressure of executive action. The analyst inevitably must feel the conflict between his desire to do definitive analysis and the need to get an answer in a hurry. In this situation the analyst has little choice but to present the best possible analysis of the decision within the time available. If he does not, the decision will probably be made without the benefit of his work. On the other hand, deadlines are sometimes not as absolute as they are made to seem, and it may be that a decision can be held up while better analysis is made available.

In the next section we will try to point out some of the effects of time pressure on the decision process, and offer some highly simplified examples of how one might react to this pressure.

EFFECTS OF PRESSURE

In the absence of any very general evidence on the nature of the effects of pressure on decision making in the firm, we will suggest some hypotheses. These hypotheses can best be viewed as suggestions of things to be watched for in particular situations, rather than general statements of facts.

As we have pointed out, the general effect of time pressure is to reduce the available information and the extent of analysis accomplished in preparation for an actual choice. This means that fewer alternatives will be identified under conditions of time pressure. It means also that less evidence will be obtained on the outcomes, their probabilities, and their values. In the absence of this evidence, it is increasingly difficult to do analysis. This leads to the formulation of a simple, but possible revealing, principle of a tentative nature: *Pressure favors intuition as against analysis.*

We might also say that as pressure increases we are more likely to find the firm making its decisions on the basis of judgment, unorganized experience, and implicit processes of choice. All these are, of course, arrayed in contrast to our attempts to move toward rationality through data collection and analysis. This may mean that, in some firms, the only decisions on which anything like effective staff assistance can be given, are those which provide sufficient time for the staff to perform its routine functions. One of the major differences between staff organizations is their ability to do nonroutine analysis in the face of executive decision deadlines. It is perhaps true that the most difficult aspect of staff work is to put knowledge into the hands of those who make decisions, under the conditions of pressure which characterize these decisions.

Control decisions, such as those relating to quality control, production control, or inventory control are inherently time-pressure decisions. If management hopes to control a production process, it must be able to make quick decisions as to what action to take when something goes wrong with the process. It is hypothesized that relatively simple policies are established to cover the common repetitive situations in which a control choice must be made. These policies are then followed almost automatically through to the selection of an alternative. This indicates the obvious way of reacting to repetitive decisions made in the face of time pressures. This way is, of course, the formulation of policy which effectively predetermines the choice.

Finally, we suggest two well-known problems which will indicate some of the relevant considerations.

THE PISTOL PROBLEM

Consider two persons determined to fight a duel with single-shot pistols. When one of them fires, the shot is either fatal or a miss. Having fired and missed, one duelist can only stand there until his assailant walks up and delivers the fatal shot. For each duelist a function is given which tells the probability of a hit as a function of the distance between the persons. One form of this problem is to ask, "When is the optimal time to fire?" There is an advantage in delaying the decision to fire, since this improves the probability of a hit. However, the longer the delay, the more likely the opponent will fire, perhaps with devasting effect. The pressures of time are obvious.

THE FIANCÉ PROBLEM

A young lady has determined that N gentlemen are potential husbands, but she knows none of them. She proposes to become engaged to them one at a time. She begins by selecting one man at random and becoming engaged. The question is, then, should she marry him, or discard him in the hope of finding a more suitable mate. If she becomes engaged a second time, she will perhaps discard the man if he is not more desirable than the first man, but otherwise she faces the same problem again. Here pressures are again in evidence. She is quite ignorant of those men to whom she has not yet been engaged. The supply of men is limited because, after breaking an engagement, it is diffiult to take up again with a man. Time presses also, since this process leaves her a little older at each stage. The question is, "To how many men should she become engaged before marrying one?"

DEALING WITH PRESSURES

There is a real need for some method of dealing with the pressure which will be effective in the context of management decisions. Modern statistics has, of course, recognized the financial pressures involved by introducing considerations of the cost of taking data and the costs associated with say type 1 and type 2 errors. Little has been offered so far as to how one should take into account the pressure of time, and it is the purpose of the discussion which follows to explore an approach to this problem.

Before proceeding, a word of caution is necessary. These very pressures themselves may make it impossible for the analyst to behave optimally under pressure, if the rules for optimal behavior are complicated, costly, and time consuming. Thus, the analyst faces a sort of double dilemma. He would like to know the rules for rational behavior under pressure, but if the answer you give him is too complicated, pressure will prevent him from using it. Ideally what is sought is some rough guide to behavior in making decisions under pressure which can be economically applied. If a missile is in flight in our general direction, we are unlikely to be interested in a complicated scheme for calculating the best direction in which to run. These kinds of results are not generally available at present.

We suggest here a hypothetical problem which is intended to illustrate three basic notions.

1. The principal reason for postponing a decision is to gather additional information. If no additional information can be obtained, the choice may as well be made, and the time available before the deadline used for advance preparation or early action.
2. The basic problem of dealing with deadlines is knowing when to stop gathering additional information and make the choice. In this respect the problem is much like a statistical sequential sampling plan.
3. In order to deal rationally with decisions in the face of deadlines, a great deal must be known about the characteristics of the information which has not yet been obtained. Here, as in the problem of searching for alternatives, reasonable behavior seems to require more information than is likely to be available in most situations.

AN EXAMPLE

This is the problem of the political opportunist who tries to pick the candidate who will win the election, attach himself to this candidate, and thus obtain a comfortable appointment as a reward for his loyalty. If he picks the wrong candidate, the loser, of course all is wasted, for the loser has no jobs to distribute to his followers. The earlier in the campaign that the opportunist becomes associated with a candidate, the greater his reward if his man wins the election. The election is, of course, a rather definite deadline, because no elected official has much sympathy for followers who only declare themselves after the returns are in. The time between the present and election day is divided by the opportunist into three periods. He has the possibility during any of these periods of making a survey of voter opinion which will presumably reveal to him something of the way in which the election will go. Let us suppose that his payoff is given as a function of the time he declares his support, as shown in the following matrix.

	Present	Period 1	Period 2	Period 3	After Election
He supports the winner	10	9	8	7	0
He supports the loser	0	0	0	0	0

The surveys of voter opinion which he may wish to make not only take time, but cost money. In the same units as the payoff data, the cost of a survey will be taken as .25, no matter in which period it is made. To make things simple, let us further assume that the result of a survey is simply a statement, "Candidate A will be elected" or "Candidate B will be elected." A survey gives no other information. From past experience with surveys, our political opportunist knows that, as the surveys are made closer to the time of the election, they are more and more likely to be correct. In fact, he estimates the probability that a survey will be correct as follows:

Period	1	2	3
Probability of a correct prediction	.60	.70	.90

For simplicity we will assume that the outcomes of the surveys are probabilistically independent.

At the present time the information which the opportunist has in hand leads him to the opinion that the probability of A being elected is .55; thus the probability of B being elected is .45, since this is a two-party contest.

The political opportunist is thus faced with the choice of whether to go ahead with one or more surveys before declaring his choice, or to associate himself with a candidate immediately. Whoever decides to declare for a candidate must, of course, decide which one.

Assume for the moment that he decided to dispense with any future surveys and declare a choice immediately. His decision is then represented by the following matrix:

	$p_1 = .55$ A is elected	$p_2 = .45$ B is elected
Support A	10	0
Support B	0	10

It may readily be shown that the application of the expectation principle will lead him to support A, with an expected payoff of 5.5. We will continue to use the expectation principle throughout the analysis of this decision.

Now what might happen if he were to take one or more surveys of voter opinion during the three future periods available to him before the election? After any survey, he will want to consider the information thus obtained and decide once more whether to stop or continue. Let us assume that he contemplates the possible outcomes of a series of three such surveys. These outcomes are listed below. The letter A indicates the survey results in the statement, "A will be elected."

Period 1	Period 2	Period 3
A	A	A
A	A	B
A	B	A
A	B	B
B	A	A
B	A	B
B	B	A
B	B	B

The effect of these surveys will clearly be to change his probabilities of the possible futures. Our first step will be to show for each possible result how the probabilities would be changed. Given these probabilities, the expectations for various alternatives of stopping or continuing may be computed, which will finally suggest a method of dealing with the time pressure to maximize expectations.

To simplify our symbolism let

$S_1 = A$ is elected

$S_2 = B$ is elected

$p_1 =$ probability of S_1 at present (prior)

$p_2 =$ probability of S_2 at present (prior)

$f_k(S_j) =$ probability of S_j given the results of k surveys (the posterior probability) $k = 1, 2, 3$

$p(K|S_j) =$ the conditional probability of the survey results represented by K, given S_j (for example, K may stand for A or AB, or ABA)

Using Bayes' theorem we may write

$$f_k(S_j) = \frac{p(K|S_j)p_j}{\sum_j p(K|S_j)p_j}$$

which gives us the posterior probability of S_j, given its prior probability p_j, and k surveys with the result K. This will tell us then how the political opportunist's probabilities change as the result of his surveys.

Suppose, as before, that the first survey gives the result $K = A$. The prior probability of S_1 is $p_1 = .55$. Now if we assume that S_1 is true, namely that A will be elected, the probability of the first survey yielding the result A is the probability of the first survey being correct in its prediction. Thus

$$p(A|S_1) = .60$$

Substituting in Bayes' theorem we obtain

$$f_1(S_1) = \frac{(.60)(.55)}{(.60)(.55)+(.40)(.45)} = .65$$

Thus, if the first survey is made and the result is A, the probability of S_1 is increased to .65 and the probability of S_2 is decreased to .35.

Now suppose the first survey has been taken with the result A as before, and the second survey is made also yielding the result A. Given that S_1 is true, the conditional probability that both surveys will yield A is simply the probability that both will be correct. This is the product of their individual probabilities of being correct.

$$p(K = A, A \mid S_1) = (.60)(.70) = .42$$

Again using Bayes' theorem we have

$$f_2(S_1) = \frac{(.42)(.55)}{(.42)(.55)+(.12)(.45)} = .81$$

Finally, if three surveys are made and all yield the result A, similar calculations yield

$$p(K = A, A, A \mid S_1) = (.60)(.70)(.90) = .38$$

$$f_3(S_1) = \frac{(.38)(.55)}{(.38)(.55)+(.012)(.45)} = .97$$

Similarly, the probabilities of S_1 may be calculated for all possible results of one, two, and three surveys. These are shown in Table 11-1.

Table 11-1

Survey Results	$f_1(S_1)$	$f_2(S_1)$	$f_3(S_1)$
A A A......................	.65	.81	.97
A A B......................	.65	.81	.32
A B A......................	.65	.44	.88
A B B......................	.65	.44	.08
B A A......................	.45	.66	.94
B A B......................	.45	.66	.17
B B A......................	.45	.26	.76
B B B......................	.45	.26	.04

The probabilities of S_2 are simply one minus those given in Table 11-1.

After any survey, if the opportunist decides to declare his choice, then it is not hard to see that he maximizes expected payoff by declaring for the candidate whose probability of success is largest at that point. Let $R_k(K)$ stand for the expected return after k surveys, the result of which are given by K, if the candidate whose probability of success is greatest is chosen. For example, after one survey, which is taken at a cost of .25, if the result turns out to be A, the best choice at that point would be A. The expected payoff from such a choice is

$$R_1(A) = (.65)(9) - .25 = 5.60$$

Similarly

$$R_1(B) = (.55)(9) - .25 = 4.70$$

The expectations associated with stopping and making the best choice for other numbers of surveys with various results are as follows:

$$R_2(AA) = (.81)(8) - .50 = 5.98$$
$$R_2(AB) = (.56)(8) - .50 = 3.98$$
$$R_2(BA) = (.66)(8) - .50 = 4.78$$
$$R_2(BB) = (.74)(8) - .50 = 5.42$$
$$R_3(AAA) = (.97)(7) - .75 = 6.04$$
$$R_3(AAB) = (.68)(7) - .75 = 4.01$$
$$R_3(ABA) = (.88)(7) - .75 = 5.41$$
$$R_3(ABB) = (.92)(7) - .75 = 5.69$$
$$R_3(BAA) = (.94)(7) - .75 = 5.83$$
$$R_3(BAB) = (.83)(7) - .75 = 5.06$$
$$R_3(BBA) = (.76)(7) - .75 = 4.57$$
$$R_3(BBB) = (.96)(7) - .75 = 5.97$$

It will be recalled that the expected payoff if no survey activity is undertaken is 5.50. Thus we now know the expected payoff for a decision made at any point in the information collection process. The problem may now be posed differently. If the political opportunist wishes to maximize expectation, then wherever he is in the data collection possibilities, he must make the following choice:

a_1 = continue with more data collection, making the expectation maximizing choice at each future stage

a_2 = stop and choose the candidate associated with the larger expectation in view of presently available information.

Let us suppose that two surveys have been taken with the results A, A. If the decision maker stops at this point, his best choice is A, and the expected payoff is 5.98. The symbol $E_{AA}(a_2)$ will represent the expectation of a_2 after two surveys which resulted in A, A.

$$E_{AA}(a_2) = R_2(AA) = 5.98$$

If he decides to go on, taking the third survey, it may result in either A or B. The probability that the third survey will yield A is

(Prob. of S_1)(Prob. of correct survey)

+ (Prob. of S_2)(Prob. of wrong survey)

After two surveys yielding A, A, the probability of S_1 may be obtained from Table 11-1.

$$f_2(S_1) = .81$$

Then the probability that the third survey will result in A is

$$(.81)(.90) + (.19)(.10)$$

By similar reasoning, the probability that the third survey will give B as a result is

$$(.81)(.10) + (.19)(.90)$$

If the third survey is taken, the deadline forces a choice immediately afterward. If the third survey results in A, the best choice will be A with expected payoff

$$R_3(AAA) = 6.04$$

If the third survey results in B, then the best choice will be B, with expectations

$$R_3(AAB) = 4.01$$

Putting these together, the expected return if he decides to continue with the third survey is

$$E_{AA}(a_1) = \{(.81)(.90)+(.19)(.10)\}\,6.04 + \{(.81)(.10)+(.19)(.90)\}\,4.01 = 5.53$$

Thus, having two surveys with the results A, A, the best choice would be to stop immediately and declare support for candidate A. This has an expected return of 5.98, which is clearly better than an expected return of 5.53 if he decides to go on.

The same choice may be evaluated for another possible stage of information collection. These computations are shown in the following paragraphs.

It must be emphasized that these expectations are computed on the premise that the decision maker elects the expectation maximizing choice at each future stage. Thus, given one survey which resulted in A, we reason as follows in exploring the expected return from a second survey and optimal future choices. If the second survey results in A, then the decision maker would be in the position of comparing

$$E_{AA}(a_1) = 5.53$$

and

$$E_{AA}(a_2) = 5.98$$

Making the expectation maximizing choice, he would at that point elect to stop. Again starting from the position of one survey with the result A, if the second survey yields B, the comparison will be made between

$$E_{AB}(a_1) = 5.56$$

and

$$E_{AB}(a_2) = 3.98$$

Thus, after the results A, B, the choice will be to continue, with an expectation of 5.56. In summary, after A, A, stop; after A, B, continue.

Given then the single result A, the expectation from continuing is

$$E_A(a_1) = \{(.65)(.70)+(.35)(.30)\}\,5.98 + \{(.65)(.30)+(.35)(.70)\}\,5.56 = 5.79$$

Given that the result of the first survey is A, the choice would be to continue since

$$E_A(a_1) = 5.79 > E_A(a_2) = 5.60$$

The complete set of such computations is as follows:

$$E_{AA}(a_1) = \{(.81)(.90)+(.19)(.10)\}\,6.04 + \{(.81)(.10)+(.19)(.90)\}\,4.01 = 5.53$$

$$E_{AA}(a_2) = 5.98$$
$$E_{AB}(a_1) = \{(.44)(.90)+(.56)(.10)\}\,5.41 + \{(.44)(.10)+(.56)(.90)\}\,5.69 = 5.56$$

$E_{AB}(a_2) = 3.98$
$E_{BA}(a_1) = \{(.66)(.90)+(.34)(.10)\}\,5.83 + \{(.66)(.10)+(.34)(.90)\}\,5.06 = 5.54$

$E_{BA}(a_2) = 4.78$
$E_{BB}(a_1) = \{(.26)(.90)+(.74)(.10)\}\,4.57 + \{(.26)(.10)+(.74)(.90)\}\,5.97 = 5.54$

$E_{BB}(a_2) = 5.42$
$E_A(a_1) = \{(.65)(.70)+(.35)(.30)\}\,5.98 + \{(.65)(.30)+(.35)(.70)\}\,5.56 = 5.79$

$E_A(a_2) = 5.60$
$E_B(a_1) = \{(.45)(.70)+(.55)(.30)\}\,5.54 + \{(.45)(.30)+(.55)(.70)\}\,5.54 = 5.54$

$E_B(a_2) = 4.70$
$E(a_1) = \{(.55)(.60)+(.45)(.40)\}\,5.79 + \{(.55)(.40)+(.45)(.60)\}\,5.54 = 5.67$

$E(a_2) = 5.50$

All of these calculations are brought together in Figure 11-2, which shows the possible evolutions of the information collection process, and indicates at each stage whether the political opportunist should stop or continue. Several points may be drawn from the example of the political opportunist.

1. The example, though highly simplified, does in fact suggest a rational method of reacting to time pressure so as to maximize the expected return. Thus, the question of how to face time pressures is not unanswerable.
2. The example includes the interesting features of more realistic time pressure problems. A deadline is in evidence at a known point in time. In some cases, the deadline itself may be unknown. When two opposing military forces are moving to occupy a strategic position, the deadline for force A's arrival is the time of force B's arrival, which is not definitely known. The example also includes a benefit for early choice which may arise through advance preparation for the deadline. This is the familiar concept "Time is money." It leads also to a more general notion of deadlines. Instead of a definitive point in time at which the payoffs change dramatically, one may think of simply the payoff being a nonincreasing function of time. The example also includes directly the cost of information collection, which is reckoned into the expected payoffs.
3. Out of this example it may be possible to formulate a rough principle for dealing with deadlines. *After each increment of information is obtained the decision is reviewed in the light of the new evidence. The cost of stopping immediately and making the best possible choice is compared with the cost of continuing. The expected cost of continuing is computed under the assumption that at each future stage of information collection, the optimal choice between stopping and continuing is made. On the basis of expected payoff, stop or continue the process.*

To apply this principle quantitatively it is necessary to be able to enumerate the possible outcomes of future data collection efforts, and further, to compute the probabilities of these outcomes. In addition, it must be possible to indicate just how the information will quantitatively change the decision maker's view of his choice. In the example this was done by means of Bayes' theorem. It is essential also to begin with some prior probabilities.

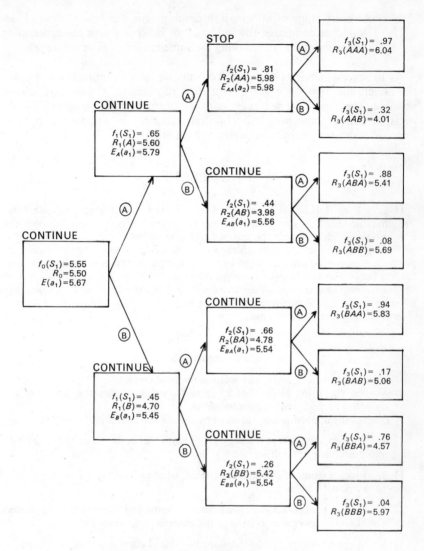

Figure 11-2   The Political Opportunist

4. It is probably true that, in most actual situations of decision making under pressure within the firm, the foregoing method requires more information and computation ability than will be available. The principle then may best serve as a rough guide for sharpening judgments about how to deal with deadlines. In this rough form it might suggest the following:
   a) Study information as fast as it becomes available.
   b) If no more information can be obtained, there is little point in waiting and the choice should be made.

c) At every stage of information development, the best present choice should be compared (by judgment or however) with the expectation from continuing and making the same choice at each future stage.

As in several previous decision problems we have examined, one reaches the conclusion that an exact quantitative response to deadline is seldom possible. The study of exact analysis of the problem does, however, give the decision maker some possibility of sharpening his intuitions and perhaps improve his responses in nonquantitative situations.

PROBLEMS

11-1.* Large lots of solid-fuel rocket engines are received from a manufacturer. They may be tested only by actually firing a sample of a few engines. Suppose that it is known in advance that the engines will come from a process which is either producing 8 percent defective product or one which is producing 3 percent defective product. Suppose we are permitted to take a sample of two engines from each lot for test firing. For purposes of analysis, the cost of testing an engine is taken to be $1,000, the cost of accepting a defective engine is $15,000 and the cost of rejecting a good engine is $1,000. Assume a lot size of 50.

a) If the prior probabilities are

$$p' = .03 \qquad \text{probability} = .50$$

$$p' = .08 \qquad \text{probability} = .50$$

analyze the decision as a statistical decision under uncertainty.

b) Assume the prior probabilities are unknown and treat the problem as a statistical decision without probabilities.

c) Discuss the application of various principles of choice in part (*b*).

11-2. Explain the process whereby prior probabilities are transformed by sampling into posterior probabilities.

11-3. From a study of statistical decisions, what general guides for decisions of all sorts can be derived?

11-4. Outline the general steps in a sequential statistical decision-making process. How would such a process be related to the analysis of Chapter 7?

11-5. Suggest how the model developed in this chapter might be interpreted as

a) A model of learning.

b) An adaptive control system.

c) An illustration of decision making as a sequential process.

d) A model of how people's beliefs are changed by experience.

e) A model of how staff results are integrated into a manager's conceptualization of a decision.

11-6.* Show that if observations are independent, the posterior probability resulting from a given prior probability and a sample of size two is the same as that resulting from obtaining the same observations in two samples each of size one.

11-7.* A businessman must make travel plans in advance and the success of these plans depends heavily on the weather. Let S_1 represent the condition "good weather on the day of travel" and S_2 stand for "bad weather on the day of travel."

In the businessman's opinion, the chances of good weather on the day in question are .70. His utilities are shown in the matrix below.

	S_1	S_2
Air	1.0	0
Rail	.25	.75
Auto	.50	.25

A long-range weather prediction is available which is right 60 percent of the time. (The prediction is either "good" or "bad.") Assume that the results of the long-range weather forecast can, for simplicity, be considered independent of the business-man's opinion. What would be a consistent choice
a) Without the prediction?
b) Given the prediction?
c) What is the value of the prediction to him?

11–8.* Four men examine a potential oil property. Their respective probabilities for the event "oil will be found if a well is drilled on this property" are .01, .20, .80, and .99. They agree that there are three methods of testing for the presence of oil, one of which is right half of the time, one of which is right 90 percent of the time, and one of which has never been wrong. If the results from the use of each of these testing methods were to be processed according to Bayes' theorem, how would the belief of each man change?

11–9. Consider a manager whose firm places new consumer products on the market from time to time. Suppose for simplicity that he considers a product which at least breaks even, a success, and a product which does not break even, a failure. When a new product possibility is brought to his attention he makes his own estimate of its chance of success. He may then submit the item to a consumer test panel. Again for simplicity, the results of the panel test are either "success" or "failure." The product may be either discarded, marketed, or submitted to a test marketing at this point. The results of the test marketing are also either "success" or "failure." It is known that the result of the test marketing is *not* independent of the consumer panel result. Show symbolically how the statistical decision model might be adapted to this situation. What data would be required for its application? What difficulties would you expect to encounter in obtaining this data?

11–10.* A manufacturer is considering the possibility of introducing a new product and the advisability of a test marketing prior to making the final decision. His alternatives are

$$a_1 = \text{market the product}$$

$$a_2 = \text{do not market the product}$$

For simplicity, only three possible futures are considered which are shown below together with his prior probabilities associated with them.

	Profit	Prior Probability
S_1: the product captures 10 percent of the market	$10,000,000	.70
S_2: the product captures 3 percent of the market	$ 1,000,000	.10
S_3: the product captures less than 1 percent of the market	− $ 5,000,000	.20

If the test marketing is made, three possible results are considered:

Z_1 = test sales of more than 10 percent of the market

Z_2 = test sales of 5 to 10 percent of the market

Z_3 = test sales of less than 5 percent of the market

The conditional probabilities of the test results are given in the table below.

	Z_1	Z_2	Z_3
$P(Z\mid S_1)$	.60	.30	.10
$P(Z\mid S_2)$	.30	.60	.10
$P(Z\mid S_3)$	.10	.10	.80

Assume that utility is linear in money.
a) What is his best alternative before the test?
b) How much would it be worth to have perfect knowledge of the outcome?
c) What action is best for each possible result of the test marketing?
d) What is the value of the test marketing?

11–11.* If one were betting a dollar on red, black or 0 and 00 at an ordinary roulette wheel, what would be the expected value of perfect information?

11–12.* The manufacturer of a missile claims it is 98 percent reliable. The missile has been evaluated by an independent agency which suggests that it is only about 90 percent reliable. The decision maker, who is buying the missile, is about to conduct his own tests on the missile which will consist of two actual firings. Suppose our decision maker, based on his experience, is uncertain about the claims of the manufacturer and the testing agency. (If he was certain that one of them was right, he would need no further tests.) We suppose that he can express this uncertainty based on his experience in a statement like, "The probability that the manufacturer's claim is right is .40, and the probability that the independent agency's claim is correct is .60." (They might both be wrong, but we neglect this to achieve the utmost simplicity.)
Suppose the two missiles tested are both failures, what would be the decision maker's resulting opinion?

11–13.* Solve the problem of the political opportunist under the following conditions: Two periods are available in which to collect data on voter intentions. The payoffs are:

	Now	End of Period 1	End of Period 2	After the Election
Correct choice	100	80	70	0
Wrong choice	0	0	0	0

The cost of each survey is 2 units. The prior probabilities held by the opportunist are .60 for candidate R and .40 for candidate D. The probabilities of correct inferences from the surveys are

Period	1	2
Probability	.80	.90

11–14. Formulate some rough guides for decision-making behavior in the following situations:
a) A limited time option to purchase a potential plant site.
b) Getting a cigarette on the market which contains no tobacco.

c) Deciding to repair or replace a machine which has failed and is vital to the operation of the plant.

11–15. Formulate some guides to decision-making behavior in the following situations:

a) Which supplier to choose in the face of a fast-approaching deadline for the delivery of a new part for a firm's product.

b) Deciding whether to hold or to sell a stock in a presently declining market.

11–16. Suppose in the example of the political opportunist, the results of the surveys were not taken to be independent. Show symbolically what data would be necessary and how they would enter into the calculations of the posterior probabilities.

SUGGESTIONS FOR FURTHER STUDY

Howard, Ronald A. "Information Value Theory." *IEEE Transactions on Systems Science and Cybernetics*, Vol. SSC-2, No. 1 (August 1966), pp. 22–26.

Howard, Ronald A. "Bayesian Decision Models for Systems Engineering." *IEEE Transactions on Systems Science and Cybernetics*, Vol. SSC-1, No. 1 (November 1965), pp. 38–39.

——————————. "The Foundations of Decision Analysis." *IEEE Transactions on Systems Science and Cybernetics*, Vol. SSC-4, No. 3 (September 1968), pp. 211–219.

Pratt, John W., Howard Raiffa, and Robert Schlaifer. *The Foundations of Decision Under Uncertainty: An Elementary Exposition.* Cambridge: Harvard University, pp. 353–375.

Raiffa, Howard. *Decision Analysis.* Reading, Massachusetts: Addison-Wesley, 1970.

Raiffa, H., and R. Schlaifer. *Applied Statistical Decision Theory.* Boston: Graduate School of Business, Harvard University, 1961.

Schlaifer, Robert. *Analysis of Decisions Under Uncertainty.* New York: McGraw-Hill, Inc., 1969.

MULTIPLE CRITERION DECISION ANALYSIS 12

Is there any point in taking considerable trouble to learn about a manager's preferences so that we can tell him what he already knows—what his own preferences are? The answer to this is twofold.

THE SCIENTIFIC STUDY OF VALUES

In the first place, managers are not always sure what their own preferences are. The assumption that, if an analyst presented a manager with predictions of the outcomes associated with various courses of action, the manager would clearly be able to evaluate the outcomes for himself may not be entirely warranted. Indeed, one of the important tasks of the analyst may be that of helping the manager to clarify his objectives and values. The method may involve making preferences explicit, checking their self-consistency, and encouraging the explicit and careful consideration of trade-offs. The need for value clarification is, as we have said, the motivation for management to respond to a decision by exploring its goals more carefully before making a choice.

Secondly, the analyst is deeply interested in having the manager accept his recommendation as to the appropriate course of action. Management acceptance is the primary means by which the analyst may demonstrate achievement and thus justify his efforts. Further, with increasing management acceptance, the analyst finds greater opportunities to perform his basic function of relieving the manager of some of the hard work of making a decision. If, from the study of a manager's preferences among simple outcomes, one is able to predict his preferences among more complex outcomes, and if these predictions turn out to be correct, then the analyst will be increasingly able to make recommendations which the manager will accept, and the manager will be increasingly inclined to delegate various aspects of the decision process. If one could ever succeed in completely understanding a manager's preferences, the imaginary ultimate accomplishment would be to read these preferences into a computing machine. The manager could then rely on the machine to make all his decisions, since the machine would achieve the same results as if he himself had made the choices. While it is hardly likely that this will be accomplished, it illustrates the basic point of the scientific study of values.

One might summarize this program in a form such as that of Figure 12-1. The values of the manager are taken to be the basic phenomena under study. These values are observed and measured by obtaining preference statements from the manager, perhaps using a method like the method of paired

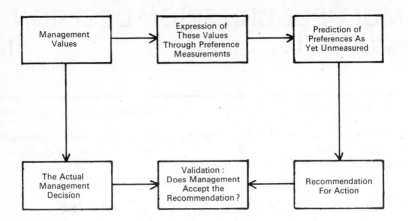

Figure 12-1 The Scientific Study of Values

comparisons. The results of this observation program covering some simple preferences are organized into a logical structure, perhaps in the form of an indifference map. This permits the analyst to predict the manager's preferences among outcomes which have not been studied and among outcomes far more complex than those for which the original data were obtained. These predictions of a manager's preferences are then used as a basis for making recommendations with respect to various courses of action. Such a recommendation is interpreted as a prediction of how the manager himself would choose if his preferences were well described by our indifference map, and if he acted in a consistent fashion. If the decision actually made by the manager agrees with the recommendation made by the analyst, then the prediction is confirmed. In this sense, knowledge of the manager's values may be validated.

Setting goals or objectives for an organization has traditionally been *the* management prerogative, and it should be clear that science proposes no challenge to this tradition. Goals have, however, been largely matters of implicit understanding and agreement among the top managers, and few attempts have been made to explicitly transmit these objectives throughout the organization. Goals were spoken of in broad and general terms, but there was seldom any clear statement of just what combinations of risk and profit expectation were or were not acceptable to the firm, for example. The objectives are not transmitted to new managers by explicit statement, but rather by an extended process of assimilating "the way things are done in this company." Science has thus found it difficult to go beyond studies in which expected cost or expected profit were treated as the explicit goals. The final reports of such studies must go to top management who integrate them with their implicit views of the firm's objectives.

There are now some interesting reasons for altering this situation and suggesting to the manager that goals be made more explicit. What is sought are not more elaborate general pronouncements about the firm's value system, but rather specific statements sufficiently operational to permit decisive application to actual decision situations. That is, science would like to get at the organization's indifference maps.

There are three purposes which may be served if managers are willing to make their goals explicit in this way. First, is the increased possibility for the delegation of decisions. As long as the firm's value system is implicit, top managers must make the value system operative by giving personal attention to decisions. Not even ordinary inventory control decisions can be delegated without some explicit rendering of values. Here, indeed, is where the current movement toward greater delegation appears to be stalled. Secondly, as we have earlier suggested, the decision process may be blocked because the manager is not clear abou this value system. When offered an opportunity to install a machine accounting system which will require the dismissal of x persons and promises a net savings of y per year, he may not be at all clear that "y justifies x." One of the less developed possibilities of management science is that of helping him become clear by offering a conceptual structure within which to make his values explicit, to see their interrelationships, and to formulate in his own mind the trade-offs which he feels are appropriate for the firm. Explicitness is simply offered as a possible means for assisting in the resolution of value conflicts.

Perhaps the most difficult aspect of goal setting is that of coming to grips with the multiple, conflicting nature of most value structures. In deciding which of two houses to buy, compare them on the basis of price, number of rooms, tax rate, style, location, and so on. It is relatively easy to compare the houses one attribute at a time, but the difficulty arises when these comparisons must be aggregated into an overall preference. Similar problems occur when one must choose between development projects, plant locations, candidates for vice-president, and, in fact, in nearly all interesting decisions. Here the early results of some experiments in the division of labor have been especially suggestive. It has been proposed that the multiple goal problem be approached by having the manager compare his opportunities on the basis of one attribute at a time, evaluating the houses first on the basis of price, second on the basis of number of rooms and so on. These simple comparisons, judgments, or ratings are easy to make. It is then proposed that these be combined, not by the manager, but by the analyst and his computer into an overall evaluation. The surprising result is that even if the logic used to aggregate the basic preference statements is simple and straightforward, the results seem to meet with two responses. Managers seem to appreciate this sort of assistance with the difficult part of making the firm's value system operative, and secondly, they seem to be at least as satisfied with the final result of this method as with their usual ones. If this sort of result were to be further confirmed, then we might look toward the formulating of a principle to guide in the division of labor.

Use analysis to accept as inputs simple judgments or decisions well within a manager's experience, and to extend logically the consequences of these inputs to situations not within his experience and easy intuition.

We are suggesting with this principle that the assumption that these subtle combinations of multiple and conflicting values could be made only by experienced persons may warrant a careful examination. Perhaps they can be made with more satisfactory results using some rather simple analytical models.

TERMINOLOGY

There is a variety of terminology associated with models which reflect the complexity of decision-maker value systems. Models which emphasize explicit evaluation of the various attributes of outcomes or consequences are often called "multiple attribute" models. Those which emphasize explicitness as to the various objectives which a decision maker may be seeking may be called "multiple objective" models. We will use the more general term "multiple criterion" to describe all of these methods.

OBJECTIVES

The analyst of management decisions aims at evaluating outcomes as far as possible in terms of explicit criteria or measures of value such as cost or profit. When the resulting conceptualization of a decision is presented to management, their response is nearly always to modify the analyst's work through the addition of various judgments. Perhaps the most significant and difficult judgments are those pertaining to value. The necessity for these judgments arises in two ways. First, it is usually not possible for the analyst to be fully aware of the objectives of the firm since these are often implicit in the thinking of management, rather than explicitly stated. Second, most outcomes contain aspects which are relevent to the objectives of the firm but cannot be readily evaluated by the analyst in terms of cost, profits, or whatever measures of value are being employed. While it is very useful to use cost or profit as a measure of value for most firms, not all aspects of an outcome can be directly measured in these terms, and most firms have other objectives, such as customer service, good will, community reputation, job satisfaction, safety, employment stability and so on. These factors, which cannot be directly expressed in cost or profit terms, are called "intangibles" or "irreducibles."

The ultimate aim of the analyst with respect to these intangibles is to develop objective methods of evaluating them, so that a single measure of value may be associated with each outcome in a decision. This measure would have the property of objectively reflecting not only the cost of profit represented by the outcome, but also the worth of the intangible values associated with it.

It must be immediately pointed out that the study of decisions and value measurement is a very long way from this goal at the present time. This means that in most instances intangibles must be evaluated by some process of judgment exercised by the decision maker and based upon his perception of the objectives of the firm. (If his personal objectives differ from those of the firm, there may be little to prevent their inclusion in the decisions he makes.) The analyst often finds little opportunity to influence or even gain insight into this judgment process. Nevertheless, it is important to try to understand why it is necessary and to be able to seize whatever opportunities present themselves for improving these judgments.

In attacking the problem of evaluating intangibles it is very easy to get embroiled in questions which could only be answered by lifting the top of the decision-maker's head and looking inside. Thus, if management decides to forego profit in return for something rather vaguely called "good will," we cannot ask if they really mean this or if this really represents the objectives of the firm. If a decision maker indicates that laying off an employee is equivalent in his judgment to a loss of $1,000, little can be done to validate his statement in any ordinary sense. What can be done with respect to the evaluation of intangibles is to make the judgments explicit and consistent.

In terms of our objectives of rationalizing decisions, explicitness and consistency are of basic importance. In this chapter we will explore briefly the origin of intangible values within the firm and some of the attempts to make value judgments both explicit and consistent. The reader should be warned that this is not only the most important part of the analysis of decisions but also the most difficult and most primitive with respect to scientific development. Indeed, some people believe that science can never make much of a contribution to the problem, while others strongly disagree.

VALUES AND OBJECTIVES OF THE FIRM

One way to think about the problem of value measurement is to begin by looking at the objectives or goals of the firm. The outcomes in a decision are then evaluated in terms of how far they advance the firm toward its objectives, or their efficiency for the objectives. Conceptually at least, if the objectives of the firm were explicitly stated, the analyst would attempt to predict how well the outcomes served these goals, and the outcomes could be evaluated more or less directly. It is true that for most firms a great deal of useful analysis can be done based on the assumption that the most important goal is profit maximization.

Without maintaining that profit maximization is in fact the objective of all managers, several arguments are commonly given to suggest it serves adequately as a measure of value for management decision making:

1. Although management has other goals, the attainment of these is well correlated with the attainment of profits. Profits thus serve as a useful proximate measure of value.
2. Profits constitute a rule of thumb by which the busy manager simplifies very complicated affairs. He need not absorb all the details of the operations of his firm nor the complexities of the decisions he must make. Profit predictions provide him with a useful basis for simplifying his environment. Managers find it easiest to decide questions which they believe are decidable in terms of accounting dollars. They thus welcome any attempt to express the values of events in dollars and any ideological exercise which supports the convention that dollars are indeed the appropriate measure.

3. If one goes about looking toward the maximization of profits, other objectives will "take care of themselves." This may be interpreted as saying that profit is in some rough sense the most important objective and certainly the most easily quantified. Specific attention to other goals may be surpressed and dealt with in an implicit fashion. This in turn supports the conventional position that the staff should concern itself with predictions of cost and profit exclusively. The staff, on this view, has not the competence to go beyond these considerations, and the evaluation of events relative to other goals, showing where staff work stops and managerial judgment takes over. With this common view of the problem, no great surprise attaches to the refusal of management to accept the staff recommendations. Unfortunately, however, the experimental feedback from such refusals seldom indicates whether the differences are concerned with other aspects of the decision. This view simply suggests another way in which management science models simplify the management situation. They try to be of service by answering questions as to how a manager might choose if profit were his objective.

4. Profit is simply an intermediate goal. It provides a mechanism for greatly simplifying the way in which a variety of objectives are brought to bear on a choice problem. This is to argue that if the firm makes plenty of profit it is clearly in a place to accomplish whatever other objectives it may have. This position argues that while it may be impossible to specify the relationship between, say, research and development and profit, it is possible to argue that if the firm has plenty of profit it can if it wishes undertake R and D. Profits represent the power to achieve other goals, including public service and so on. Typically, it is argued that an objective of the firm is to survive and grow, and that profit is a necessary condition for this.

5. The most important and subtle argument in favor of the use of cost and profit in decision making suggests that it is a basis for achieving decentralization or delegation of decision making without loss of coordination. To run a business of any size it is necessary to delegate, but to avoid burdensome costs of coordination some effective control scheme must be devised. If every decision maker is given a score in the form of profit or cost and told to maximize or minimize his score, it is hoped the problem of coordination among decision makers will automatically be solved, resulting in effective operation of the firm. The use of cost and profit calculations in the firm's decision making thus provides an internal price system. By analogy the allocation of resources in the firm is to be handled by a "market mechanism" similar to that of the economy. This raises all the fascinating questions of the possibility of a rationally designed system of decentralized decision making. Cost accounting makes a beginning in this direction but great difficulties remain which require the attention of management science.

On the other hand, there are a wealth of arguments to the point that a simple theory of profit maximization will not, in fact, predict the choices made by managers. While profit can be made operational it presents some difficulties in the process. One of the most troublesome of these is the allocation of overhead, which requires judgment on the part of the calculator of profit. Many other such judgments are required to produce an operational definition, giving it a rather arbitrary character. One must couple with assertions of the profit motive the answers to several difficult questions:

1. How far in the future are profits to be calculated in a given decision? How are future profits to be related to present profits?
2. What is the relation between profit and uncertainty? How can profits and probabilities be combined in making a choice? To understand decisions it may become necessary to translate profits into utilities. The theory of diminishing marginal utilities suggested it was necessary to consider both the mean and the variance of the probability distribution of profit in making a decision. On the other hand, if in a decision relatively small sums are involved profits may reasonably be assumed to be linearly related to utilities and the latter may be neglected.
3. What explanation is to be given for the three following instances of management decision-making behavior?
   a) Managers do not select the profit-maximizing alternative and engage in policies apparently antithetical to the maximization of profits.
   b) It is possible to show a manager ways of making more profit which he will decline. Not all means of making a given amount of profit are equally acceptable to a manager.
   c) Managers explicitly use other goals than profit in their work. For example, they are concerned with such measures as sales volume, rate of growth, share of the market, and industry position. They also consider such objectives of a less operational character as the good corporate image, satisfactory labor relations, job security and satisfaction, and public service. Either these are objectives quite distinct from profit maximization, or they are simply intermediate goals which managers believe will lead ultimately to profits.

EXPLICITNESS

If it were possible to obtain an exact statement of the objectives of the firm, the problem of evaluation would be practically solved. Several intervening factors make this very difficult.

1. It is often quite difficult to obtain from any manager an explicit statement of the firm's goals. Managers may find themselves unable or unwilling to render such an explicit definition of objectives. Even if we obtain it from one manager, the other members of management may see the objectives differently, and the stockholders may in turn hold still a different view. We have only a primitive understanding of how these differing views of the firm's objectives are, or could be, aggregated into what we might wish to call "the objectives" of the firm. Still another level of difficulty arises when we consider the

possibility that each decision maker may from time to time interject his own personal objectives, which may be somewhat different from those of the firm.

2. Generally the firm will have several objectives rather than a single one. Thus, we are confronted with a multiplicity of objectives, some of which may be in conflict with others. The firm may, for example, wish to make as much profit as possible, but at the same time be a "good place to work." When the decision is to be made to keep on or lay off some employees who are temporarily not needed, these goals are seen to be in conflict with each other. In theory this is taken care of by assuming some higher-level objective which subsumes both profit and stability of employment and permits them to be evaluated on a common measuring scale. This is usually rather difficult to do in practice. In general, however, the firm does have conflicting goals, and evaluation of outcomes which serve more than one objective requires some knowledge of the relationship among them.

3. It is likely that as management, ownership, business conditions, competitive pressures, and so on, change, the objectives of the firm may also change. Thus, we must think of the firm's objectives as being dynamic in some vague sense.

Still other features complicate the problem of measuring values in terms of the objectives of the firm. In spite of these difficulties, it is instructive to examine the logical structure of the value measurement problem in these terms. This will help to make clear the steps that would have to be taken to measure intangible values and will indicate those few steps that we know something about, as well as the many steps which still present great difficulties.

THE BASIC STRUCTURE OF MULTIPLE OBJECTIVES

Let us assume that a firm has a set of objectives or goals represented by $G_1, G_2, ..., G_n$. G_1 might represent maximization of this year's profit; G_2 maximization of next year's profit; G_3, the maintenance of favorable employee attitudes; G_4, the maintenance of satisfactory relations with the community; and so on. Now suppose the problem is to analyze a decision within the context of this firm, and that several outcomes are connected with the alternatives in the decision. The outcomes are represented by $\theta_1, \theta_2, ..., \theta_m$. If we were to carry out the full process of value measurement explicitly, it would be necessary first to evaluate each outcome in terms of each objective. To do this we must have complete predictions of all the aspects of each outcome which are related to any of the objectives. For a given outcome it would be necessary to know what it would represent in terms of this year's profit, next year's profit, its effect on employee attitudes and so on. Granting all this one could then speak of the value of each outcome with respect to each objective. We might symbolize the value of outcome θ_a with respect to objective b by $V_b(\theta_a)$. Our next step would be to define a function which would weight these evaluations according to the relative importance of the various objectives, and combine them into a single measure which would be the value of the outcome with respect to the firm's complex objectives. The result might be expressed as

$$V(\theta_a) = V\{V_1(\theta_a), V_2(\theta_a), ..., V_m(\theta_a)\}$$

These final measurements would then appear in the decision matrix, and some principle of choice could be applied. This process, carried out in detail, might be called "explicit value measurement."

The antithesis of explicit value measurement is implicit measurement, wherein the outcome is evaluated as a whole by the process of judgment. In most decisions, it is possible to use a value measurement process that is partly explicit and partly implicit. The analysis of management decisions has traditionally attempted to evaluate outcomes in terms of cost or profit explicitly, and then rely on judgments for the implicit determination of the complete evaluation.

METHODS—AN EXAMPLE

In many value measurement problems it is helpful to think in terms of three basic methods of measurement. The most common method used to evaluate outcomes in cost or profit terms is based simply on the accountant's synthesis of values from the expenses of the firms. This method is founded on the exchange value concept which suggests that something is evaluated in terms of what it will cost to buy, or what it will bring if sold on the market. The accountant merely synthesizes these expenses into a measure of cost or profit for the particular outcomes involved in a decision.

Suppose, for example, an economic lot size decision is to be made and that the problem of measuring the cost of setting up for a production run is under consideration. Starting with estimates of the direct labor and machine time involved in setting up, the accountant would apply labor costs and machine costs based directly on expense estimates to produce a measure of this setup cost. This of course assumes that no other considerations are involved, such as the confusion, delays, and administrative problems associated with the setup process. It would also assume that total setup cost over the planning period is linear in the number of setups.

A second method of obtaining this cost is simply to ask someone presumably experienced in these matters to make a judgment. This judgment might be in part based on the measurements produced by the accountant; nevertheless it would primarily be a judgment.

The third method involves the study of past decision-making behavior and the inference of values from this behavior. Although this method does not lend itself yet to wide use in the analysis of management decisions, it is suggestive of some interesting possibilities. To illustrate, suppose we ask the decision maker to review his past decisions with respect to economic lot sizes and to select one or several which he feels were satisfactory decisions. We are asking him to make a judgment about the effectiveness of past decisions. From a study of such a satisfactory past decision we might obtain the lot size decided upon, the storage cost, demand, and planning period used. If the decision maker judges this decision to have been satisfactory, we might assume that the lot size was close to optimal. Thus, the factors involved might approximately satisfy the relation (see problem 9-19).

$$L = \sqrt{\frac{2C_1 D}{C_2 T}}$$

In this relation we have assumed that everything is measured except the setup cost, C_1. We could then solve it for C_1.

$$C_1 = \frac{L^2 C_2 T}{2D}$$

The result would be a measure of setup cost, inferred from a past decision which was judged to be optimal. Such an inference is filled with possible pitfalls; however, it does provide an approximate evaluation of setup cost which could be used in future decisions. Clearly, if we infer setup costs in this way from a series of decisions, all of which are judged to be satisfactory, and these costs turn out to be markedly different, some questions of importance could be raised. We might, for example, inquire of the decision maker whether the setup cost had actually changed in these situations, or if he had simply committed errors of inconsistency. This method is a useful guide to consistent decision making in the sense of our original objectives.

SCALES

All problems of measurement, including that of the measurement of values, involve the construction and use of scales. Everyone is familiar with the ordinary scales used in physical measurement, such as length, weight, temperature, and so on. The values of outcomes in most management decisions are measured on a scale of dollars which is so common as to be taken completely for granted. To understand more clearly the problem of value measurement it is necessary to introduce a more general picture of the kinds of scales which might be used and then to show that different decision problems require different types of scales for value measurement.

Three basic types of scales are relevant in the analysis of decision problems.

1. An ordinal scale is simply a ranking. If we rank outcomes according to our preference for them, we have measured them on an ordinal scale. Sometimes we will say that an outcome, A, is "preferred or equivalent to" another outcome, B. This relation defines a partly ordered scale.
2. An interval scale has an arbitrary zero point and a constant unit of measurement. Temperature is often measured on the Fahrenheit or Centigrade scales, which are interval scales.
3. A ratio scale has an absolute zero point and a constant unit of measurement. When we measure weight we use ratio scales, which have absolute zero points. When we evaluate an outcome in dollars of profit, we are also using a ratio scale.

RANKING AND RATING WITH AN ADDITIVE MODEL

A simple and direct method has turned out in actual practice to be very useful and to lead to excellent results. Excellent results here means that the method has been found by decision makers to be easy to use, has led to evaluations which they found useful, and has produced rank orderings which seemed to correspond closely to their actual ultimate choices.

We will illustrate the method of ranking and rating with an additive model using a simplified example of a person who is concerned with deciding which university to attend. The method makes particular attempts to accommodate itself to the cognitive style of the decision maker. The basic steps involved are:

1. The decision maker is asked to develop a list of several, possibly as many as ten, factors which are important in evaluating a university which he or she might attend. Perhaps this results in a list of such factors as

   • Annual tuition and living expenses
   • Size of institution
   • Distance from home
   • Strength in the biological sciences
   • Strength in the physical sciences and mathematics
   • Variety of degree programs
   • Campus atmosphere
   • Physical environment, mountains, lakes, climate

2. The decision maker is then asked to rank these in their order of importance, with ties permitted. These first two steps in themselves often require considerable effort and result in the decision maker arriving at significant clarification of his or her preferences.

3. The decision maker is then asked to assign ratings to the factors on a (ratio) scale from 0 to 1.0. The highest ranked factor is rated 1.0, and the second ranked factor is assigned a rating of .9 if it is "about 90 percent as important as the first factor," or a rating of .85, .76, or whatever expresses the decision maker's attitudes.

4. Some attention is then given to how each factor might be measured or summarized for data collection purposes. Unless a substantial budget is available for the evaluation effort, some rough, approximate measures may have to suffice. For example:

Factor	Possible Measure
Annual expenses	Dollars
Size	Number of main campus students
Distance from home	Travel time or travel expenses
Strength in biological sciences	Number of courses offered
Variety of degree programs	Number of first degree programs
Campus atmosphere	A direct, implicit judgment
Physical environment	A direct, implicit judgment

This step also is likely to be difficult for the decision maker and it should be emphasized that as many revisions as desired may be made, that this is an important part of the value clarification process, and that the results involve no commitment.

5. Data on these factors for several universities under consideration by the decision maker are then obtained. The data collection process for things like costs and number of students is very specific, but for factors such as campus atmosphere, it may involve only a general, unstructured exposure to information and opinions about each campus.

6. The next step is to rank and rate the universities on the basis of each factor individually considered. For example, in considering size, the decision maker may express his preferences by ranking the university with the smallest number of students as number one, and the ranking may simply proceed in inverse relationship to number of students. In the case of "campus atmosphere" the ranking process is much more implicit. The decision maker ranks one of the universities as number one on campus atmosphere, simply on the basis of his unanalyzed impressions.

7. For each factor, the ranked universities are then rated. The smallest institution is assigned the rating of 1.0, and the next largest is assigned the rating of .95 if the decision maker feels that it is "95 percent as desirable or attractive" as the top ranked university.

8. At this point we have judgments or expressions of preference which might be summarized as follows:

w_i = the weight or rating assigned to the ith factor as a result of step 3 $(i = 1, ..., n)$

x_{ij} = the weight or rating assigned to university j for its particular level of factor i as a result of step 7

A simple additive model is then used to aggregate these expressions of preference into an evaluation of each university.

$$V_j = w_1 x_{1j} + w_2 x_{2j} + ... + w_n x_{nj}$$

These evaluations, the V_j values, are then used to rank the universities and interpreted as a prediction of the decision-maker's preference.

While ranking and rating with an additive model may appear to be highly simplified and to rest on a large number of untested assumptions, it has received strong support through wide use in actual practice.

TYPES OF VALUE CLARIFICATION MODELS

The ranking and rating process with an additive model which we have just illustrated is typical of many such models in that it neglects uncertainty. This probably makes excellent practical sense in that it reduces the complexity of the cognitive demands placed on the client by temporarily suppressing the problem of uncertainty while the multiple criterion problem is dealt with. It is typically far easier for the client to later take account of uncertainty, rather than to consider it simultaneously as another dimension of his preference structure. We will, however, shortly examine the leading example of a model which includes uncertainty as an aspect of the multiple criterion problem.

In an attempt to clarify this distinction, we have used the symbol U to designate functions or scalings which have the properties of utility functions which we explored in Chapter 3. Functions or scalings which do not necessarily have the properties of utility functions are designated by the symbol V.

The most widely used models include:

Linear Additive

$$V(a_i) = \sum_j w_j x_{ij}$$

Higher Order Additive

$$V(a_i) = \sum_j w_j \log x_{ij}$$

Multiplicative

$$V(a_i) = \prod_j x_{ij}^{w_j}$$

or

$$V(a_i) = \sum_j w_j x_{ij} = \sum_{j,k>j} W_{jk} x_{ij} x_{ik}$$

where W_{jk} is a weighting of the same general sort as w_j

There are two important results which emerge from actual applications of these and similar value clarification models:

1. The linear additive model turns out to be an excellent predictor of actual decisions in a variety of circumstances.
2. With some minor exceptions, none of the other models has been found to be significantly better than the linear additive model in predicting the actual choices of decision makers.

These observations suggest that in most applications it would make considerable sense to at least start with a linear additive model. When the costs of developing and implementing more complex models are taken into account, it is unlikely that the greater sophistication will be justified. For most practical purposes, the linear additive form is likely to be sufficient. One may, in these circumstances, choose models on the grounds that they appeal to the client's natural way of thinking about his preferences, that they have an intuitively logical form, or that they are simply easy to implement.

ESTIMATING MODEL PARAMETERS

We have already noted the basic methods of value explication, and they have direct application to the problem of estimating the parameters of models such as these. The direct or "client explicated" approach asks the client to furnish the rankings and scalings which are the model parameters. We might usefully organize this process into a series of steps.

1. Have the client, using the ranking and rating process, produce a value or satisfaction associated with each level of each attribute to be included in the model. That is, have the client produce the x_{ij}. For quantitative attributes, such as colors, the client is asked to identify the most preferred level and assign it a value of 1.00 or 100. He is then asked to indicate his relative value, or relative satisfaction for the other levels with respect to the most preferred level.

   If the attribute levels are quantitative, the analyst's approach may be to help the client to draw a graph of value on the ordinate and attribute levels on the abscissa, plotting answers to questions such as, "What is your relative satisfaction with level x as compared to the most preferred level of this attribute?"

2. Check for consistency by feeding back to the client questions having to do with the ratios of the values obtained. "Since x_{ij} is twice x_{pq}, you appear to feel twice the satisfaction associated with level i over that associated with level p. Does that really reflect the way you feel?" Experience suggests that with a little practice, these steps are not especially difficult to carry out with most clients.

3. The steps involved in obtaining the weights, the w_j values, are identical with those just given—ranking, rating, and then some checks for internal consistency. Some clients, of course, experience difficulty in these efforts, and we will consider the import of these difficulties subsequently.

The results are ratio-scaled attribute value and weights which may then be used as model parameters. Experience has shown that clients often are able to grasp the sense of linear additive models and participate confidently in the explication of meaningful parameters. This is not, however, generally the case for more complex models such as the multiplicative, and in these cases parameters must be inferred.

INFERRED PARAMETERS

The steps involved in the inference of parameters using regression methods might be organized as follows:

1. As in the direct explication process, the x_{ij} are obtained and checked for internal consistency.

2. The client is asked to consider a set of alternatives similar to those we seek to evaluate. Each alternative is described as naturally as possible, including in the description all of the attributes which are to to be included in the model. The client is asked to rank and rate these alternatives, expressing his overall value or satisfaction for each on a ratio scale. The results of this step are a set of values, $V(a_i)$.

3. Using the $V(a_i)$ and the x_{ij}, we may now obtain the values of the w_j as the coefficients of a multiple regression model. The resulting values for the w_j coefficients are least squares estimates based on the observed

data. Here again, experience indicates that, while complex regression models involving interaction terms may be used in this method, the usual linear models work very well indeed for most practical purposes.

BOOTSTRAPPING

One of the most interesting results in the field of decision aiding emerged when experiments were made involving the substitution of a value explication model obtained in one of these ways for the client himself. That is, a model was obtained for a client's preference structure, either by direct explication or by inference. The unaided behavior of the client was then compared with the choices that would have been made using the model alone. The result has quite regularly been that the model has performed better than the unaided client. This is another demonstration of the inconsistency, the variability, the response to irrelevant cues which characterizes unguided human behavior. This inconsistency, when evaluated in terms of the client's preferences as captured by the model, turns out to be a serious detriment to good decision-making behavior. The possibility then emerged that a client could improve his decisions by creating a model of this sort and relying on the model completely for guidance in choosing. This process of improving decision-making consistency has come to be known as "bootstrapping."

MULTIPLE CRITERION DECISION MODELS AND UNCERTAINTY—KEENEY'S METHOD

Recently a subtle and powerful method has been developed by Keeney for the assessment of utility functions, or really utility surfaces, in complex situations where the outcomes or consequences are not limited to a single dimension as in Chapter 3. In principle, there is no logical reason why we could not simply apply the methods of that chapter directly, generating a utility assessment in the form of a multivariate expression based on the decision maker's expression of preferences over lotteries in which the outcomes were given corresponding multi-dimensional descriptions. To take a simple example, suppose we consider a decision maker who characterizes jobs in terms of salary and location. He considers $20,000 to be the smallest salary that would even warrant attention, and $40,000 to be the largest that could be anticipated as a possibility. He regards the worst possible alternative as a job at $20,000 in city B, and we could conventionally assign this job a utility of 0. The best possible alternative would be a job at $40,000 in city G, the utility of which we would assess at 1.00. We could then establish a point on his utility surface by asking him to specify a value of p for which he would be indifferent between

> A salary of x dollars in city Y and
> $20,000 in city B with probability $1-p$ or
> $40,000 in city G with probability p.

The resulting value of p would, as usual, be the utility assessment for a job involving x dollars in city Y. This perfectly logical multi-dimensional extension of our earlier method fails in application simply because it has been found repeatedly that, once we go beyond varying two attributes simultaneously, the responses required of the decision maker become so difficult as to be virtually impossible. The cognitive load imposed makes the process impractical and unacceptable to most decision makers.

Keeney's Method shows the conditions under which we may get around this practical difficulty and assess utility functions which have all of the properties of those developed earlier, including most importantly, applicability in uncertain situations. The basic strategy of this method is to use the previous approach of Chapter 3 to assess utility functions for each attribute, one at a time. Keeney has then shown how these individual attribute utility functions may be combined, either by addition or multiplication, to produce the utility surface outlined above. The decision maker is thus faced with the much simpler task of considering his preferences for only one attribute at a time, all of the others being held constant for assessment purposes. This method has been applied with considerable success in such situations as water resource project evaluation and in the selection of alternative airport locations for a major city.[1][2] We may best illustrate the method with a simplified airport site selection decision. This example is given without proof of several of the complex mathematical results on which it depends. The interested reader will find these in reference given below (1).

We suppose that in choosing among alternative airport locations a decision maker (which may be a government agency, a commission, or a constituency) considers three attributes to be of concern; cost (x_1), safety (x_2), and capacity (x_3). There may be severe measurement difficulties in specifying, for example, a variable which measures the safety of a location. We will assume, however, that it is reasonable to use some measure such as the number of people, passengers and nonpassengers killed or seriously injured per aircraft accident. Questions about the usefulness of this measure might later be resolved by exploring the sensitivity of the resulting site preferences to the use of alternative measures.

Using our previously developed methods, the decision maker is asked to respond to questions about preferences with respect to gambles involving costs, assuming that safety and capacity are held constant at satisfactory levels. In this way, a conditional utility function for cost is assessed, say $u_1(x_1)$. In just the same way, conditional utility functions for safety and capacity are obtained. Experience indicates that this may be a very reasonable task for the decision maker to perform.

What we would like at this point is a way of combining these conditional utility functions into a utility function for airport sites as a whole, $u(x_1, x_2, x_3)$. Keeney has provided a rather complex proof that if the decision maker's preferences exhibit properties called preferential independence and utility independence, then this process of combination may be logically

[1] R. de Neufville and R. L. Keeney, "Use of Decision Analysis in Airport Development for Mexico City," Chapter 23 in *Analysis of Public Systems*, A. W. Drake, R. L. Keeney, and P. M. Morse, eds., Cambridge, M.I.T. Press, 1972.

[2] C. S. Shih and J. H. Dean, *Decision Analysis on Water Resources Planning and Management for an Arid Metropolitan Center in West Texas*. Texas Water Resources Institute, Texas A and M University, Technical Report No. 54, October 1973.

carried out by either addition or multiplication. His method further permits one to actually carry out the combination process, whenever the necessary conditions hold. We first illustrate the concepts of preferential independence and utility independence, and then outline the process of combining the conditional utility functions.

Suppose that the three attributes are restricted by the decision maker to consideration of the following ranges:

Cost: 100 to 500 million dollars
Safety: 1 to 1000 persons killed or seriously
           injured per aircraft accident
Capacity: 50 to 150 operations per hour

Preferential independence means simply that the decision maker's willingness to trade cost for safety does not depend on the level at which capacity is fixed. Similarly it means that the willingness to trade cost for capacity does not depend on the level at which safety may be fixed, and so on. Preferential independence may be tested with questions of the following form: suppose we fix capacity at 100 operations per hour and consider two sites, one with a cost of 200 million dollars and a safety of 800 persons per accident, the second with a cost of 400 million dollars and a safety of x_2 persons per accident. For what value of x_2 would these sites be indifferent to the decision maker? Suppose, for example, the answer is 600 persons per accident. If we then change the level of capacity to, say, 50 operations per hour and repeat the question, and if the answer remains at 600 persons, we have an initial indication that cost and safety may be preferentially independent.

Utility independence is similar in concept and in approach to the decision maker. The basic question is whether the utility function for cost is independent of the levels at which safety and capacity are set. This can be tested by assessing a few utilities for cost at various levels of safety and capacity. If the conditional utilities thus obtained do not depend on the other attribute levels, utility independence may be said to hold.

Given that these conditions are satisfied, then it can be shown that the utility function for sites will be of one of two forms. The additive form is

$$u(x_1, x_2, x_3) = k_1 u_1(x_1) + k_2 u_2(x_2) + k_3 u_3(x_3)$$

and the multiplicative form is

$$u(x_1, x_2, x_3) = k_1 u_1(x_1) + k_2 u_2(x_2) + k_3 u_3(x_3)$$
$$+ Kk_1 k_2 u_1(x_1) u_2(x_2) + Kk_1 k_3 u_1(x_1) u_2(x_2)$$
$$+ Kk_2 k_3 u_2(x_2) u_3(x_3) + K^2 k_1 k_2 k_3 u_1(x_1) u_2(x_2) u_3(x_3)$$

The k_i and K are coefficients or scaling constants which we must determine in order to complete the assessment of utilities for sites.

Examination of the multiplicative form of the utility function shows that if K is 0, it reduces to the additive form; thus the additive form may be considered a limiting case of the more general multiplicative model. Analysis of the multiplicative model, which we will not undertake here, yields the result that if the k_i sum to 1, the value of K is 0, and the appropriate combination method is additive. If the k_i do not sum to 1, then the multiplicative model will be appropriate.

We may illustrate the assessment of the k_i scaling factors using cost, x_1, as an example. The decision maker is asked to consider a_1 which is an outcome having cost at its most preferred level and the other two attributes at their least preferred level. Thus a_1 could be represented by the triple ($x_1 = 100$, $x_2 = 1000$, $x_3 = 50$), or simply by $(100, 1000, 50)$. He is asked to choose between a_1 and a second alternative, a_2, which is a gamble involving $(100, 1, 150)$ with probability p and $(500, 1000, 50)$ with probability $1-p$. That is, the gamble involves all attributes at the most preferred levels with probability p and at the least preferred levels with probability $1-p$. As before, the decision maker is asked to find the value of p for which he would be indifferent between a_1 and a_2.

For a_1, our scaling convention fixes $u_1(100) = 1$, $u_2(1000) = 0$, and $u_3(50) = 0$. Using these values in the multiplicative form yields $u(a_1) = k_1$. In the gamble, our convention suggests that $u(100, 1, 150) = 1$ and $u(500, 1000, 50) = 0$. Equating the utilities for a_1 and a_2 leads directly to the result that $k_1 = p$. Similarly, the other k_i are obtained. If they sum to 1, the additive model is appropriate since K will be 0. If not, we set all of the attributes at their most preferred levels, making their utilities 1, and substitute these utilities along with the known values of the k_i into the multiplicative model. It may then be solved for K which will assume a value greater than -1 but less than 0.

We would then have a complete, multi-dimensional utility function which would have the important and useful properties of those we studied in earlier chapters and would be obtainable by methods which have been shown to place a reasonable cognitive load on the decision maker. Of course, if preferential independence and utility independence do not hold, the model may only be an approximation whose usefulness will depend on the sensitivity of the predicted preferences to these assumptions.

VALUE CLARIFICATION IN PRACTICE

The published experience with the actual application of multiple criterion decision-making methods is, if limited, quite encouraging. There is, however, another body of practical experience, given little visibility in the literature, which tends to indicate that the direct assessment of preference structures in multiple criterion situations is very often a matter of considerable difficulty. The experience of numerous attempts at value assessment by analysts engaged in similar efforts, suggests that there are indeed troublesome problems associated with these transactions between the client and the decision analyst. This experience, although not the product of formal, controlled laboratory experimentation, is the result of actual attempts to assess directly the preferences of subjects who make decisions in the world outside the laboratory. It suggests that there may be a substantial number of decision makers who experience confusion, uncertainty, and blocking when asked to:

- Rank attributes or objectives, even with the aid of such decomposing techniques as paired comparisons,
- Rate attribute levels and assign weights across attributes on ratio scales,
- Indicate indifference trade-offs,
- Specify indifference probabilities in decisions involving standard gambles.

While this experience is difficult to document usefully, it seems to suggest the need for more careful attention to this basic encounter between the analyst and the decision maker, and a greater sensitivity to the difficulties of many clients in the task of value explication through direct assessment methods.

The objective of the analyst is to develop cost-effective methods of making client preferences explicit. This effort has generally proceeded by:

1. Proposing axioms which imply that the client can make explicit certain "simple" preferences
2. Developing the deductive consequences of these axioms to indicate the sorts of predictions and recommendations they would make possible
3. Translating the axioms rather directly into inquiries to which the client is assumed to be capable of responding

When the client appears to encounter difficulties in responding to these opportunities to express simple preferences, it may be that:

1. The analyst has somehow not been very skillful in managing the transaction.
2. The client has failed to understand what he is being asked to do.
3. The client simply finds himself unable to give a meaningful response.

From the analyst's as well as the client's point of view, the term "meaningful" denotes a response which will be both predictive of client behavior and provide acceptable norms for decision making when its deductive consequences are elaborated.

Analysts have tried to deal with the first two possibilities by seeking ways of involving the client, of interesting him in value explication, and of explaining more clearly what he is supposed to do. It may be that we have not faced adequately the possibility that the client does not find himself able to respond with full conviction to the simple decision problems which provide the basic data on his preference structure. It is quite possible that the decisions we put to the client are not so simple as their "simple" structure might imply. We may unwittingly transmit to the client the implication that surely any self-respecting decision maker ought to be able to immediately furnish indifference probabilities, trade-offs, or scalings of relative importance. It may even be that clients, sensing this, feel forced to respond, and in doing so, express preferences about which they have little confidence. We strongly suspect that:

1. To the extent that an experienced decision maker feels forced to express preferences in the face of reluctance and uncertainty, the results will not be meaningful in the sense suggested above.
2. One reason why applications of value explicating methods sometimes seem at first to "succeed" but later fall into disuse, is the client's uncertainty about the input responses which have been to some extent "forced" and his lack of confidence in their long-term effectiveness and meaningfulness.

Our experience suggests the need for openness to the possibilities that clients may be characterized by incompletely developed cognitive value structures, by lack of familiarity and experience on which to base confident expressions of preference, and by a degree of self-awareness which implies a less than perfect understanding of one's own goals and preferences.

Our basic hypothesis then is that, given procedures which are open and neutral to difficulties in value explication, a considerable amount of client reluctance and uncertainty will become evident. This seemingly uncharacteristic behavior on the part of experienced professional decision makers makes it useful to consider briefly the rationalist position; if people can decide and act then, in some sense they must know their preferences. This suggests a number of possibilities.

1. Given sufficient data on decision-making behavior, we can impute preferences. Linear regression models have been quite successful in this respect. Our concern here, however, is with the more common case in which such data are not available and direct assessment methods are required.
2. The data from psychology suggest that although value conflicts commonly block choice, we develop strategies which permit the circumventing of these conflicts. In the face of such value conflicts, we respond by searching for acts which are free of conflict, suppressing some aspects of our value structure, suppressing some aspects of acts or outcomes thus effectively remaking our perceptions, simplifying our preference structure to one or two important dimensions, or taking refuge in such precedents as platitudes, rules of thumb, and socially accepted preferences. Many of these responses appear to occur without our being aware of them. If clients were more self-aware in this respect, it seems likely that this sort of behavior would not meet the standards of reasonableness by which they would like to judge their decision making. Perhaps one of the more useful contributions that an analyst may make with direct assessment techniques is to increase the client's sensitivity to such nonrational responses to value conflicts.
3. Alternatively, we may entertain the hypothesis that a perfectly clear view of goals is not essential to action. As one may act in the face of uncertainty about the future, so one may also in the face of uncertainty about goals and preferences. Indeed, from a cost-benefit point of view, the effort required to eliminate uncertainty about individual or organizational preferences may not be warranted by the resulting

benefits. From this point of view, the central issues of value assessment are the questions of how best to clarify (rather than simply explicate) uncertain values and the questions of how much effort can reasonably be devoted to the reduction of client uncertainty about preferences.

The essence of the decision analysis approach is embraced by this third view. It supposes that a closer look at the data on the direct assessment of client preferences will support the conclusion that it is not so much that clients do not know what they want as it is that they are uncertain about what they want. It proposes to make this uncertainty explicit using the Bayesian structure and concepts for encoding and reducing uncertainty. It recognizes that the more uncertain we are about our preferences, the more valuable will be efforts to clarify them. The value of clarifying objectives is related directly, in this view, to the chances of changing our minds enough to change the courses of action we choose. The Bayesian structure provides at least the conceptual tools for thinking about the worth of value clarification and the degree of uncertainty about preferences that it is reasonable to tolerate.

The decision analysis approach seeks to:

1. Permit the client to express clear confident preferences if they seem natural and thus take advantage of convention methods of value explication
2. Permit the client to express uncertainty, doubt, lack of confidence if that is natural
3. Direct attention toward the problem of value clarification as opposed to value explication, in cases where that attention appears to have some constructive potential
4. Sacrifice rigor grudgingly in order to cope with the realities of practical application

Clients are permitted and encouraged to express uncertainty about their own (or their organization's) preferences if this seems a comfortable and valid reflection of their state of knowledge. If x and y are acts, outcomes, or attributes, for example:

1. If the client is uncertain whether x is preferred to y, this uncertainty is encoded in a probability statement. The probability that x is preferred to y is p. This may be interpreted as the client's degree of belief in the declarative statement, "I prefer x to y." Uncertainty is to be understood here as imperfect knowledge of preferences and is modeled in the usual Bayesian fashion using the language of probability theory. It supposes that, just as one may be uncertain about external events, so one may also be uncertain about one's own state of mind or preference structure.
2. If the client is uncertain about the number of units, k, of x he would be willing to give up in return for an increase of one unit of y, this uncertainty is encoded in the form of a probability distribution on the random variable k.

3. If the client is uncertain about the value of q which would leave him indifferent between

   x with probability q; nothing with probability $1-q$, and y with probability 1

   this uncertainty is modeled by means of a probability distribution on the random variable q. This result is the assessment of a utility for y which is a random variable $U(y) = q$.
4. If x is given a value or utility of 1 and the client is uncertain as to the assignment of a utility to y which will express the relative desirability of y, this uncertainty is encoded in the form of a probability distribution on the random variable $U(y)$.

The real point of the decision analysis approach, however, is not a concern with the rigor or precision of such models. It aims rather at using these models as a guide for a necessarily more qualitative consideration of the problem of whether it would be worthwhile to engage in various value clarification activities. These models are typically far too formal to describe real situations, yet they may still function usefully by providing structure and direction to the necessarily far less exact patterns of analysis which actual situations demand.

The advantages of this approach include the following:

1. It reflects an attempt to adhere to the principle that the usefulness of decision aids depends on their costs and benefits, and these in turn depend on the experience, information, and personal style of the client.
2. By trading effort devoted to forcing client choices for effort devoted to making value uncertainty explicit, we may be increasing both the predictive and the normative quality of the resulting models.
3. It transforms the problem of value explication into the problem of value clarification, thus motivating efforts toward learning and uncertainty reduction.
4. It clarifies the simplifications taking place when uncertainty about preferences is suppressed.
5. It provides at least a rough basis for the design of reasonable processes of value clarification. At very least, it raises the possibility that some effort toward value clarification might be worthwhile.
6. It is, for some clients, "natural," and aids in the achievement of greater self-objectification. It is a process which may add credibility to the results of value explication efforts. The elimination of all uncertainty about goals is perhaps seldom warranted, and the realistic question is that of what degree of uncertainty can reasonably be tolerated.
7. It directs attention to what may be the key problem for the analyst; how to be of assistance to the client in clarifying goals, objectives, and preferences. We turn to this problem briefly in the following section.

This line of thought leads to a concern for effective value clarification methods. A number of investigators have reported that in the process of attempting to apply conventional value explication methods, a significant amount of client learning takes place. Indeed, a number of post-experiment interviews with clients seem to be characterized by the reaction, "While for their intended uses, these methods may not be too practical, they do have the interesting effect of increasing my understanding of my goals and preferences." This general reaction from clients is sufficiently common to suggest that value explication techniques may be of some considerable use in value clarification. There are, of course, other approaches which address the problem of clarification more directly.

1. The analyst may try to motivate the client toward greater clarity about goals without supplying any structure for the process. The client is urged to introspect, to be analytical, or to "select" goals for his activities. This is the approach of much of the conventional management literature. Since managers commonly aspire to the cultural norm of decisiveness and knowing what one wants, urging in this direction may be to some degree effective.
2. The analyst may supply some sort of structure or designed experience which aims at clarifying preferences. The examples here include the development of scenarios and simulations aimed at broadening the range of the decision maker's experience.
3. The analyst may attempt to assist the client in being analytical about his goals, in exploring the decomposition and integration of various goal hierarchies.

The most interesting point, however, is that we need evidence on both the costs and the benefits of these methods of goal clarification, and attention must be given directly to the problem of developing such methods of clarification, as opposed to explication.

PROBLEM

12–1.   Design and test on two or three subjects an explicit value clarification process which yields a multiple criterion decision-making model. Select a situation or context of personal or professional interest. Consider, for example, designing a building, allocating funds for health care programs, designing a university day-care program, selecting experiments for a space mission, new product design, choosing a job, buying a new car, writing a pollution control regulation, setting up an air pollution monitoring station network, formulating a public health program for a city, choosing sites for nuclear power plants, measuring the productivity of a computer center, monetary policy planning, deciding whether to modify the weather, or locating an urban freeway.

SUGGESTIONS FOR FURTHER STUDY

Fishburn, P. C. *Decision and Value Theory*. New York: John Wiley & Sons, 1964.
Fishburn, Peter C. "Lexicographic Orders, Utilities and Decision Rules: A Survey." *Management Science*, Vol. 20, No. 11 (July 1974), pp. 1442–1471.

Geoffrion, A. M., J. S. Dyer, and A. Feinberg. "An Interactive Approach for Multi-Criterion Optimization, with an Application to the Operation of an Academic Department." *Management Science*, Vol. 19, No. 4 (December 1972), pp. 357–368.

Huber, George P. "Methods for Quantifying Subjective Probabilities and Multi-Attribute Utilities." *Decision Sciences*, Vol. 5 (1974), pp. 430–458.

Huber, George P. "Multi-Attribute Utility Models: A Review of Field and Field-Like Studies." *Management Science*, Vol. 20, No. 10 (June 1974), pp. 1393–1402.

MacCrimmon, K. R. "An Overview of Multiple Objective Decision Making." A chapter in Cochrane, J. L. and M. Zeleny (eds.), *Multiple Criteria Decision Making*. Columbia, S.C.: University of South Carolina Press, 1973.

Warfield, J. N. "Intent Structures." *IEEE Transactions on Systems, Man, and Cybernetics*, Vol. 3, No. 2, (March 1973), pp. 23–41.

PERSONAL STYLE IN DECISION MAKING   13

Discussions of decision aiding lead naturally to the subject of mathematical models and digital computers which have been associated with many of the interesting developments of the past twenty years. In this discussion, however, we explore a somewhat different hypothesis—that the very success of models and computers may have distracted our attention from some of the basic realities of making decisions.

THE SIGNIFICANCE OF STYLE

It is well known that the benefits of analysis and computation are not to be had unless at least two basic conditions can be realized. To be the subject of analysis, a decision must be anticipated so that the sometimes extensive process of modeling it can be carried out in sufficient time for the results to be useful in the actual context of affairs. In addition, a person must have the skill to take an ill-defined research problem so that the concepts involved are operational and the crucial steps of mathematical representation and measurement become possible. Those whose chief professional activity is the making of decisions need not be reminded that these conditions are not readily met, for they are constantly aware of the difficulty of achieving them. Analysts who study and support professional decision makers might profit from the reminder that, first, in the world of authority and responsibility not all important decision situations can be usefully foreseen and must be regarded as "decisions of encounter" rather than "programmed decisions." Further, analysts might well explore the possibility of viewing the decision maker's all too frequent unwillingness or inability to be explicit about the decision situation as a datum rather than an annoyance. In other words, instead of concentrating on the decision maker's difficulty in communicating to others the values and predictions he is accustomed to handling implicitly, one might ask what can be usefully done without the need for explicitness.

These "facts of life," the inability to anticipate and the inability to be explicit, suggest that a good deal of professional deciding lies beyond the present frontier of decision analysis. One can simply accept this as a fundamental limitation, or one can turn to the world of unanticipated decisions and implicit decision processes, asking if there is a contribution that science might make in this world. Can decision-aiding methods be developed which enhance the effective intuitive skills built up by professionals through years of ill-organized experience? Do the methods of science preclude it from contributing to those decisions of encounter which must be made under the pressure and pace of daily affairs?

DECISIONS OF ENCOUNTER

A decision of encounter, an unanticipated decision, is one which precludes much delegation, much seeking of "outside" assistance, and perhaps even precludes much reflection on the part of the decision maker himself. These decisions must be taken on the basis of what we will call the subject's own implicit or intuitive methods. Indeed, we will say that whenever a decision maker does not, or cannot be explicit about some aspect of a situation, the aspect is intuitive or implicit. This definition of "intuitive" is not very satisfying because it fails to suggest our personal introspective appraisals of intuitive deciding and because it deliberately sets aside the distinction between inability and unwillingness to be explicit. It turns out, however, to be a useful definition for the purpose at hand. Intuitive, implicit, or judgmental decision making is the mainstay of the experienced decision maker. Intuitive, unaided methods have typically served the decision maker well, and he can reflect on some personal history of productive reliance on his developing intuition. Until very recently there has been little to choose from except implicit methods, and even now aids tend to be available only in well-defined situations to those with special training. Effective professionals in many fields including management, the sciences, and the arts are usually highly implicit deciders and find this way of working not only reliable and habitual, but satisfying since it utilizes their unique skills and sensitivities. It is especially important that intuitive methods appear well suited to meet the pressure of ongoing affairs, permitting rather immediate responses on the basis of limited information. There is considerable evidence to show that unaided human decision making is reasonable, effective, and reliable within at least a modest range of decision-making challenges. There are, obviusly enough, some very serious ways in which implicit methods fail and mislead us, and it is these which concern us here.

OBJECTIVES

It is now well established that one objective of decision aiding is to extend the capacity of the human mind to remember and perform simple logical operations. Much of the mathematical analysis and computer application of recent years has been an attempt to extend the "logical" limitations of the decision maker in extensive repetitive tasks involving storing and processing information. We wish, however, to turn in a different direction, facing other difficulties which might be characterized as "psychological" rather than "logical" limitations on perceptual and cognitive activity. These difficulties appear when intuitive methods lead us astray, trap us, and, sometimes to our great surprise, fail to merit the confidence we have come to place in them. The particularly difficult situations are those in which the limitations of intuitive methods are not obvious to us at all but occur at the subconscious level of decision processes. It is our hypothesis that if one were to investigate aids for decisions of encounter, the most productive area of study is likely to be these psychological limitations rather than the more conventional logical ones.

CONVENTIONAL METHODS

There is, of course, a long history of attempts to overcome these psychological problems by means of highly rationalistic and pseudo-logical modles requiring one to externalize the decision process in terms of some seemingly sensible steps. It has often been suggested that one should "define the problem, develop alternate solutions, . . ." or perhaps, "list the goals or objectives, develop alternate courses of action, evaluate the degree to which each action accomplishes each goal, . . ." These recipes are the subject of numerous articles and books on how to make decisions. They are appealing in that they sound reasonable and obviously "the right way to do it." There appears to be very little evidence, however, that they have any interesting effect on the actual decision-making behavior of experienced persons. Although the evidence is largely experiential, the best hypothesis appears to be that if one really wanted to alter the behavior of an intuitive decider, these pseudo-logical schemes are not going to be very effective. The reasons which might be advanced in support of this hypothesis are useful in guiding the search for other methods of dealing with perceptual and cognitive shortcomings.

We would suggest that the failure of these methods might involve a failure to recognize that every experienced decision maker develops his own personal style which cannot be radically reformulated in the short run. It may also be a failure to meet what appear to be the really difficult and troublesome problems of decision making. These "define the problem" formulations have a kind of pious ring, telling one what he should do in making a decision but not how he should do it nor what it will gain him if he does. They say little of the great problem of division of labor in decisions. What aspects should be delegated, what aspects should be handled by the computer, and what should be turned over to staff specialists for analysis? They seem to say that the amount of mental effort or cognitive strain which they require ought to be invested in every decision, failing to recognize that some decisions warrant more time than others and that, in some, experience is far more highly developed than in others. They say nothing of the relative costs and benefits of the type of explicitness they require. They seem to assume that all intuition is bad and ought to be immediately replaced. These methods contribute little to the handling of uncertainty, yet these are surely the central difficulties in many decisions. They almost equate uncertainty with irrationality, failing to help the decision maker resolve the serious question of how much uncertainty to tolerate and how much effort to devote to gathering additional information to reduce the uncertainty. They require one to know his own mind with full clarity, which he clearly does not. They suppose that one cannot act without being perfectly clear about one's objectives, a requirement which would bring most organizations to a standstill.

Such pseudo-logical methods simply do not represent the sort of thing which is "done" in most professional circles. To use these methods explicitly is not really "socially acceptable" and might even betray some degree of incompetence. Their deliberateness fails to meet the time constraints which surround many decisions of encounter. They require more self-discipline and self-awareness than most of us find comfortable, and imply a radical reformulation of one's habits. In short, they do not appear to be worth their cost.

THE PERSONAL STYLE HYPOTHESIS

If even a few of these reasons turn out to be confirmed through the study of efforts to influence decision making, they will provide the incentive to develop a basic hypothesis which may lead us in a new direction. One might call this the "Personal Style Hypothesis" because it involves the premise that each decision maker's personal style of deciding is the fundamental point of departure. Simply stated the hypothesis is this: *More is to be gained from attempts to apply natural enhancements to the decision maker's personal style than from equivalent efforts to radically reformulate and externalize his style in the image of some pseudo-logical model.* We view this, not so much as a novel and completely untested hypothesis, but rather as a fairly obvious interpretation of the data which is already in, and a suggestion that we pay more careful attention to what really goes on in the making of actual decisions. We see it as a very rough specificaton of the direction one must take to influence and assist the intuitive professional facing an unanticipated decision problem. The Personal Style Hypothesis can be understood if we make clear the somewhat special meanings of the concepts of "personal style" and "natural enhancements."

THE DIMENSIONS OF STYLE

One might quickly develop a host of dimensions for describing decision-making style, and this may be well worth doing for we have two purposes in mind. First and most important is the development of self-consciousness, self-awareness, or self-knowledge. One reading of a great deal of the evidence turned up by modern psychology is that the key to the improvement of the intuitive, implicit decision process is self-awareness, and that this must begin by motivating the subject to explore the various dimensions of his own style of deciding. We will return shortly to this most fundamental notion. Our second purpose supposes that by exploring the dimensions of style we will be able to suggest more or less specific ways of enhancing that style. We would thus like to find ways of looking at style which are useful in the sense that they lead us to such enhancements. We might begin to lay out some of these dimensions as a series of questions. For example:

1. To what extent is one's style of decision making intuitive, implicit, and private? To what extent is it analytical, explicit, and public?
2. To what degree is one tolerant of ambiguity in a decision situation? Can we decide in the face of ambiguous notions about objectives or ambiguous statements of the alternative courses of action? Some studies suggest that experienced decision makers are highly tolerant of ambiguity and capable of resolving that ambiguity in their own ways.

3. Similarly, to what degree is one tolerant of uncertainty as to the consequences of one's actions? Some of us require considerable information and assurance before we will act, others are far more willing to act on the basis of limited information and substantial uncertainty. We should not imagine that one such style is always "better" than the other.

4. How reasonable is our hindsight? How effectively do we learn from our past decisions? Do we regret decisions which turn out badly or do we suppress these feelings and look to the future? Do we distinguish clearly between a good decision that depends on reason and logic, and a good result or outcome which always depends on some degree on chance, luck, and circumstances beyond our control?

5. How much cognitive effort does one invest in a decision? Some decision makers are careful and deliberate thinkers, others tend to proceed "off the top of their heads" or "by the seat of their pants."

6. To what degree does one delegate or seek external aids to deciding?

7. To what extent is there a need for coherence between one's beliefs, actions, and objectives? We may seek coherence by becoming more optimistic about a course of action after we have chosen it, than before. Sometimes we adopt the belief that what we have become committed to is the best possible course of action, while we had no such conviction prior to our commitment. We achieve coherence or reduce "cognitive dissonance" by revising our perceptions.

8. How sensitive are one's unaided decision-making abilities to conditions of stress? There is considerable evidence that most of us become distinctly poorer decision makers when we are under stress or pressure.

9. To what extent are our perceptions and thoughts influenced, not so much by the external world, as by our own needs and desires. One of the great discoveries of modern psychology is that what we see and what we think are influenced *subconsciously* by our needs and tensions.

10. To what degree is one clear about his own decision-making process? How much self-knowledge or self-consciousness does one have in this connection? It is well established that we seldom understand the reasons we do what we do, nor the goals we are striving to attain.

11. To what degree are our perceptions of the external world distorted because of distortions shared by our associates? Science is full of instances of socially shared distortions, often going about under the heading of "common sense." Indeed, one of the best definitions of common sense pictures it as that kind of sense which tells us when we look out the window that the world is flat.

12. To what degree does one abstract or simplify the external world in making a decision?

13. To what degree does one rely on rules of thumb or policy categories for disposing of decision problems?

14. To what degree does one look ahead in a decision? Is the planning horizon in the relatively near, or relatively distant future? One of the skills of a good chess player is his ability to look ahead to the future consequences of his moves. The ability of computers to play chess is directly related to their "look-ahead" ability.

Proposals for various dimensions of personal style could go on, and it may be important for a decision maker to consider dimensions which might be useful for understanding his own style; however, we turn now to the concept of "natural enhancements" which appeared in our Personal Style Hypothesis.

ENHANCING PERSONAL STYLES

We are looking for ways of enhancing, complimenting, supplementing, or assisting the decision process which are well adapted to the nature of that process. We want to develop enhancements which do not arise from some rationalistic view of choice, but rather from a specific study of decision-making style. Such techniques must be well suited to the context of affairs, in that they meet the time constraints within which one must act, and can be shown to have benefits that will match the cognitive efforts required of the user. The techniques which are likely to succeed are those which do not require a great amount of special training or "selling" and which the decision maker finds "naturally assimilable" into his own personal style. Such a set of specifications may seem difficult if not impossible to meet, but there are some grounds for optimism. The decision-aiding techniques we seek are more likely to be concerned with the implicit and intuitive aspects of deciding than with the explicit aspects. They are more likely to be the sort of thing which a decision maker is able and willing to do for himself, rather than things that must be done for him by others.

Let us try to illuminate these general notions by means of specific examples of possible relationships between aspects of personal style and enhancement techniques. As we have mentioned, there is considerable psychological evidence to support the notion that under conditions of stress, the effectiveness of one's intuitive, implicit decision-making skills is likely to be degraded. It raises directly the question of what individual or organizational efforts might be undertaken to remove the stressful conditions which may lead to intuitive degradation. This leads in turn to the larger question, "What are the best conditions for the flourishing of effective intuitive skills?" There are, of course, some very obvious answers to the question of "stress relieving" the decision maker, involving the rearrangement of workload, taking the problem home, or a quiet retreat for necessary reflection.

There are some less obvious answers as well. We know that it is sometimes effective, when one has a large number of things to do and feels "pressured," to write the tasks down and progress through the list one at a time. This simple way of handling stress has the effect of making the pressure explicit and thus reducing one's internal anxiety. It also has the effect of concentrating attention on one decision at a time, thus making the situation intuitively manageable. Similarly, we begin to notice that when a decision maker is faced with a decision which involves a considerable degree of uncertainty, the pressures and anxieties are to some extent relieved by making those uncertainties explicit, perhaps even by expressing them in the language of probability theory. This tends to depersonalize the uncertainty, to relieve the decision maker from being its sole bearer, and to allow him to concentrate his intuition on other aspects of the decision problem. One should note here that these techniques are things the decision maker can do for himself and things which generally depend on his own self-consciousness and self-awareness in decision making.

It is also of some interest to notice that the more general question of the conditions under which one's intuition can function most effectively has not been widely studied in management situations. In fact, those who seem to have had the most interest in this problem are the sages who developed Eastern religions such as Buddhism and Taoism. These men gave considerable thought to "freeing the mind" or creating the conditions under which one's intuition could work most effectively. The familiar progression in yoga from concentration to meditation and contemplation is aimed at freeing the mind from irrational passions, unconscious needs, and all manner of distractions so that it may be most reasonable. It is of special interest that many of the contemporary findings of psychology tend to confirm the notions developed by these ancient thinkers. Again we come around to the point that what is needed is self-knowledge or self-awareness in the decision process.

NEED DETERMINED THINKING

Wishful thinking is our common phrase for the sort of distortion that creeps into perceiving and conceptualizing as a result of basic needs and desires. Psychologists have been much interested in this need-determined sort of distortion because we ourselves are often not conscious of it. We consider three hypotheses about the effects of needs in the decision process.

1. Habitual ways of viewing a decision situation arise because a conception which meets the needs of one situation is uncritically applied to others. Habits might be thought of as ways of economizing the limited capacity of the mind. Rather than develop a conception which tries to account objectively for each individual choice situation, one simply resorts by analogy to customary conceptions or tends to fit decisions into categories previously developed. Organizations develop such habits, and they tend to get formalized into policies or routines for decision making. These habitual conceptions are perpetuated because they satisfy one's need to respond to the pressure of affairs which overtax the conceptualizing capacity of the mind. Habits also help to satisfy the need for being able to defend a decision in an organization. Certainly a widely used defense for an unsuccessful decision is the claim that it was based on "the way we always do it," or that it was placed in a category for which a policy was already determined.

2. One's conceptions of choice situations tend to move toward a view of the situation as the person would like to see it, and not necessarily as it is. Expectations are not independent of desires, and conceptions play a part in satisfying needs when actions prove inadequate to the task. If a person finds himself in very limited control of a situation, to some extent powerless to act in a satisfying way, then at least he can

remake his conceptualization of the situation to view it more satisfactorily. If the need for certainty and confidence in decision making cannot be achieved through predictive knowledge and the ability to control events, then perhaps conceptions will become subjectively free of doubt and uncertainty in response to this need.

Perception is a selective process which tends to give structure to the vastly complicated situations encountered in experience. In perceiving a situation, some elements of it "stand out" more clearly than others. The term is "figure and ground," the figure being those elements perceived most clearly against the suppressed background of the remainder. The psychologist goes on to hypothesize that the elements which tend to stand out as figure are at least in part controlled by needs, in the sense of having previously been perceived in satisfying situations. This, of course, works as the result of fears as well as desires.

3. Finally, conceptions of choice situations get distorted because of the social and organizational processes which lead a person to view things in ways accepted by his associates. Socially shared views, which come not so much from contact with reality as from the need to belong, or to avoid questioning the views of a group, are part of most decisions.

An individual decision maker in an organization experiences a demand from his superiors that his behavior be reliable, predictable, and in a general sense within control. They need to know how he is going to make decisions so they can account for, and plan on, the basis of his behavior. He thus finds it increasingly necessary to conform to the organization's way of conceptualizing decision situations or to follow the organizational rules. The rules and conventions tend to become important, no longer because of their original objective effectiveness for achieving organizational goals, but for their own sake. It becomes less important to make a decision to advance the objectives of the organization and more important to make a decision acceptable in the organizational process. This leads to viewing decisions as falling into one of a relatively small number of organizationally sanctioned categories. Thus, conceptualization of choice situations becomes a rigid process. This may mean the decisions are less and less successful at the same time they are becoming more reliable, predictable, and defensible within the organization.

It may be that the influences of our needs on our perception and thinking constitute one of the most serious sources of difficulty in our intuitive or implicit decision processes. Our needs for wish-fulfillment, escape, or self-defense may be sources of difficulty largely because we are not aware of their distorting effects on our decision making. This leads us again to what we take to be the essential conclusion of psychological research in this connection. Vigilance, self-knowledge, self-awareness or self-consciousness constitute the basic strategy for freeing ourselves from the subconscious sources of distortion. Knowing oneself makes it easier to see decision situations accurately, but knowing oneself in this sense is not easy.

One obvious suggestion, which may turn out to amply reward the effort required, is simply to keep an explicit record of one's predictions or decisions in repetitive situations. It may be surprisingly effective, for example, to explore one's thinking for the systematic effects of needs by "keeping score." Suppose, for example, we had occasion to repeatedly estimate the cost of doing particular jobs and later had an opportunity to learn the actual costs. It is important to keep a written record of one's estimates because the memory also is subject to need-determined distortions. Comparing the estimate with the actual may reveal systematic biases and unreliability. Knowledge of these is the first step in disciplining the intuition. An interesting experiment is to repeatedly predict where the stock market will be a week or a month in the future, and then to compare these predictions with what actually happens. It is likely that a large number of investors would profit from a knowledge of the systematic optimistic or pessimistic biases on which their market decisions are based.

EVALUATION

Certainly one of the most difficult aspects of choosing is coming to grips with the multiple, conflicting nature of most value structures. In deciding which of two houses to buy, we compare them on the basis of price, number of rooms, tax rate, style, location, and so on. It is relatively easy to compare the houses one attribute at a time, but the difficulty arises when these comparisons must be aggregated into an overall preference. Similar problems occur when one must choose between development projects, plant locations, candidates for vice-president, and, in fact, in nearly all interesting decisions. The basic kernel of self-knowledge is this: the one dimensional comparisons are easy for the unaided intuition, but the multi-dimensional comparisons are difficult. We have sometimes been disdainful of the decision maker who gives a "check mark" to the house which has the lower price, another to the house which has the greater number of rooms, and so on, making the decision in favor of the house which receives the greater number of check marks. On second thought, however, this decision maker has worked out for himself a simple decision aiding device which moves toward a very sensible division of labor. He uses his unaided intuition to make the easy one dimensional comparisons, but then employs a very simple, logical model to do what his intuition finds difficult, the task of aggregating these judgments into an overall preference. Now it is obvious that a little more effort on his part might lead to a more sophisticated logical model in which he ranked the attributes of houses in order of their importance to him and then gave each house a numerical score for each attribute. Finally, the model would combine ranks and scores into an overall measure of the desirability of each house. The principle of division of labor remains the same.

There is currently a renewed interest in this type of decision-aiding scheme, and a number of careful studies have yielded interesting results. We know that if someone else designs a complex ranking and rating system and tries to "sell" it to a decision maker, only the most limited success can be expected. On the other hand, many decision makers seem to develop and use such logical models for themselves rather naturally. While these tend to be simple, rather than sophisticated, logical models, we are discovering that such simple models are surprisingly effective. One meaning of effectiveness is that decisions reached by laborious, unaided, intuitive methods are in many cases the same as those reached by surprisingly simple, logical models for combining one dimensional judgments. In this sense, simple models "work" for many decision makers who have been studied as they worked on rather difficult decision problems. There are other ways to assess the effectiveness of these methods as well. Decision makers seem to develop them easily, find their use appealing, and have less cause to later regret decisions made with such aids. We suspect also that these methods serve to increase the reliability of the resulting decisions by reducing to some degree the effects of the unconscious distractions we have previously examined.

These three examples of the relations between dimensions of personal decision-making style and natural enhancements may lend some credence to our basic hypothesis, or at least suggest some justification for studying it further. The notion of self-directed change is important here. Outsiders may show a decision maker that his behavior is not as satisfactory as he may have supposed, suggest to him the sorts of things that may be unconsciously influencing it, and offer some suggestions as to the way in which it might be changed. If, however, change is actually to occur, it must be the work of the decision maker himself. Coming to know one's own mind as the basis of self-motivated change is, so far as we can now tell, *the* effective way of disciplining the intuition. There are also other obvious advantages. Nobody has to sell a decision maker on the use of decision-aiding techniques he has developed himself. There is none of the traditional resistance to change to overcome. The process is also well adapted to the context of affairs, serving to enhance the intuitive powers of the manager to deal with unanticipated decisions. It encourages him to evolve decision-aiding techniques particularly suited to his own style and circumstances.

Our conclusion is that the contribution of science to the intuitive decision processes which operate to some degree in all decisions and to a very great degree in decisions of encounter, is to encourage the process of achieving self-consciousness which will lead to self-directed change. Self analysis, we are suggesting, will form the basis for self-motivated change leading toward the achievement of an effective and disciplined intuition. This is, after all, the basic conclusion of modern psychotherapy and ancient Buddhism. Once a person becomes aware of the inner sources of his behavior, the needs which have unconsciously driven him, he will be able to free himself of their influences. To enhance the intuition, one must have feedback not only from the results of his decisions, but also from his own appraisal of the internal sources of his behavior.

SUGGESTIONS FOR FURTHER STUDY

Bruner, Jerome J., J. Goodnow, and George A. Austin. *A Study of Thinking*. New York: John Wiley and Sons, Inc., 1956.
Calkins, Robert D. "The Decision Process in Administration." *Business Horizons*, Fall 1959.
Clarke, T. E. "Decision Making in Technologically Based Organizations; A Literature Survey of Present Practice." *IEEE Transactions on Engineering Management*, Vol. EM-21, No. 4 February 1971.

Doktor, R., and W. Hamilton. "Cognitive Style and the Acceptance of Management Science Recommendations." *Management Science*, Vol. 19, No. 8, April 1973.

Duncan, W. J. "The Researcher and the Manager: A Comparative View of the Need for Mutual Understanding." *Management Science*, Vol. 20, No. 8, April 1974.

Lindbloom, Charles E. "The Science of Muddling Through." *Public Administration Review*, Vol. XIX, No. 2 (1959).

APPENDIX
SOLUTIONS FOR SELECTED PROBLEMS

CHAPTER 3

3–1. $U(\$1,000) = (.40)(.10)+(.60)(.50) = .34$

3–3. *a*) In the relevant region the utility function exhibits diminishing marginal utility.

b) In the relevant region the utility function exhibits increasing marginal utility.

3–5. Increasing marginal utility in the relevant region.

3–6. Constant or increasing marginal utility in the relevant range.

3–7.

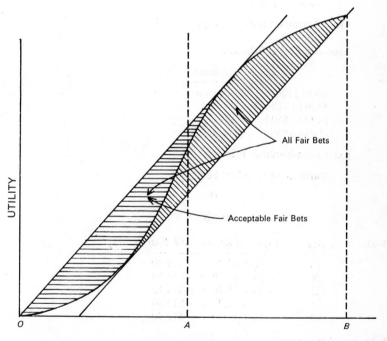

DOLLARS

3–9. *a*) Increasing or constant marginal utility in the relevant region.

b) Decreasing marginal utility in the relevant region.

c) First increasing, then decreasing marginal utility.

3–15. $U(B) = .72$
$U(D) = (.16)(.60) + (.48)(.73) + (.36)(.80) = .7344$
Thus choose D.

3–16. For each person, the utility of his share will be
$(.50) U(-\$25,000) + (.50) U(\$50,000) = (.50)(.64) + (.50)(.78) = .71$
while the utility of accepting no contract is .70.

3–17. $U(A) = .65$

$U(A \text{ twice}) = (.25) U(\$400,000) + (.25) U(\$100,000) + (.25) U(\$100,000)$

$\qquad + (.25) U(-\$200,000)$

$\qquad = (.25)(1.00) + (.25)(.83) + (.25)(.83) + (.25)(0) = .665$

3–18. *a*) \$6,000 with probability p; 0 with probability $1 - p$
b) \$2,000
c) $U(a_1) = .70 \qquad U(a_2) = .865$

3–20. Expectation Principle:

$E(a_1) = \$194$

$E(a_2) = \quad 190$

$E(a_3) = \quad 194$

Most Probable Future Principle:
Choose a_2
Aspiration Level Principle:

A	Choice
up to \$120	a_2 or a_3
\$120 to \$190	a_2
\$190 to \$500	a_3
above \$500	a_1

Expiration-Variance Principle:

Variance of $a_1 = 151,800$

$\qquad\qquad a_2 = \quad 0$

$\qquad\qquad a_3 = \quad 61,800$

3–31.

Age	Expected Return for 1 Year
25	$-30 + 15.30 = -\$14.70$
26	$-30 + 15.50 = -\$14.50$
27	$-30 + 15.90 = -\$14.10$
28	$-30 + 16.40 = -\$13.60$
29	$-30 + 17.10 = -\$12.90$

3–32. *a*) 3,000 units
b) 3,000 units
c) 1,000, 2,000, or 3,000 units
d) 3,000 units
e) 1,000 units

3–33. *a)* $p = .10$
b) Do Not Propose, Indifference, Propose
c) $-\$10,000 < A \leqslant 0$ Do not propose
$0 < A \leqslant \$90,000$ Propose

3–39. $p_R < .485$

3–41. Expected Return $= \dfrac{1}{2} \cdot 2 + \dfrac{1}{2^2} \cdot 2^2 + \dfrac{1}{2^3} \cdot 2^3 + \cdots$

$$= 1 + 1 + 1 + \cdots$$

$$= \infty$$

If the person has 2^{20} cents expected return is given by

$$= \frac{1}{2} \cdot 2 + \frac{1}{2^2} \cdot 2^2 + \cdots \frac{1}{2^{20}} \cdot 2^{20} + 2^{20} \sum_{n=21}^{\infty} \frac{1}{2^n}$$

$$= 20 + 2^{20} \left\{ \frac{1}{2^{20}} \right\} = 21$$

3–43. *a)* $U(0) = .60$
b) Indifference
c) $\$25,000$

CHAPTER 4

4–1. Let: G, G = first casting good, second casting good
G, B = first casting good, second casting bad etc.
The decision might be made explicit as follows;

	$(1-p)^2$ G, G	$(1-p)p$ G, B	$p(1-p)$ B, G	p^2 B, B
a_1: Make 1	$C_1 + C_2$	$C_1 + C_2$	$2C_1 + 2C_2$	$3C_1 + 3C_2$
a_2: Make 2	$C_1 + 2C_2$	$C_1 + 2C_2$	$C_1 + 2C_2$	$2C_1 + 3C_2$

a) $E(a_1) = (.25)(7C_1 + 7C_2)$
$E(a_2) = (.25)(5C_1 + 9C_2)$
a_2 will be preferred to a_1 if $C_1 > C_2$
b) $E(a_1) = (1.11)(C_1 + C_2)$
$E(a_2) = (1.01)C_1 + (2.01)C_2$
a_2 will be preferred to a_1 if $C_1 > 9C_2$

d) If a_1 had been chosen on the basis of available knowledge, the value of immediate knowledge of casting quality would be

$$p(1-p)C_1 + 2p^2 C_1$$

If a_2 had been chosen, the value would be

$$(1-p)^2 C_2 + 2p(1-p)C_2 + p^2 C_1$$

4-2.   The expected value of stopping is

$$E(\text{stop}) = P_B$$

and the expected value of continuing is

$E(\text{go} \mid P_B) = $ expected value of continuing search with the best available project having present worth P_B.

$$= \int_{P=P_B}^{\infty} Pf(P)\, dP + P_B \int_{P=0}^{P_B} f(P)\, dP - C$$

where $P = $ the present worth of the opportunity discovered.
Let $A = $ the value of P_B for which

$$E(\text{stop}) = P_B = E(\text{go} \mid P_B)$$

Then one could formulate a policy of the form, "Stop if $P_B > A$, otherwise continue."

4-4.   a) $$E(m) = C_1 \int_{x=0}^{L_1} f(m,x)\, dx + C_2 \int_{x=L_2}^{\infty} f(m,x)\, dx$$

$$\frac{dE(m)}{dm} = C_1 \int_{x=0}^{L_1} \frac{\partial f(m,x)}{\partial m}\, dx + C_2 \int_{x=L_2}^{\infty} \frac{\partial f(m,x)}{\partial m}\, dx = 0$$

b) $$\int_{x=0}^{L_1} \frac{\partial f(m,x)}{\partial m}\, dx + \int_{x=L_2}^{\infty} \frac{\partial f(m,x)}{\partial m}\, dx = 0$$

4-5.   Let: $f(m,x) = \dfrac{1}{2k}$, $m - k \leqslant x \leqslant m + k$

$$E(m) = C_1 \frac{L_1 - m + k}{2k} + C_2 \frac{m + k - L_2}{2k}$$

If $m - k \leqslant L_1$ and $m + k \geqslant L_2$

$$E(m) = C_1 \frac{L_1 - m + k}{2k}$$

if $m - k \leqslant L_1$ and $m + k \leqslant L_2$

$$E(m) = C_2 \frac{m + k - L_2}{2k}$$

if $m - k \geqslant L_1$ and $m + k \geqslant L_2$

Thus if $C_1 > C_2$, let $m \geqslant L_1 + k$
if $C_1 < C_2$, let $m \leqslant L_2 - k$

4-7.

Stage	No. of Components
1	3
2	2
3	2

4-8.   Bet \$100.
If you win, stop, if you lose, bet \$200.
If you win, stop, if you lose, bet \$400.

Probability of Success:

$$p + (1-p)p + (1-p)^2 p$$

where $p = \dfrac{18}{38}$

4-11. Choose a_2.

4-12. Based upon the expectation principle, one could say that the person was behaving as though the cash equivalent of his life was

$$\frac{.07}{39p}$$

where p is the probability of a fatal accident per mile of auto travel.

4-13. a) yes
b) If $0 \leqslant A \leqslant \$1,000$, choose no standby machine, otherwise purchase the machine.

4-14. $p = 3/35$

4-15. $E(a_1) = \$2,000$
$E(a_2) = \$1,450$
$E(a_3) = \$1,455$
Probability that a_1 is best = Probability of seven or more breakdowns = .24
Probability that a_2 is best = Probability of six or less breakdowns = .76
Probability that a_3 is best = 0

4-16.

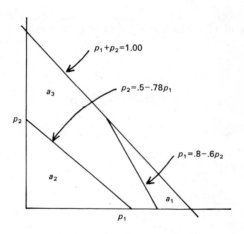

4-17. Maximum number of calls should be 3.

4-18. Probability of waiting $= \displaystyle\int_{x=0}^{c} me^{-mx}\,dx = k$

4-19. Choose λ so as to minimize the function

$$C(\lambda) = C_1 \mu + C_2 \frac{\lambda}{\mu - \lambda} + 8C_3 \left(\frac{1-\lambda}{\mu} \right)$$

4–26. Replace every 5 or 6 periods, yielding a cost of approximately $171.

4–27. Replace every 200 hours, yielding an average cost of $77.50 per hundred hours.

4–29. $T = 4$

4–31. $E(a_1) = \$957$
$E(a_2) = \$882$ (approximate)

4–35. 1.002

4–38. a) For a given n

$$EAC(n) = \left\{ I + \sum_{j=1}^{n} \frac{Cj}{(1+i)^j} - \frac{Sn}{(1+i)^n} \right\} \left\{ \frac{i(1+i)^n}{(1+i)^n - 1} \right\}$$

The expected value of $EAC(n) = \sum_{n=0}^{\infty} \{EAC(n)\} f(n)$

b) No.

4–39.

t	Capacity for Risk of 50%	Capacity for Risk of 25%
0	20,000 units	20,973 units
1	22,000	23,080
2	24,000	25,200
3	26,000	27,352
4	28,000	29,518

The number of machines required in each case is equal to the smallest multiple of 1500 which is equal to or greater than the indicated capacity requirement.

CHAPTER 5

5–1. The number to be stocked is that value of I which satisfies the relation

$$1 - p = \sum_{x=0}^{I_0 - 1} \frac{e^{-m}m^x}{x!}$$

5–2. 24 or 25 units

5–6. a) $I_0 = 100 + 1.22\sigma$
b)

C_1/C_2	I_0
.10	112.9
.25	108.4
.50	104.3
1.00	100.0
1.50	97.5
2.00	95.7
2.50	94.0
3.00	93.3

5–7.

C_2	I_0
.01	0
.10	0
.15	1
.50	1
1.00	2
2.00	2
4.00	3
8.00	3

5–8. 2155 gallons

5–10. $P(I_0) = \displaystyle\sum_{d=d_0}^{I_0} e^{-mt}\frac{(mt)^{I_0-d_0}}{(I_0-d_0)!}$

5–11. 136 units

5–12. $P(I_0) = \dfrac{R-C_0}{R+C_1}$

5–13. Let C = total cost

$$\text{Prob}(C \leqslant A) = \int_{I-(A/C_1)}^{I+(A/C_2)} p(D)\,dD \qquad 0 \leqslant A < C_1 I$$

$$\text{Prob}(C \leqslant A) = \int_{0}^{I+(A/C_2)} p(D)\,dD \qquad A \geqslant C_1 I$$

5–14. If expected profit is given by

$$E(I) = \int_{D=0}^{I}\{RD - C_1(I-D)\}\,p(D)\,dD + \int_{D=0}^{\infty}\{RI - C_2(D-I)\}\,p(D)\,dD$$

Then

$$P(I_0) = \dfrac{R+C_2}{R+C_1+C_2}$$

5–15. If $\quad \text{Profit} = RD - C_1(I-D) \qquad$ for $D \leqslant I$

$\qquad\qquad\quad\; = RI - C_2(D-I) \qquad$ for $D > I$

then

$$\text{Probability(Profit} \leqslant 0) = P\left\{\frac{C_1 I}{R+C_1}\right\} + 1 - P\left\{\frac{(R+C_2)I}{C_2}\right\}$$

5–16. a) $P(I_0) = \dfrac{C_2-C_1}{C_2}$

5–17. To minimize expected costs, let $I = 4$.
To maximize probability that costs are less than or equal to $400,000,
let $I = 5$.

5-18. To minimize expected costs, find z_0 such that

$$\int_{-\infty}^{z_0} N(z)\, dz = \frac{C_2}{C_1 + C_2}$$

where $N(z)$ is the Normal distribution with mean of 0 and standard deviation of 1. Then

$$I_0 = A + Bt + z_0(C + Dt)$$

5-19. a) $I = 1,800 + 400p$

b) Probability $(C(I) \geqslant A) = \dfrac{I - 200A - 1,800 + 2,200 - I - 25A}{400}$

$$= 1 - \frac{A}{2} - \frac{A}{16}$$

if $I - 200A \geqslant 1,800$ and $I + 25A \leqslant 2,200$

If the first of these conditions holds, but the second does not, then

$$\text{Probability}\,(C(I) \geqslant A) = \frac{I + 200A - 1,800}{400}$$

If the second condition holds, but the first does not, then

$$\text{Probability}\,(C(I) \geqslant A) = \frac{2,200 - I - 25A}{400}$$

5-20.

p	I
.10	1,256
.09	1,268
.08	1,282
.07	1,296
.06	1,310
.05	1,328
.04	1,350
.03	1,376
.02	1,410
.01	1,466

5-21.

If starting inventory is	make
0	3
1	2
2	0
3	0

5-22. a) $I_0 = 4$ or 5 $E(I_0) = \$2,000$
b) $I_0 = d + 1$ or $d + 2$ $E(I_0) = \$1,000$
Thus the prediction is worth $\$1,000$.
c) $\$2,000$

5-23. a) $I_0 = $ mean demand
b) $I_0 = $ mean demand if distribution is symetrical about the mean

5–24. a) $I_0 = 100$
b) $U(I_0) = 100k$

5–25. $I_0 = \dfrac{m}{1-p}$

CHAPTER 6

6–1. The best bid is approximately 1.03 times the cost estimate, yielding an expected profit of .00163 times the cost estimate.

6–3. The best bid is approximately 1.09 times the cost estimate, yielding an expected profit of .0255 times the cost estimate.

6–6. The best bid is approximately $10,000, yielding an expected profit of about $188.

6–8. There is no bid which will yield a positive expected profit.

6–10. Let: Profit $= Z$
For any bid B,

$$\text{Prob}\{Z \le A\} = \int_{C=B-A}^{\infty} f(c)\, dcp(B), \quad \text{for } A < 0$$

$$\text{Prob}\{Z \le A\} = \int_{C=B-A}^{\infty} f(c)\, dcp(B) + 1 - p(B), \quad \text{for } A \ge 0$$

6–11. $B = 1.175c$

CHAPTER 7

7–1. $A = E(y)$

7–2.

Day	Critical Price Level
1	1126
2	1130
3	1137
4	1150

7–3.

Period	Critical Price Level
1	$1,019
2	$1,071
3	$1,123
4	$1,180
5	$1,250

Total expected cost $= \$969$

7–10.

Draw Number	Stop if Result Is
1	3 or more
2	3 or more
3	2 or more
4	0 or more

7-14. a) $\int_x \dfrac{d}{x^2} f_j(x)\, dx$

b) $\displaystyle\sum_{j=1}^{N} \int_x \dfrac{d}{x^2} f_j(x)\, dx$

c) $\int_x \dfrac{d}{x} f_j(x)\, dx$

d) $\displaystyle\sum_{j=1}^{N} \int_x \dfrac{d}{x} f_j(x)\, dx$

e) $\dfrac{\sum_{j=1}^{N} \int_x (d/x)\, f_j(x)\, dx}{\sum_{j=1}^{N} \int_x (d/x^2)\, f_j(x)\, dx}$

f) $\dfrac{ln(b/a)}{(1/a)-(1/b)}$

g)

(b/a)	Average Unit Cost
2	$1.39a$
3	$1.65a$
4	$1.85a$

7-15. $X_2 = \$100$
$X_1 = \$97.50$

7-16. On day 1

$E(\text{stop}) = x_1$

$E(\text{go without option}) = E(x)$

$E(\text{go with option}) = -k + \displaystyle\int_{x_2=0}^{x_1} x_1\, f(x_2)\, dx_2 + \int_{x_2=x_1}^{\infty} x_2\, f(x_2)\, dx_2$

7-17. $X_2 = \$12.50$
$X_1 = \$11.48$

CHAPTER 8

8-7. Laplace: choose a_5
Minimax: choose a_5
Hurwicz: choose a_5 for $\alpha = 0$ to $\alpha = 14/19$
            a_3 for $\alpha > 14/19$
Regret: choose a_5
When the values in the matrix are modified by addition and multiplication, the choices remain the same.

8-13. Laplace: choose 0 and 00
Minimax: indifference among all three alternatives
Hurwicz: choose 0 and 00 for any α
Regret: choose 0 and 00

8–20. With two possible futures:
$$E(\text{Bet}) = .5(\$4) + .5(-\$2) = \$1$$
With six possible futures:
$$E(\text{Bet}) = \frac{4-2-2-2-2-2}{6} = -\$1$$

CHAPTER 9

9–1. It is first necessary to set bounds on the production quantity x. Then the various principles of choice may be applied directly.

9–2. One way to treat this decision is to consider two possible futures:
s_1: the new site will be more profitable than the one under option by an amount x
s_2: the new site will be less profitable than the one under option by an amount y

Laplace: Take up option if $\dfrac{x-y}{2} < 0$

Minimax: Take up option. (Maximin)

Hurwicz: Take up option if $\alpha(x+y) < y$

Savage: Take up option if $x < y$

9–3. *a)*
$$A = \sqrt{\frac{C_2 K_2}{C_1 K_1}}$$

b)
$$\text{Expectation: } A = \sqrt{\frac{C_2 E(K_2)}{C_1 K_1}}$$

Most Probable Future:
let $K_2' = $ most probable value of K_2
$$A = \sqrt{\frac{C_2 K_2'}{C_1 K_1}}$$

Aspiration Level:
let: $F = $ Probability $(TC(A) \geqslant L)$
$\quad = $ Probability $(K_2 \geqslant K_2{}^*)$
where $L = $ aspiration level

$$K_2{}^* = \frac{AL - C_1 K_1 A^2}{C_2}$$

$$F = \int_{K_2{}^*}^{\infty} f(K_2)\, dK_2 \qquad \frac{\partial F}{\partial A} = -f(K_2{}^*)\left\{\frac{L - 2C_1 K_1 A}{C_2}\right\} = 0$$

if $f(K_2{}^*) \neq 0, \quad A = \dfrac{L}{2C_1 K_1}$

Variance of $TC(A) = \left(\dfrac{C_2}{A}\right)^2 \sigma_{K_2}^2$

c)

Laplace: $A = \sqrt{\dfrac{C_2 \, E(K_2)}{C_1 \, K_1}}$, $\qquad E(K_2) = \displaystyle\int_0^\infty K_2 \, f(K_2) \, dK_2$

here $f(K_2) = \dfrac{L}{K_{2U} - K_{2L}}$ $\qquad$ for $K_{2L} \leqslant K_2 \leqslant K_{2U}$

Minimax: $A = \sqrt{\dfrac{C_2 \, K_{2U}}{C_1 \, K_1}}$

Hurwicz:

$\qquad$ Assuming pessimism is associated with low values of K_2

$\qquad K_2(\alpha) + K_{2U}(1 - \alpha) \, K_{2L}$

$$A = \sqrt{\dfrac{C_2 \, K_2(\alpha)}{C_1 \, K_1}}$$

Regret:

$\qquad$ let: $A_i =$ optimal A for K_{2i}

$\qquad$ For a given K_{2i}, the regret associated with any area A is

$$C_1 \, K_1 \, A + \dfrac{C_2 \, K_{2i}}{A} - 2\sqrt{C_1 \, C_2 \, K_1 \, K_{2i}}$$

For a given A this will be maximized either when $K_2 = K_{2L}$ or when $K_2 = K_{2U}$. To find the value of A for which the maximum regret is minimized, let

$$C_1 \, K_1 \, A + \dfrac{C_2 \, K_{2L}}{A} - 2\sqrt{C_1 \, C_2 \, K_1 \, K_{2L}}$$

$$= C_1 \, K_1 \, A + \dfrac{C_2 \, K_{2U}}{A} - 2\sqrt{C_1 \, C_2 \, K_1 \, K_{2U}}$$

Solving; $A = \dfrac{C_2 \, K_{2U} - C_2 \, K_{2L}}{2\sqrt{C_1 \, C_2 \, K_1 \, K_{2U}} - 2\sqrt{C_1 \, C_2 \, K_1 \, K_{2L}}}$

9-4. If we continue the simplifying assumption that a third casting, if made, will be good, and if we take the possible futures to be values of p such that

$$p_1 \leqslant p \leqslant p_2$$

then the following is a possible analysis.

Laplace: Let: $E(a_i, p) =$ expected cost for alternative i given p

$$E(a_i) = \int_{p=p_1}^{p_2} E(a_i, p) \, f(p) \, dp$$

where $f(p) = \dfrac{1}{p_2 - p_1}$

$$E(a_1, p) = (1 + p + p^2)(C_1 + C_2)$$

$$E(a_1) = (C_1 + C_2)\left(1 + \dfrac{p_1 + p_2}{2} + \dfrac{p_2^2 + p_1 p_2 + p_1^2}{3}\right)$$

$$E(a_2, p) = (1+p^2) C_1 + (2+p^2) C_2$$

$$E(a_2) = (C_1 + C_2)\left(1 + \frac{p_2{}^2 + p_1 p_2 + p_1{}^2}{3}\right) + C_2$$

$$E(a_1) < E(a_2) \text{ if } p_1 + p_2 < \frac{2C_2}{C_1 + C_2}$$

Minimax: Choose so as to minimize $E(a_i, p_2)$
Hurwicz: Choose so as to minimize

$$(\alpha) E(a_i, p_1) + (1-\alpha) E(a_i, p_2)$$

Regret: The maximum regret for a_1 is

$$E(a_1, p_2) - E(a_2, p_2)$$

and for a_2 is

$$E(a_2, p_1) - E(a_1, p_1)$$

assuming both these differences are non-negative.

9-5. Let $a_1 = $ Stop

$a_2 = $ Search for one more opportunity

Assume $P_L \leqslant P \leqslant P_u$
Laplace: $E(a_1) = P_B$

$$E(a_2) = \int_P^{P_B} P_B f(P)\, dP + \int_{P_B}^{\infty} P f(P)\, dP - C$$

Maximin: Stop
Hurwicz: $H(a_1) = P_B$
$\quad\quad\quad H(a_2) = \alpha P_u + (1-\alpha)(P_B - C)$
Regret: For a_1: $P_u - C - P_B$
$\quad\quad\quad a_2$: C

9-7. One approach to this decision uses the following matrix of expected values:

	fire	no fire
a_1: insure	\$ 1,040	\$40
a_2: no insurance	\$10,000	0

Laplace: $E(a_1) = \$540$
$\quad\quad\quad E(a_2) = \$5,000$
Minimax: choose a_1
Hurwicz: The alternatives will be equally preferred for $\alpha = .995$
Regret: choose a_1

9-8. Laplace: buy spare
Minimax: buy spare
Hurwicz: The alternatives will be equally preferred for $\alpha = .914$
Regret: buy spare

9–10. Assume the alternatives are numbered in the order of presentation in the problem statement.
Laplace: a_2
Minimax: a_1
Hurwicz: a_1 and a_2 will be equally preferred for $\alpha = .138$.
Regret: a_2

9–11. Laplace: a_3
Maximin: a_1
Hurwicz: for $\quad 0 \leqslant \alpha \leqslant .20 \qquad a_1$
$\qquad\qquad\quad .20 \leqslant \alpha \leqslant .36 \qquad a_3$
$\qquad\qquad\quad .36 \leqslant \alpha \qquad\qquad a_2$
Regret: a_2 and a_3 are equally preferred

9–12. Laplace: One possible approach is to take $p(t) = .25$ for each month. The policy which minimizes expected costs is one of replacement every month.
Minimax: replace every month
Hurwicz: replace every month
Regret: replace every month

9–14. Let a_1: $c = 2$, $N = 50$
$\qquad\;\; a_2$: $c = 1$, $N = 100$
Laplace: choose a_2
Minimax: choose a_2
Regret: choose a_2
Hurwicz: The plans are equally preferred for $\alpha = 554/604$.

9–18. If $C_1 > C_2$, $m = L_1 + K$
$\qquad\; C_1 < C_2$, $m = L_2 - K$

9–19. a) If P were exactly known, the economic purchase quantity is

$$L = \sqrt{\frac{2C_1 D}{C_2 PT}}$$

b) Applying the Laplace principle under our assumption that

$$P_1 \leqslant P \leqslant P_2$$

implies assuming that the density function of price is

$$f(P) = \frac{1}{P_2 - P_1}$$

The expected cost of procurement is then

$$E\{C(L)\} = C_1 \frac{D}{L} + C_2 \frac{LTE(P)}{2}$$

where $E(P)$ is the expected price, which is given by

$$E(P) = \frac{P_1 + P_2}{2}$$

Taking the first derivative of the expected cost, setting it equal to zero, and solving for L yields:

$$L = \sqrt{\frac{4C_1 D}{C_2 T(P_1 + P_2)}}$$

If we wished to be conservative, the minimax principle might be applied to minimize the maximum cost of procurement. For any lot size L, the maximum cost will occur when price takes its upper limit, P_2. This maximum cost will then be

$$C(L) = C_1 \frac{D}{L} + C_2 \frac{LTP_2}{2}$$

and the lot size which minimizes the maximum cost is simply

$$L = \sqrt{\frac{2C_1 D}{C_2 TP_2}}$$

To apply the Hurwicz criterion it is only necessary to note that, for any alternative lot size, L, the maximum possible cost will be

$$C(L) = C_1 \frac{D}{L} + C_2 \frac{LTP_2}{2}$$

and the minimum possible cost will be

$$C(L) = C_1 \frac{D}{L} + C_2 \frac{LTP_1}{2}$$

The Hurwicz criterion then takes the form

$$\alpha \left\{ C_1 \frac{D}{L} + C_2 \frac{LTP_1}{2} \right\} + (1 - \alpha) \left\{ C_1 \frac{D}{L} + C_2 \frac{LTP_2}{2} \right\}$$

which reduces to

$$C_1 \frac{D}{L} + C_2 \frac{LTP_2}{2} + \alpha C_2 \frac{LT(P_1 - P_2)}{2}$$

The value of L which minimizes this function is

$$L = \sqrt{\frac{2C_1 D}{C_2 T\{\alpha P_1 + (1 - \alpha) P_2\}}}$$

c) To apply the Regret principle note first that for any price P_i, if the optimal lot size L_i is used, the minimum total cost will be

$$C(P_i, L_i) = C_1 \frac{D}{L_i} + C_2 \frac{L_i TP_i}{2} = \sqrt{2C_1 C_2 TDP_i}$$

For some price P_i, the regret associated with a lot size L is

$$C(P_i, L) - C(P_i, L_i) = C_1 \frac{D}{L} - C_1 \frac{D}{L_i} + C_2 \frac{LTP_i}{2} - C_2 \frac{L_i TP_i}{2}$$

$$= C_1 D \left\{ \frac{1}{L} = \frac{1}{L_i} \right\} + C_2 \frac{TP_i}{2} \{L - L_i\}$$

Inspection of this function may serve to convince us that the maximum regret for any L will occur either when $P_i = P_1$ or when $P_i = P_2$. The maximum regret for any L is either

$$C_1 \frac{D}{L} + C_2 \frac{LTP_1}{2} - \sqrt{2C_1 C_2 DTP_1}$$

$$C_1 \frac{D}{L} + C_2 \frac{LTP_2}{2} - \sqrt{2C_1 C_2 DTP_2}$$

For values of L near L_1 the maximum regret will be given by the second of these quantities, and for values near L_2, by the first. To find the L for which the maximum regret is minimized, one may set these two quantities equal and solve for L. This yields

$$L = \frac{\sqrt{2C_1 C_2 DTP_2} - \sqrt{2C_1 C_2 DTP_1}}{(C_2 T/2)(P_2 - P_1)}$$

9-20. The Laplace principle suggests the assumption that

$$f(P) = \frac{1}{5.50 - 4.50} \text{ for } 4.50 \leqslant P \leqslant 5.50$$

The expected price is

$$E(P) = \frac{5.50 + 4.50}{2} = 5.00$$

The best lot size is given by

$$L = \sqrt{\frac{2C_1 D}{C_2 TE(P)}} = \sqrt{\frac{(2)(500)(60,000)}{(.02)(12)(5.00)}}$$

$$= 7,071 \text{ units}$$

The minimax principle suggests that costs will be maximized when price is at its highest, \$5.50. To minimize costs for this price we take

$$L = \sqrt{\frac{(2)(500)(60,000)}{(.02)(5.50)(12)}}$$

$$= 6,742 \text{ units}$$

The Hurwicz principle suggests that the best lot size for a given α is

$$L = \sqrt{\frac{2C_1 D}{C_2 T\{\alpha P_1 + (1 - \alpha) P_2\}}}$$

Considering α as an unknown, this yields

$$L = \sqrt{\frac{(2)(500)(60,000)}{(.02)(12)\{\alpha(4.50) + (1 - \alpha)(5.50)\}}}$$

The optimum lot size as a function of α is given in the following table:

α	L
1.00	7,454
.90	7,372
.80	7,293
.70	7,217
.60	7,143
.50	7,071
.40	7,002
.30	6,934
.20	6,812
.10	6,804
.00	6,742

For the regret principle we have

$$L = \frac{\sqrt{2C_1 C_2 DTP_2} - \sqrt{2C_1 C_2 DTP_1}}{(C_2 T/2)(P_2 - P_1)}.$$

$$= \frac{\sqrt{2(500)(.02)(60,000)(12)(5.50)} - \sqrt{2(500)(.02)(60,000)(12)(4.50)}}{(.02)(12)(.5)}$$

$$= 7,083 \text{ units}$$

9–21. $I_0 = 1,167$

9–22. $I_0 = 125$ units

If $C_2 = kC_1$, $\quad I_0 = 80 + 50\dfrac{k}{1+k}$

9–23. $I_0 = \dfrac{10C_2}{20 + C_2}$

$I_0 = \dfrac{NC_2}{C_1 + C_2}$

9–24. $I_0 = 2155.5$

9–25. Laplace: If no purchase has previously been made, the expected price paid on Wednesday is \$21.

Using the rule: If Tuesday's price is less than or equal to \$21, buy, otherwise wait, the expected price paid on Tuesday is

$(7/13)(\$21) + (1/13)(\$16 + \$17 + \$18 + \$19 + \$20 + \$21) = \$19.84$

Thus no purchase would be made on Monday.

Minimax: Buy Monday.
Hurwicz: $H(\text{Monday}) = $ Monday's Price
$H(\text{Tuesday}) = \alpha(28) + (1 - \alpha)(16)$
$H(\text{Wednesday}) = \alpha(30) + (1 - \alpha)(12)$

Regret:

Monday's Price Is	And His Action on Monday	Regret if Wednesday's Price Is $30	Regret if Wednesday's Price Is $12
$20	Buy	0	8
20	Wait	10	0
21	Buy	0	9
21	Wait	9	0
22	Buy	0	10
22	Wait	8	0
23	Buy	0	11
23	Wait	7	0
24	Buy	0	12
24	Wait	6	0

9-27. Laplace: $f(y) =$ uniform

$$A = E(y)$$

Maximin: Given the highest price quoted on day 1, sell as long as it is possible for the price on day 2 to be lower.

Hurwicz: $A = \alpha y_{max} + (1-\alpha) y_{min}$

Regret: Suppose x_1 is the highest price quoted on day 1. If x_1 is accepted, the maximum regret is

$$y_{max} - x_1$$

If x_1 is not accepted, the maximum regret is

$$x_1 - y_{min}$$

9-29. Laplace:

$$E(B) = (B-C)\frac{1.35-(B/C)}{.40}$$

$$B_0 = 1.175C$$

Maximin: Choose any B in the range

$$.95C \leqslant B \leqslant 1.35C$$

Hurwicz: $B = 1.35C$ for any $\alpha > 0$

Regret: For any bid B, the maximum regret may be either $1.35C - B - \Delta_1$, (if the smallest competing bid is $1.35C$) or $B - \Delta_1 - C$ (if the lowest competing bid is $B - \Delta_2$, where $\Delta_1 > \Delta_2$).

Letting $1.35 - B - \Delta_1 = B - \Delta_1 - C$

$$B = 1.175C$$

9-31. Laplace and Regret:

$$I_0 = \frac{(R-C_0)\bar{D}}{R+C_1}$$

Maximin: $I_0 = 0$

Hurwicz: $I_0 = \bar{D}$ if $\alpha \geqslant \dfrac{C_0+C_1}{R+C_1}$

$$I_0 = 0 \text{ otherwise}$$

CHAPTER 10

		Red	Blue	Value
10–1.	*a)*	2/5, 3/5	4/5, 1/5	23/5
	b)	1, 0	1, 0	4
	c)	1, 0	1, 0	4
10–2.	*a)*	1, 0	0, 1, 0	12
	b)	1, 0	0, 0, 1	13
10–3.	*a)*	1, 0	1, 0, 0	5
	b)	0, 1, 0	0, 0, 1, 0	8
10–4.	*a)*	3/11, 8/11	9/11, 2/11	− 5/11
	b)	5/6, 1/6	0, 1/2, 1/2	13/2
10–5.	*a)*	0, 0, 1	Blue 1 with prob. .40 to .80; Blue 2 the remainder	4
	b)	4/11, 7/11, 0	6/11, 5/11, 0	46/11
10–6.	*a)*	3/11, 8/11	0, 9/11, 2/11	60/11
	b)	Red 1 with prob. 2/9 to 3/5	0, 1, 0	3
10–7.	*a)*	1/3, 1/3, 1/3	1/3, 1/3, 1/3	1/3
	b)	1/20, 2/20, 4/20, 13/20 (after 20 plays)	9/20, 3/20, 7/20, 1/20, 0	2.83 ≤ value ≤ 3.20

10–8. Both manufacturers must make major model changes each year.

10–9. value = $240,000

10–11.
Red   1/4, 3/4
Blue   1/4, 3/4
Value   − .125

10–12. Consider a simple instance in which $N = 4$, $C = 4$ and $B = 0, 1, 2, 3, 4$.

The matrix for this example may be written:

	0	1	2	3	4
0	0	−1	0	1	2
1	1	0*	0*	1	2
2	0	0*	0*	1	2
3	−1	−1	−1	0	2
4	−2	−2	−2	−2	0

For this example the game has four saddle points indicated by the starred values in the matrix. The value of the game is zero.

CHAPTER 11

11–1. Given x_1 (both good)

$$E(a_1) = \$40,060$$

$$E(a_2) = 47,160$$

Given x_2 (one good, one bad)

$E(a_1) = \$49,370$

$E(a_2) = 46,710$

Given x_3 (both bad)

$E(a_1) = \$55,370$

$E(a_2) = 46,310$

If no samples are taken and the lot is accepted, the expected cost is \$41,250. The expected cost if samples of size two are taken is \$42,777.

The matrix for a decision under uncertainty is shown below. The rules are defined as in the example given in the text.

	S_1	S_2
R_1	\$22,500	\$60,000
R_2	22,470	59,610
R_3	21,370	57,940
R_4	24,030	57,840
R_5	46,960	48,150
R_6	46,980	48,060
R_7	48,460	46,710
R_8	48,500	46,000

11–6. Let x_1 = the first observation

x_2 = the second observation

If observations are independent,

$$P(x_1, x_2 \mid S_j) = P(x_2 \mid x_1, S_j) = P(x_2 \mid S_j) P(x_1 \mid S_j)$$

For two samples of size 1:

$$P(S_j \mid x_1) = \frac{P(x_1 \mid S_j) p_j}{\sum_j P(x_1 \mid S_j) p_j}$$

$$P(S_j \mid x_1, x_2) = \frac{P(x_2 \mid S_j) P(S_j \mid x_1)}{\sum_j P(x_2 \mid S_j) P(S_j \mid x_1)}$$

$$= \frac{P(x_2 \mid S_j) P(x_1 \mid S_j) p_j}{\sum_j P(x_2 \mid S_j) P(x_1 \mid S_j) p_j}$$

Thus:

$$P(S_j \mid x_1, x_2) = \frac{P(x_1, x_2 \mid S_j) p_j}{\sum_j P(x_1, x_2 \mid S_j) p_j}$$

11–7. *a)*

	Utility
Air	.70
Rail	.40
Auto	.425

b)

	Utility if Prediction Is Good	Utility if Prediction Is Bad
Air	.78	.61
Rail	.36	.445
Auto	.445	.42

c) The value of the prediction is zero.

11-8.

A Priori Probability	A Posteriori Probability given a report indicating oil from a testing method which is		
	50% Correct	90% Correct	100% Correct
.01	.01	.083	1.00
.20	.20	.692	1.00
.80	.80	.972	1.00
.99	.99	.998	1.00

11-10. *a*) a_1: market the product

b) $(.70)(\$10,000,000) + (.10)(\$1,000,000) + (.20)(0) = \$7,100,000$

c) If test result is   Best action is

$$Z_1 \qquad\qquad a_1$$
$$Z_2 \qquad\qquad a_1$$
$$Z_3 \qquad\qquad a_2$$

d) \$89,000

11-11. Expected value of perfect information

$$(18/38)(\$1) + (18/38)(\$1) + (2/38)(\$17) - (-2/38)$$

11-12. The posterior probability that the reliability is 90% is .97.

11-13.

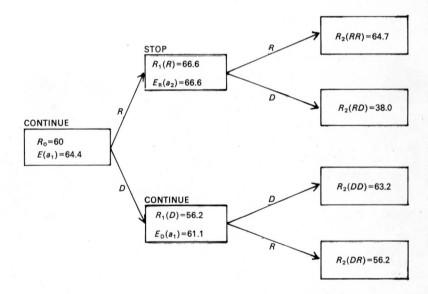

11-16. It would be necessary to have conditional probabilities fo the following form:

Let: X_k = the result of the kth survey

$$p(X_1 \mid S_j)$$
$$p(X_2 \mid X_1, S_j)$$
$$p(X_3 \mid X_1, X_2, S_j)$$

These probabilities could then be used in Bayes' theorem in place of the conditional probabilities used in the text example.

INDEX